HOW
THE CONSERVATIVES
RULE
JAPAN

STUDIES OF
THE EAST ASIAN INSTITUTE
COLUMBIA UNIVERSITY

HOW
THE CONSERVATIVES
RULE
JAPAN

NATHANIEL B. THAYER

PRINCETON UNIVERSITY PRESS

PRINCETON, NEW JERSEY

The East Asian Institute at Columbia University

THE EAST ASIAN INSTITUTE at Columbia University was established in 1949 to prepare graduate students for careers dealing with East Asia, and to aid research and publication on East Asia during the modern period. The faculty of the Institute are grateful to the Ford Foundation and the Rockefeller Foundation for their financial assistance.

The Studies of the East Asian Institute were inaugurated in 1962 to bring to a wider public the results of significant new research on modern and contemporary East Asia.

STUDIES OF THE EAST ASIAN INSTITUTE

The Ladder of Success in Imperial China by Ping-ti Ho. New York, Columbia University Press, 1962; John Wiley, 1964.

The Chinese Inflation, 1937-49 by Shun-hsin Chou. New York, Columbia University Press, 1963.

Reformer in Modern China: Chang Chien, 1853-1926 by Samuel Chu. New York, Columbia University Press, 1965.

Research in Japanese Sources: A Guide by Herschel Webb with the assistance of Marleigh Ryan. New York, Columbia University Press, 1965.

Society and Education in Japan by Herbert Passin. New York, Bureau of Publications, Teachers College, Columbia University, 1965.

Agricultural Production and the Economic Development of Japan, 1873-1922, by James I. Nakamura. Princeton, Princeton University Press, 1966.

The Korean Communist Movement, 1918-1948 by Dae-Sook Suh. Princeton, Princeton University Press, 1967.

The First Vietnam Crisis: Chinese Communist Strategy and United States Involvement, 1953-1954 by Melvin Gurtov. New York, Columbia University Press, 1967.

Japan's First Modern Novel: Ukigumo of Futabatei Shimei by Marleigh Grayer Ryan. New York, Columbia University Press, 1967.

Cadres, Bureaucracy, and Political Power in Communist China by A. Doak Barnett with a contribution by Ezra Vogel. New York, Columbia University Press, 1967. *The Japanese Imperial Institution in the Tokugawa Period* by Herschel Webb. New York, Columbia University Press, 1968. *The Communists and Chinese Peasant Rebellions: A Study in the Rewriting of Chinese History* by James P. Harrison. New York, Atheneum, 1969.

Foreword

SO FAR in life, both my pleasure and profession have been to talk politics. This book is the result of conversations held in Tokyo during the years 1965 and 1966 and briefly on my return from Burma in the winter of 1968. There are four groups of men to whom I am particularly indebted: newsmen, scholars, politicians, and their secretaries.

For slightly more than three years, from 1962 to 1965, I acted as press attaché of the American embassy in Tokyo. Before that assignment, I served two years in what was then the Bureau of Far Eastern Affairs in the Department of State. Both these jobs brought me into contact with some of Japan's most talented reporters. When I decided to write this book, I turned to these men. Their response was overwhelmingly generous. At the start, they spent long hours explaining to me the fundamentals of Japanese politics. Later, they opened the doors to the offices of politicians I had not met. Finally, they provided me with a critical sounding board for my ideas about the Japanese political process. This book could not have been written without their assistance at every stage.

After I had learned enough about Japanese politics to be able to ask sensible questions, I turned to the politicians themselves. My days were spent talking to them in their offices, in the outer chambers of the Diet, in the party or faction headquarters, or, in the evenings, in the restaurants of Akasaka or Shimbashi. I am grateful for the many hours they gave me, for the forthrightness with which they expressed their opinions, for the inside view they allowed me of the political process. It has not always been possible to reduce their cordiality and candor to the footnotes. I use this foreword to advise that the politicians themselves were my principal source for this book.

Newsmen like to look under political rocks. Politicians are inclined to watch the stars. I found recourse to the secretaries of the Dietmen helpful. The secretaries are an extraordinary group. Most of them are young. Many plan to run for office themselves some day. All have a thorough knowledge of Japanese politics. Few hesitate to speak out so long as it does not involve their boss. Sometimes they confuse the woods with the trees. After all, their principal tasks are to insure that constituents' sons find jobs, that the bureaucracy does not get too finicky in interpreting laws, that political funds are gathered (and partially reported), that voters get enough to eat and drink before going to the polls. Even if they sometimes forget that the ultimate goal of politics is the welfare of the nation, they reminded me continually that politics is the art of dealing with people.

Another source was scholars, both Japanese and American. Japanese scholars believe that power not only corrupts but contaminates and they stand aloof from the politicians, particularly the conservative politicians. I therefore relied on them chiefly for researches into the elections and for studies in the history of political parties. Since most of this help was drawn from written sources I have been able to pay my intellectual debts in the footnotes. American scholars helped me keep my perspective when I was in danger of becoming too engrossed in Japanese politics. They reminded me that political science was a discipline not an emotion, that what seemed self-evident within the Japanese context was sometimes incomprehensible outside of it, and that my chief value would be to remain disinterested.

These are the four principal groups upon which I drew most heavily, although other groups should not be overlooked. The Japanese bureaucracy is one, particularly the specialists in the election bureau of the Home Ministry and the librarians in the national Diet library.

Certain individuals gave so unstintingly of their time and energies that they must be singled out and thanked by name.

Among the newsmen, Yoshimura Katsumi,[1] who is now an assistant managing editor of the Sankei newspaper, deserves special mention. He has been active as a reporter since the end of the Pacific war. His chief contribution was his sense of history and his ability to put things in perspective. He was always able to direct me to another source for the other side of the story.

Among the secretaries, I would like to particularly thank Kobayashi Katsumi. He was an invaluable political source (through his good offices I was able to study closely the regional organization of his Dietman, Nakasone Yasuhiro), a patient listener and trenchant critic of my various theories, a meticulous proofreader of the manuscript as it went through several drafts, and finally, a precise translator of its Japanese edition. Except for the errors, the book has become as much his as mine.

Among the scholars, my greatest debt is to James Morley, formerly the director of the East Asia Institute at Columbia University, now a special assistant to the ambassador in the United States embassy in Tokyo. When I started writing this study, Professor Morley was on sabbatical leave in Tokyo. He read the first chapters as they came off the typewriter. More chapters were mailed to him after he went back to New York. Finally, when I returned to the United States with a complete manuscript, he read that. He has therefore been in on the study from the beginning and his advice and criticism did much to shape it. His blue pencil gave the book whatever style it has and his insistence on academic precision gave the book whatever scholarly value it has.

Among the politicians, I must single out Shiina Etsusaburo, senior statesman, who during the period of this study served variously as foreign minister, chairman of the executive council of the Liberal Democratic party, and minister of international trade and industry. Although we are a generation apart

[1] Japanese names are written in their Japanese order: surname followed by first name.

(his daughter and my wife are college classmates), I feel that we operate on a common wavelength. It was he who showed me that Japanese politics were rich, exciting, sophisticated, and not always what they seemed on the surface. Looking over my footnotes, I find that I have quoted Minister Shiina only once. His impact on this book and on my thinking is far greater than that.

Finally, though I open myself to charges of having been brain-washed, I should like to say a kind word about the Department of State. State usually likes its officers to be seen but not heard. In my case, it not only relaxed this attitude but relieved me from all other duties in the embassy and continued my salary while I was making this study. Edwin O. Reischauer, presently university professor at Harvard, then American ambassador to Japan, may have urged State to be this broad-minded, but I am not sure. But even ambassadors don't readily change traditions in the State Department. My fellow officers, all too familiar with a more penurious and high-handed policy, are still amazed at State's largesse.

No doubt some reader, who has seen a bit more of the world than these diplomats, will suggest State had its interest in seeing this book published and that State should be held responsible for the contents. I, of course, would be delighted to go along with any scheme whereby I gracefully accepted the plaudits for the book and State bore the onus for the errors. But I don't think I could get away with it. State's only role was to give permission to write it in the beginning and to pay for it in the end. True, after I had gotten well on in the manuscript I asked several colleagues in the Tokyo embassy to read chapters, but as usual we fell to squabbling, and I never did incorporate all their criticism into the text. When the manuscript was complete, I sent several copies to Washington and asked for permission to publish. Six months later, I received a brief letter saying the manuscript had been cleared. There were no suggestions of any deletions or revisions. Unfortunately, I find that I must be solely responsible for the book's content.

FOREWORD

The final editing of the manuscript took place in New York after I had assumed duties at the Japan Society. I am indebted to its officers and directors for their patience and forbearance. In particular, I wish to thank one of the society's vice presidents, Hugh Borton, whose course on Japanese history started my formal studies on this fascinating country many years ago, and the society's president, John D. Rockefeller 3rd, whose interest and concern have done so much to better relations between Japan and the United States.

NATHANIEL B. THAYER
New York City
September 3, 1968

Note to the Paperback Edition

ONCE PUBLISHED, a book lives its own life. The author can become quite objective. He would make an excellent reviewer, but tradition precludes anyone from soliciting his views. Occasionally, that tradition falls to the publisher's desire to put out a paperback edition. I find myself in that position now.

Looking over the original manuscript, I recall all the things I wanted to do but never got done. I had intended to write at length about relations between the bureaucrats and the politicians since the LDP politicians do things that bureaucrats normally do and Japanese bureaucrats do things normally reserved to politicians. The intent remains unfulfilled. I had wanted to write about ideology. How conservative are the conservatives? The answer is best given negatively. The conservatives are not Marxists, but their ranks include just about every other shade in the political spectrum. I had also wanted to write about the newsmen and the newspapers. I am currently doing that, but the researches will go into another book, not this one.

I have second thoughts about many of the chapters.

Recently, I have been reading in small group theory. I find that it offers apt concepts for analyzing the factions. I had explained a faction as a creation of a faction leader to bring him to power. I now realize that the faction leader is the captive of his faction. He is perhaps the only one who cannot violate the rules under which the factions play their games. I had pointed out the "normal" size of a faction to be twenty-five members. Larger factions tended to break down into units of twenty-five members each. The reason, I suggested, was that a faction leader found it hard to provide funds for a larger faction. Small group theory points out that direct contact cannot be maintained among all members in groups larger than twenty-five. That observation rather than economics may provide the better explanation for determining the normal size of a faction.

Events have demonstrated that the economic community has limited powers. And I now find that I cannot describe those powers without reference to the press. Originally I had suggested that the power of members of the economic community derived from their ability to supply the politicians with funds. My opening quotation from the bestseller, *Corona of Gold*, suggested that the members of the economic community worked in the tea houses quietly. During Yoshida's days, and perhaps until Ikeda's early days as premier, my description might have been true. I now believe that their power comes from their ability to articulate business interests to the government and government interests to the other businessmen and that they exercise this ability in public communication. One criterion for deciding who the most powerful member of the economic community is is to determine who can command the most column inches in the newspapers. The newsmen decide whom they shall quote as members of the business community and how much space they will give to each. Nobody challenges their decisions. These decisions do much to determine the shape of the economic community.

I believe more strongly than ever that further researches should be made into the typology of the *kōenkai*. It is no longer just a rural form of organization. It has come to the cities. I have made some electoral projections which suggest that the conservatives will hold a majority in the Lower House throughout the decade of the seventies. But whether they continue to hold a majority the following decade will depend on whether the *kōenkai* proves to be the most effective means of organizing the urban vote.

New challenges to the conservatives are coming from above and below. The House of Councillors offers the challenge from above. The Liberal Democrats may lose control of this House, if not in the 1974 elections then in the 1977 elections. In the past, the Councillors have regarded their role as moderating the excesses, correcting the mistakes, and filling the oversights of the House of Representatives. Now they seem to be asserting a more positive role in the legislative process.

The challenge from below comes from the local institutions. It is threefold. First, governors, mayors, and local assemblymen, heretofore allies of the conservatives, have proved more and more willing to identify with the progressive forces. Second, the local institutions are no longer willing to accept the limited role of administrators of the central government but claim a constitutional right to some measure of self-rule if not a complete separation of power from the central government. Finally, the electorate is becoming more conscious of the importance of local institutions.

In the first edition, I paid little attention to either the House of Councillors or the prefectural, city, and town assemblies. Clearly, they need closer scrutiny.

In July 1969, shortly after this book was published, I argued in *Asian Survey* that the rules for electing the party president worked well for putting a man into office but failed badly in removing him. I noted that no incumbent president had yet been voted out of office. I doubted that an incumbent president ever could be. Prime Minister Satō kindly buttressed my argument by running for and winning the presidential office four times. After the fourth election, with Prime Minister Satō's concurrence, the party revised the rules.

I have discussed these new rules in a postscript to Chapter VI.

In the chapter on the making of a cabinet I overemphasized the role of the Cabinet formation staff. I had thought that this group would lose its *ad hoc* nature and become a permanent, if informal, institution. Such has not happened. The making of a cabinet remains very much a solo performance of the prime minister. I had explained factional balance was the principle which guided a prime minister in appointing officers to his cabinet. I think that explanation should be refined. It seems to me that there is an inner and an outer cabinet, though no politician or scholar uses those terms. Key economic and foreign posts make up the inner cabinet. The prime minister appoints their ministers on the basis of experience and ability, and he makes these appointments first. These inner cabinets resemble prewar cabinets in that the same men show up time and again in the same chairs. The prime minister uses the appointments to the outer cabinet as a balance to his appointments to the inner cabinet. Thus, the prime minister gets the men he wants in the places he wants them, though the ultimate cabinet looks to be nothing more than a compromise between the various factions' demands.

The last three chapters of the book are the weakest. In my eagerness to point out the importance of the LDP policy affairs research council, I downgraded the committees in the House of Representatives. These committee chairmen are the principal vehicle for introducing opposition ideas into conservative legislation. Their role is becoming more important.

In my discussion of decision-making, I failed to establish a typology of decisions. There are decisions to do something. There are decisions to do nothing. Some decisions require consultation with a single ministry. Other decisions require consultations among several ministries. Each decision is made differently. I used the last chapter to list all the responsibilities of the Secretary General. Lists do not make exciting reading. What I should have done is describe how various politicians have answered the challenges of this office.

I still, however, subscribe to the conclusions of the book. The party is a balance between personal and institutional authority. In the past, personal authority has been dominant.

The trend, however, is toward the strengthening of institutional authority. The party has yet to achieve its most important goal: to secure the support and loyalty of the people. Since the conclusions still seem valid, I believe the paperback edition may serve a useful purpose.

NATHANIEL B. THAYER
New York City
August 15, 1973

Contents

List of Tables

HOW
THE CONSERVATIVES
RULE
JAPAN

CHAPTER I

Introduction

THIN clouds scudded across the autumn sky, and a northern wind brought a hint of rain and a promise of cold later in the afternoon to the campus of Chūo University. The students were out in force: they clustered in the paths, lined the windows and stood on the roofs of the dormitories, their eyes focused on the black limousines nudging their way through the crowds in front of the auditorium. Today was November 15, 1955, and all the important politicians of the nation were gathering to inaugurate formally a new conservative party—the Liberal Democratic party.[1]

Party workers were pinning peach-colored ribbons on the lapels of the Dietmen to single them out from the rest of the people. But there was little need for this special attention. The students knew who most of the politicians were by sight. Look, over there is Ōno Bamboku of the Liberal party! Ōno had left his car and was pushing his way on foot up the stone steps, baleful eyes glaring under bushy white eyebrows, muttering through thick lips something that sounded like, "Damn students." And here comes Miki Bukichi of the Democratic party! Miki, as usual, wore formal black Japanese robes and carried a thin cane, though all the other politicians were attired in business suits. Finally, Hatoyama Ichirō, the prime minister, arrived. He was slightly late because he had dawdled too long in his rose garden after lunch. With his arrival, the

[1] All names of organizations, if feasible, have been translated into English. For the prewar period, I have used the translations found in the glossary published in Robert Scalapino, *Democracy and the Party Movement in Prewar Japan* (Berkeley: University of California, 1953), pp. 401-419. For other names, including those in the postwar period, I have used translations found in English language newspapers published in Japan, or English language publications of the Japanese government, or I have translated them myself. A glossary of the English equivalents and the original Japanese is appended at the end of the text.

3

conference started, and the students began drifting away. They were more interested in the men than the event.[2]

The Japanese have always placed greater stress on personality in government than they have on institutions. Indeed, the institution has often been little more than an extension of personality. As Robert K. Reischauer noted of the two original parties started in Japan in the 1880's:

> . . . the Liberal Party and the Constitutional Progressive Party, were established by Itagaki and Ōkuma respectively because these gentlemen were angry at the way the samurai of Chōshū and Satsuma were monopolizing all the good positions in the government. They used their parties as tools to pry open posts in the administration for themselves and their loyal henchmen.[3]

Both Itagaki and Ōkuma had previously been part of that small elite which ruled Japan at the time the parties were formed. They had been maneuvered out and they wanted to get back. The formation of the parties was at least partly a tactic in an intra-elite fight for power and position of a sort which had characterized Japanese history over the centuries. If the fight between the government and the parties had hinged solely on personality and the right to rule, however, the parties might have been defeated and forgotten long ago.

Japan had been relatively isolated from the rest of the world for three hundred years. When she had closed her doors, she had been as advanced as any other nation of the day. When she opened them again, she found herself in many ways far behind. The nations of the West were strong; they were advancing into Africa, starting to carve up the Chinese melon, indeed, threatening Japan herself. Young Japanese were sent abroad to discover from where this strength had come; and some of these returned with the answer that the strength of the West lies in her representative institutions.

[2] *Asahi Shimbun*, November 16, 1955, p. 3.

[3] Robert K. Reischauer, *Japan: Government—Politics* (New York: Thomas Nelson and Sons, 1939), p. 95.

4

"The people whose duty it is to pay taxes to the government possesses the right of sharing in their government's affairs and of approving or condemning."[4] These young men demanded a constitution, a parliament, and suffrage. The political parties became the means to gain these demands. Initially, the oligarchs in the government adamantly opposed the parties. But the party movement was infused with the imperatives of nationalism and ultimately proved too powerful to oppose. In 1889, a constitution was granted. Although "political realists are apt to see in the document a selfish attempt to perpetuate the political power of the oligarchs,"[5] the constitution did provide for a legislature, the Diet, with elected representatives. Its lower house was to prove to be the stronghold of the parties.

The political parties reached their ascendancy shortly after the end of World War I. The constitution had insured that the ultimate source of authority in Japan was the emperor, but now he exercised more and more of this authority through the prime minister, and during the period from 1918 to 1932, he designated the presidents of the two conservative political parties, the Friends of Constitutional Government Association and the Constitutional Association (which in 1927 was to become the Constitutional Democratic party) to lead nine of the twelve cabinets.[6] Party government had been brought to Japan by imperial edict.

Perhaps this was the fatal flaw. The Japanese politicians

[4] "Japanese Government Documents: Memorial on the Establishment of a Representative Assembly," trans. W. W. McLaren, *Transactions of the Asiatic Society of Japan*, Vol. 42, pt. 1 (1914), p. 428.

[5] Takayanagi Kenzō, "A Century of Innovation: the Development of Japanese Law, 1868-1961," *Law in Japan*, ed. Arthur Taylor von Mehren (Cambridge: Harvard University Press, 1963), p. 6.

[6] The Friends of Constitutional Government Association on the one hand and the Constitutional Association (later the Constitutional Democratic party) on the other hand were the two mainstreams of conservatism in the prewar period. We shall have occasion to refer to them again in later chapters. The latter two parties we shall lump together and call the Constitutional Democratic party for stylistic ease. They were, for our purposes, identical in organization.

looked up, not down, for their source of authority. No one had bothered to create the institutions to tap the strength, support, and sympathy of the people. Robert Reischauer, in Japan at the time, noted, "Among the party politicians, there is no systematic organization but only temporary obedience to a few very powerful leaders."[7] Membership in a political party meant loyalty to a man, not allegiance to an institution or a set of political ideals. When the men leading the parties failed to respond to the challenges of the day, it was not difficult to dismiss the parties.

Japan faced just such a challenge in the beginning of the thirties. The world-wide depression had struck Japan particularly hard. The Japanese military services, or at least the headstrong young officers, were demanding a more active foreign policy. The politicians had proved themselves all too human. "Corruption and malversation both in and out of office have become much identified with the idea 'politician' in Japanese society."[8] The emperor turned to other men in other segments of Japanese society for leadership of the nation. After 1932, he was never again to call upon the parties to furnish a prime minister until the end of the Pacific war. Hamaguchi Ōsachi, one of the last party prime ministers, wrote: "No sooner had the people recognized the establishment of party government, than they were greatly disillusioned with its evils. . . . The people did not take time to discern whether the faults lay with the system or with the politicians. They quickly lost faith with the present and despaired of the future."[9] The parties continued to exist and occasionally elections were held. But party government had clearly failed.

The political party movement was reconstituted following Japan's defeat in World War II and the arrival of American

---

[7] Reischauer, *Japan*, p. 133.   [8] *Ibid.*, p. 95.

[9] Hamaguchi Ōsachi, *Zuikanroku* [Record of Random Thoughts], quoted in the *Asahi Shimbun*, September 2, 1962, p. 2. Translations, unless otherwise noted, are by the author.

6

occupation forces. These soldiers were charged with encouraging the Japanese people "to form democratic and representative institutions" among which were to be "democratic political parties with rights of assembly and public discussion."[10] It required little more than this expression of purpose to put the Japanese politicians back into action. On November 2, 1945, the Japan Socialist party was formed, soon to be followed by the Japan Communist party. The conservatives created the Japan Liberal party on November 9, the Japan Progressive party on November 16, and the Japan Cooperative party on December 18.[11]

The occupation forces, however, were not satisfied with the reconstitution of forces as they existed before the war. One of their first moves was to see that a new constitution was drafted "which diametrically changed the basic philosophy of Japan's government. . . . Power and the right to rule were . . . given to the people." Parliament, "not the Emperor, was the highest organ of state, . . . [and] the Prime Minister was selected by the Parliament."[12] A new framework for party government was created.

The Occupation also initiated a purge of undesirable men from public office. "The purge program," claimed the occupation authorities, "served the Japanese people who were enabled by it to choose new leaders capable of charting the nation's course toward a more hopeful future."[13] Although the parties of the left escaped almost unscathed, the conservative politicians were hard hit. Almost eighty percent of them were affected by the orders and the survivors were further depleted

10 Supreme Commander of the Allied Powers [hereafter SCAP], "United States Initial Post Surrender Policy in Japan," *Political Reorientation of Japan* (Washington: Government Printing Office, 1950), pp. 429-439.
11 Tsuji Kiyoaki, ed., *Shiryō—Sengo Nijūnen Shi* [A History of the Twenty Years after the War—Documents] Vol. 1 (Tokyo: Nihon Hyōronsha, 1966), p. 333.
12 Hugh Borton, *Japan's Modern Century* (New York: The Ronald Press, 1955), p. 410.
13 SCAP, *Political Reorientation*, p. 44.

by the first elections, which were held in April 1946.[14] Over eighty-one percent of the successful candidates in this election were men who had never served in national office, although some had served in regional assemblies.[15] In subsequent elections, bureaucrats began resigning and running for office.

But the old politicians could not be completely counted out. From October 1950 until August 1951, the purge orders were lifted and in the general elections of 1952, many of these men returned to the political arena. Of the 352 successful conservative candidates, 111 came from these ranks.[16] These old politicians tried to assume control of the parties, but the new men were not willing to surrender so easily. It was a complicated fight. New politicians fought with old politicians. The old party politicians of one party fought with old party politicians of the other party. Men from the regional assemblies clashed with the ex-bureaucrats. The purge's effect was, thus, to divide the conservative leadership.

Occupation economic policies also greatly influenced the collection and distribution of political funds. Before World War II, the Japanese economy was controlled by several huge financial combines called *zaibatsu*, the most famous of which were the Mitsui and the Mitsubishi. Each of these *zaibatsu* had close ties with one of the political parties. The Mitsui was the financial backer of the Friends of Constitutional Government Association and the Mitsubishi backed the Constitutional Association, which later became the Constitutional Democratic party. Moreover, these *zaibatsu* contributed their funds to the top leaders of the party, usually the secretary general or the party president. A single source of funds

[14] Yoshimura Tadashi, "Sengo ni okeru Waga Kuni no Hoshutō [Conservative Parties in Japan after the War]," *Shakai Kagaku Tōkyū*, Vol. 1, no. 1, January 1956, p. 2.

[15] Jichishō Senkyo Kyoku, *Shūgiin Giin Sōsenkyo—Saikō Saibansho Saibankan Kokumin Shinsa—Kekka Shirabe* [General Elections of the House of Representatives—National People's Judgment of the Legal Officers of the Supreme Court—Survey of Results] (Tokyo: Jichishō Senkyo Kyoku, 1967), p. 14. Hereafter cited as *kekka shirabe*.

[16] Yoshimura, "Waga Kuni no Hoshutō," p. 8.

controlled by the top leaders of the party did much to insure loyalty and discipline, if not to the party itself, then to the top leaders of the party.

Although scholars now question the judgment, the occupation authorities firmly believed the *zaibatsu* to be intimately involved with Japan's aggression before the war and dissolved them, purged their directors, and made their stock available to the general public. Inflation was soon felt in the aftermath of the war, and in February 1948 the occupation forces imposed stringent financial restrictions. The political effect of these measures was to prevent not only the *zaibatsu* but also the other established wealthy elements of society from using their funds for political purposes. Yoshimura Tadashi of Waseda University notes, "Political funds were no longer derived from one or two, or at the most two or three large donors. Instead, political funds came from relatively numerous small contributors." These small contributors gave to many individual politicians. "Political power revolved around the various political strongmen who collected and distributed political funds."[17] The power of the purse could no longer be used to hold the parties together.

Lack of any regional organization also contributed to the weakness of the new political parties. The last election in which the political parties had vied with each other had been in 1937. It was to be nine years before the first elections were held in the postwar period, and during the interim the regional organization of the parties, such as it was, fell apart. The occupation forces contributed further to the difficulties of organizing the vote by ordering that the franchise be given to all men and women over the age of twenty years, thereby increasing the number of voters about 2.5 times.[18] Finally, the Occupation instituted a land reform program aimed at placing the ownership of the land in the hands of the men who cultivated it. This reform over the years was to alter fundamentally the traditional social structure of the villages. The

17 *Ibid.*, p. 18.
18 *Ibid.*

9

new political parties were unable to cope with these changes. Each politician who wanted a seat in the Diet had to fend for himself.

Disagreement over leadership, many new politicians, an expanded electorate, no established source of political funds, no organization in the countryside—these were not the conditions conducive to the growth of party institutions. In the decade after the war, sixteen conservative political parties were at one time or another cluttering the political stage. A party was nothing more than a clique of new politicians clustered around a leader with access to funds, political experience, and ambitions for leadership. As in the past, the personality of the leader was more important than the institution of the party.

It was against this background that the party movement in Japan began to reconstitute itself. In April 1946, the first elections were held. The three conservative parties were able to emerge with control of 248 of the 464 seats in the lower house. Of the three parties, the Liberal party was the strongest, occupying 140 seats, and its leader, Hatoyama Ichirō, confidently looked forward to forming a coalition with the Japan Progressive party, which had won 94 seats, and to becoming the prime minister.[19] But the occupation authorities stepped in and on May 4, 1946, they informed Hatoyama that he was purged. Hatoyama called upon Yoshida Shigeru to assume the prime ministership. Yoshida was a career diplomat, a former ambassador to Great Britain, and his democratic credentials were in order, as he had been arrested by the War Ministry in 1944 for opposing the war. Hatoyama claims to have extracted a promise from Yoshida to turn the party and premiership over to him when the purge charges against him were cleared.[20] If such a promise existed, Yoshida never honored it. In 1951, the purge orders against Hatoyama were lifted and in October 1952, he won a seat in

[19] *Kekka Shirabe*, 1967, p. 12.
[20] Hatoyama Ichirō, *Kaikoroku* [Memoirs] (Tokyo: Bungei Shunjū Sha, 1957), p. 55.

the lower house. The rivalry between these two men for the control of the premiership was to occupy a central place in Japanese politics for the next several years. Yoshida gave his nation long and faithful service. In the decade from 1945 to 1955, he was prime minister five times for a total of seven years. But even he could not remain in power indefinitely. In 1954, after a noxious scandal involving the conservative politicians and the shipbuilding industry, he was forced to take responsibility and resign. Hatoyama became the new prime minister.

The socialists, the chief force in opposition, were not powerless all these years. They had participated in two coalition governments, once under their own prime minister, Katayama Tetsu, and once under the conservative Prime Minister Ashida Hitoshi. They were gradually increasing their strength at the polls and in the Diet. They looked forward to forming their own government. The socialist movement, however, had always been composed of many shades of the left, and in 1951 they split to form two parties and were no longer able to offer a credible alternative to the conservatives. With the retirement of Yoshida in 1954, however, these two socialist parties patched up their differences, and again formed a single party. The conservatives, frightened that the socialists were now in a position to take over the government, also began discussing the creation of a single party.

At that time there were two conservative parties. One was the Liberal party, in which most of Yoshida's men clustered, now led by Ogata Taketora. The other was the Democratic party, led by Hatoyama Ichirō. The talks were started on May 15, 1955, by a phone call from Miki Bukichi to Ōno Bamboku. Miki was a lieutenant of Hatoyama and Ōno was a follower of Ogata. They were sworn political enemies since the days they had served together in the Tokyo Metropolitan Assembly. "In thirty years, we had never even drunk a cup of tea together," relates Ōno Bamboku. "Once in a while, I would bump into him in one of the drinking shops in the back alleys of the Ginza. But even then we would take seats far apart and drink by ourselves. . . . We wouldn't even share the same waitress."[21] The talks proceeded with mutual distrust, but progress was made. Ōno and Miki were joined by Shōriki Matsutarō, the owner of the *Yomiuri Shimbun*, and by Fujiyama Aiichirō, then a ranking official in the Japan Chamber of Commerce. After many more meetings, there was a sufficient meeting of the minds so that the parties could be brought formally into the act. In August, ten men from each party sat down to draw up a platform and principles for the new party. Another committee composed of thirty men from each party met to consider the party rules and organization. In October, a preparatory conference of all the members of both parties was held, both secretaries general pledged their efforts to making the venture succeed, and another committee was set up to work further on the terms of merger. Finally, on November 15, 1955, a formal party conference was convened in the auditorium of Chūo University and the new party—the Liberal Democratic party—was launched.

The formation of the new party marked a new epoch in Japanese political history. "When I am asked when the present political structure was put together, I always answer in 1955," Masumi Junnosuke, one of Japan's eminent political scientists, has written.[22] Not only did the relative strength of the various parties shift but there were changes within the Liberal Democratic party itself.

First, the external change. After the formation of the Liberal Democratic party, there was no opposition party in the wings with the slightest chance of assuming power. The socialists, the strongest of the opposition groups, were unable to find a common ground on which to stand and again in 1959, split into two parties, the Japan Socialist party and the Democratic Socialist party. In addition to dividing their forces, a further problem for the socialists has been their in-

21 Ōno Bamboku, *Ōno Bamboku Kaisōroku* [The Memoirs of Ōno Bamboku] (Tokyo: Kōbundo, 1964), p. 111.

22 Masumi Junnosuke, "Sen-Kyūhyaku-Gojū-Gonen no Seiji Taisei" [The Political Structure of 1955], *Shisō*, June 1964, p. 55.

ability to expand their strength through the electoral process
to any significant degree. Through three general elections
held since the split, the Democratic Socialist party has expanded its strength from 17 to 30 seats. The Japan Socialist
party won 145 seats in the 1960 elections, 144 seats in the
1963 elections, then fell to 140 seats in the 1967 elections.[23]
Since there are at present 486 seats in the lower house, the
press speaks of the socialists as being unable to break through
the "one-third barrier." Shiina Etsusaburō, a former foreign
minister, puts it more bluntly, "The socialists are the cat who
can't catch the mouse."[24]

The socialists are not the only opposition group. Besides
them, there are the communists, who reached the peak of
their legislative strength in the 1949 elections, when they captured 35 seats. In the 1967 general elections, they won 5
seats.[25] In 1960, a Buddhist organization, the Value Creation
Society, supported candidates for the Tokyo Metropolitan
Assembly, of whom 51 were elected. In succeeding years,
they have met with a certain measure of success in placing
their men in the prefectural assemblies and in the upper
house. In November 1964, the Value Creation Society finally
organized the Clean Government party[26] and in the 1967
election it entered the lower house, winning 25 seats.[27] All
four of these parties have cooperated in challenging the conservatives on specified issues. It is conceivable that these
parties may some day be able to whittle away the absolute
majority that the conservatives now hold. But few observers
are willing to predict that a coalition will be formed by them,
since they are so different in political views. Unless there is
internal dissension and splintering, the present Liberal Democratic party seems fairly certain to rule for some time to
come. The press, politicians, and scholars alike refer to it as
the "party which will rule half an eternity."

23 *Kekka Shirabe*, 1967, p. 12.
24 Shiina Etsusaburō, interview, October 13, 1965.
25 *Kekka Shirabe*, 1967, p. 12.
26 Tsuji, *Shiryō*, p. 436.
27 *Kekka Shirabe*, 1967, p. 12.

It is with the internal structure of the Liberal Democratic party that we shall be most concerned. In the years shortly after its formation, the party seemed like other conservative parties. To be sure, the conservatives had spent more time than usual in creating this party. There were formal position papers stating the party's beliefs. There was also a party law which established various party organs and offices, including the president, the vice president, the secretary general, the executive council and the policy affairs research council; and each of these organs and offices had its responsibilities. But all the previous conservative parties had had similar beliefs, laws, and organs. They had not seemed too important in the past and they did not seem too important in 1955. Real political power resided in the various strong men within the party and by 1957, these strong men had hardened their personal power into a number of factions.

The factions were all-important. The faction leaders decided who the next prime minister was going to be and who was going to enter his cabinet. Meetings of the factions in the restaurants of Akasaka could be more important than sessions of the Diet. Squabbles among the factions could upset the smooth conduct of the nation's affairs. But like the political parties before the war, the factions were unable to fulfill political hopes. In particular, they failed to generate enthusiasm among the populace, instill confidence among the economic community, or provide the political stability which the conservative politicians themselves wanted. Although the movement is halting and is barely perceptible, political power has begun to swing away from the factions and lodge in the organs of the party. The factions still exist, and are still essential to the functioning of conservative politics. But the Liberal Democratic party which exists today is an amalgam of personal power lodged in the factions and institutional power lodged in the party organs. This balance between personality and institution is the subject of this book. We turn first to an examination of the factions.

CHAPTER II

The Factions

IT WAS an evening shortly after the 1963 general elections. The Spring and Autumn Society [the faction led by Kōno Ichirō] of the Liberal Democratic party had been holding an election victory celebration at the Hotel Ōkura. The banquet over, the Dietmen began to get ready to troop out when a voice spoke up from one corner of the hall. "Wait a moment!" It was one of the lieutenants of the faction.

"Since I am in charge of the education of the recruits, I have something to say to the new Dietmen gathered here."

The freshmen Dietmen, befuddled with victory toasts, remained in their seats wondering what was coming next.

The Kōno lieutenant slowly and deliberately pulled from his pocket a newspaper clipping.

"I have here a newspaper survey taken of the new Dietmen. In it there are questions like 'What do you think of the factions?' and 'What faction do you intend to join?' There is one man who answered, 'I don't have anything to do with factions.' He is sitting in this room. This two-faced attitude of saying to the outside 'I'm a good boy' and then attending this banquet is outrageous. I don't want that sort of person in the faction."[1]

The present conservative party can be divided into a number of factions. They are formal political entities with a headquarters, regular meetings, a known membership, an established structure, and firm discipline. Many commentators refer to them as parties within a party. Few of the actions taken

[1] *Sankei Shimbun*, December 1, 1966, p. 1.

in the party's name make any sense unless the interests of the factions are taken into account.

The factions are composed of members of the Diet, the national legislature, which has a House of Councillors (upper house) and a House of Representatives (lower house). The House of Representatives is the stronger body, both constitutionally and by tradition, and the factions are much stronger in it than in the upper house, although both the representatives and the councillors belong to factions. In the following discussion I shall be thinking primarily of the lower house. Later in the chapter I shall describe the special circumstances surrounding the upper house.

The factions became a major element in Japanese politics about two years after the Liberal Democratic party was formed. Table 1 shows that in the past decade the number of factions has increased by approximately one-third. Factions differ in size: the largest faction today is Prime Minister Satō Eisaku's faction, which numbers 111 representatives. A

TABLE I. GENEALOGY OF FACTIONS 1955-1968

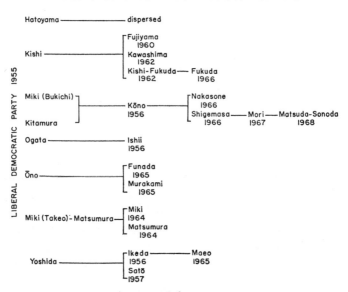

16

medium-sized faction is Fujiyama Aiichirō's faction, which numbers 28 representatives. The smallest faction is Matsumura Kenzō's faction which numbers only four representatives. Table 2 gives the factions' numerical strength.

TABLE 2. NUMERICAL STRENGTH OF THE FACTIONS, MARCH 1967

Faction	Lower House Members	Upper House Members	Total Members
Satō	57	54	111
former Ikeda	42	14	56
former Kōno	—	15	54
Matsuda-Sonoda	15	1	
Nakasone	24	—	
Miki	36	10	46
Fujiyama	17	11	28
Ishii	14	10	24
Fukuda	23	—	23
Funada	15	6	21
Kawashima	18	—	18
Murakami	10	3	13
Matsumura	4	—	4
Unaffiliated	11	4	15
Undecided	—	14	14
Total	286	131	417

SOURCE: Kikuoka Yaozō, ed., *Kokkai Binran* [Parliamentary Handbook] (42nd ed., Tokyo: Nihon Seikei Shimbun Shuppan-bu, 1967), pp. 318-325.

Through the factions, five essential party and national goals are achieved. First, the party chooses its leader through the factions. Second, through the factions the party raises and distributes most of its operating funds. Third, posts both in the government and in the party are determined by and through the factions. Fourth, through the factions comes most of the aid an individual candidate gets for the election campaigns. Fifth, the factions serve several profound psychological needs of the Dietmen, for which, at present at least, there are no substitutes.

Factions are not new to Japan. Scalapino in his study of

17

the party movement in prewar Japan quoted the grand old parliamentarian of Japan, Ozaki Yukio, as confessing in 1917 that "here in the Orient we have political factions but no political party."[2] Many of the characteristics of the present-day factions can be found in the older factions, as a brief look at history will show.

Both of the two dominant political parties before the war, the Friends of Constitutional Government Association and the Constitutional Democratic party, had factions. Infighting among them for control of their respective party was common and a great deal more rowdy than today. For example, in 1937, a dispute broke out between Kuhara Fusanosuke and Nakajima Chikuhei over who was to succeed to the presidency of the Friends of Constitutional Government Association. Kōno Ichirō, then one of the lieutenants in the Kuhara faction, describes what happened:

> We brought in about three hundred longshoremen and goon squads by truck from Yokohama, and Nakajima rolled out the workers from the Shibaura dockyards. One group took over the first floor of the party headquarters and the other took over the second floor. It wasn't too long before each faction started throwing beer bottles at the other. The police came and broke it up and placed the party headquarters off limits.[3]

The prewar factions had some degree of formal organization, because the faction leaders used to have regular meetings with their followers outside of the party caucuses. Kawashima Shōjirō, the vice president of the present conservative party, clearly remembers attending the meetings of Mori Kaku, one of the strong men of the Friends of Constitutional Government Association, who used to have a faction meeting on the 21st day of each month and forty or fifty

2 Robert Scalapino, *Democracy and the Party Movement in Prewar Japan* (Berkeley: University of California, 1953), p. 117.
3 *Asahi Shimbun*, August 2, 1964, p. 2.

of his followers would gather.[4] The widow of Hatoyama Ichirō, a postwar premier and a prewar leader of the same party, recalls, "Before the party's dissolution, my husband would invite close friends on the ninth day of every month to his home in Otowa, and ten or so . . . men in the party would come."[5]

Factions also entered into the distributing of posts in the party and government, particularly in the making of a cabinet. In 1931, for example, Inukai Tsuyoshi, the President of the Friends of Constitutional Government Association, was given the task of forming a new government. Inukai was concerned with the growth of the political power of Suzuki Kisaburō within the party and he was resolved to limit Suzuki's strength by maneuvering the factions. While he gave the post of education minister to the Suzuki faction, he counterbalanced this by awarding the post of commerce minister to an opposing faction. A member of the Suzuki faction got the post of cabinet secretary, but another faction got the post of director of the cabinet legislation bureau. Finally, Inukai refused to appoint Suzuki to the important post of the Interior Ministry, where he could exercise a decisive influence on the elections and the conduct of the police, but relegated him to the prestigious but less important post of justice minister.[6]

It also appears to have been common practice for the prewar faction leaders to give to their followers funds for elections and "pocket money" at the end of the year. "During the 1928 general elections, Tanaka Giichi, the president of the Friends of Constitutional Government Association, gave each of the party members five thousand yen [$2,500], but the rumor was out that he had given ten thousand yen [$5,000] to each of his own followers and the other faction leaders were on the lookout," says Hoshijima Nirō, who has the distinction of being the conservative politician with the longest experience in the lower house, having won sixteen elections.[7] "At the beginning of the 1930's, the going rate

[4] *Ibid.*   [5] *Ibid.*   [6] *Ibid.*
[7] *Ibid.*

for pocket money at the end of the year was between five hundred [$250] and one thousand yen [$500]," says Funada Naka, a present-day faction leader and former speaker of the lower house.[8] "Kuhara used to tell us when he handed over the pocket money that if this was not enough, to go around and see the other faction leaders," recalls Tsugumo Kunitoshi, a former secretary general of the Friends of Constitutional Government Association.[9] (This practice is a sharp departure from the present custom in which receiving political funds from another faction leader is regarded as an act of disloyalty.) "A legislator was an octopus," says Uchida Nobuya, "He had one of his tentacles stuck in the pot of each of the faction leaders."[10]

Factional fights over control of the party, regular meetings of the faction, factional balance in the making of a cabinet, factional distribution of political funds—these and other attributes have been the common property of both the prewar and postwar factions. Yet there is a consensus of political opinion that the prewar and the postwar factions are different. The prewar factions were an *addendum* to the political process. One reporter for the *Asahi Shimbun* says, "These factions were loose groupings around an important politician or were supporters of the party president of the time."[11] Masutani Shūji, a conservative politician who had been active in party politics since 1920, adds, "There were factions before the war, but they were not too important. Nobody felt obliged to belong to them. They were mostly groups which gathered for political discussion."[12] The present-day factions, however, are *integral* to the political process. Kōno Kenzō, vice speaker of the House of Councillors, says, "Everybody damns the factions, but the Liberal Democratic party and perhaps the government would not be able to move without them."[13] The factions are essential to the functioning of Japanese politics today.

8 *Ibid.*   9 *Ibid.*   10 *Ibid.*
11 *Ibid.*   12 Masutani Shūji, interview, April 12, 1966.
13 Kōno Kenzō, interview, January 25, 1966.

THE FACTIONS

The greatest stimulus to the growth of the factions in the present conservative party has been the party presidential elections. Since the present conservative party is the ruling party and the prime minister of the country is decided by a majority vote of the Diet, these presidential elections in effect decide who is to be the prime minister of the nation.

Earlier conservative parties usually chose their party leader through consultations among the party elders. But one of the terms for the merger of the present conservative party was that the party president would be decided by elections.[14] The franchise for these elections was given to the conservative members of the Diet and representatives from each of the party's prefectural federations. Although the number of conservative Dietmen varies, about five hundred men usually elect the party president. Politicians wishing to become party president, and thereby prime minister, have found that with this small number of voters, the best way to get the vote is through individual appeal to each politician. The faction then, from its inception, has been a contract between faction leader and faction follower. What the faction follower gives is his vote in the presidential election; what he gets in return is campaign support in the elections, political funds, and assistance in securing a high post in the party or government.

The success of the factional system in choosing the party president depends on long-term commitments. If a Dietman could easily shuck his factional allegiance because of dissatisfaction over the amount of financial support he received, the degree of support in the elections, or his failure to be appointed to a significant party post, the factional system would soon collapse. Each politician would go shopping shortly before the presidential elections and his vote would go to the faction leader who offered the best bargain.

These conditions existed shortly after the merger of the conservative party in 1955. Factions were as much friendship

14 Jiyūminshutō, "Tōsoku" [Party Law], in *Wagatō no Kihon Hōshin* [Basic Policies of Our Party] (Tokyo: Jiyūminshutō Kōkoku Iinkai, 1966), Art. 6.

21

clubs as they were warring bands. Their structure was dual-ringed. On the inner circle surrounding the faction leader was a cluster of lieutenants whose allegiance, because of past association, was clear. On the outer ring were other politicians whose ties to the faction leader were less clear. Sometimes the politicians on the outer ring of one of the factions fell into the orbit of the outer ring of another faction. Because of the vagueness of the relationship, a Dietman could be a member of two, or sometimes three, factions.

Take, for example, the Kōno faction. Initially, it was composed of "eight samurai," the remnants of one of the political parties in existence before the conservative merger, who through a running dispute with the prime minister had been forced to the fringes of the political world. "We had fallen almost to the point of complete extinction," writes Kōno Ichirō.[15] Political adversity breeds close friendship. The other seven samurai were identified with Kōno and were to form the core of his faction on his return to power. The drive for membership in the faction started with a series of banquets in Mukōjima, a geisha district on the far bank of the Sumida River, to which Kōno's lieutenants invited Dietmen who, they thought, would rally to Kōno's cause. The site was carefully chosen. It was far enough outside the usual haunts of the Dietmen so that any guest would not have to explain his attendance to other Dietmen, but not so distant that the invitees would have to make an undue effort to attend.

The Dietmen were probably aware that something was up by the choice of the locale, but the activities of the evening did nothing to indicate it. The Dietmen ate, drank, joked with the geisha, listened to the raconteurs, and at the end of the evening, signed a book to commemorate the occasion. This banquet was followed by others, to which substantially the same guests were invited, and finally culminated in a weekend trip to Hakone, a pleasure resort in the mountains several hours from Tokyo. Kōno's only factional membership

[15] Kōno Ichirō, *Kōno Ichirō Jiden* [The Autobiography of Kōno Ichirō] (Tokyo: Tokuma Shoten, 1965), p. 226.

list was the banquet books, and the only yardstick of factional loyalty was the distance the Dietmen were willing to travel to eat and drink with him. The other factions were formed in much the same way. In this period, any faction could be defined as a group of politicians who travelled to the resorts and hot springs for "seminars" and met for an occasional meal in Tokyo. There was no other organization.

These bonds of friendship were not firm enough to decide elections. The faction leaders were faced with the problem of making clear each Dietman's allegiance and making sure that this allegiance was permanent. They did this by creating formal organizations and making these organizations hierarchical.

From the irregularly scheduled trips and dinners it was a small step to begin to have regular faction meetings. Regular meetings meant that some sort of liaison point had to be set up; the liaison office gradually added secretaries and expanded its functions. By late 1957, most of the factions had created headquarters in one or another of the hotels in the center of Tokyo.

As the formal structure began to emerge, it also became hierarchical; politicians standing at the peak of the hierarchy got first shot at the cabinet and favored party posts. Position in the hierarchy was ultimately determined by the faction leader. He gave consideration to age and to the number of times a Dietman had been elected, common standards that are used throughout the party. But more important criteria were length of time in the faction and degree of service to the faction. A new faction member started at the bottom of the pecking order. The equation was simple: those who worked the hardest and the longest for the faction got the rewards.

With the passage of time, hierarchy and formal structure did their work in solidifying the factions. All the members of the lower house, with the exception of about a dozen men, now have factional ties. There is no longer any mystery about which Dietmen belong to which faction. Accurate member-

23

ship lists are published, and many times the newspapers will identify a Dietman by his factional affiliation. There is some movement from faction to faction by individual Dietmen, but the rate of defection is not high. "So long as the faction leader stands any chance of becoming prime minister, his followers will remain loyal to him," explains one veteran newsman.[16]

What happens to a faction when it loses its leader? This question was forcibly brought to the attention of three of the most powerful factions in 1964-65 when their leaders, Ōno Bamboku, Ikeda Hayato, and Kōno Ichirō, died.

The Ikeda faction handed over the reins of leadership to Maeo Shigesaburō, a close confidant of Ikeda for better than thirty years, since they had been young bureaucrats together in the Finance Ministry. The transition to Maeo was eased because a board of directors of about ten men had been created to watch over the faction while Ikeda was prime minister. Ikeda died in office, and it was natural for this group to remain in existence. They formed the point of continuity between Ikeda and Maeo. They are still active, meeting at least once a week. While all the faction members claim that Maeo is the leader, it is apparent that the faction is at least in part under group leadership.

The Ōno faction was not able to solve the problem of succession. Upon Ōno's death, all the faction members made the usual avowals of unity. But it was not long before the Ōno lieutenants were fighting over the mantle of leadership. Funada Naka was appointed temporary chairman of the faction and an attempt was made to compromise the various claims. The exercise proved fruitless. After an acrimonious debate lasting several days in the Hotel New Japan, the Ōno faction split in two, one group following Murakami Isamu and another group following Funada Naka. Each group has resolved itself into a separate faction. Their headquarters are in separate office buildings close to the Diet.

The Kōno faction followed much the same course as the

[16] Miyake Hisayuki, interview, October 1, 1966.

24

Ōno faction but took a great deal longer to do it. There were many eager young politicians who wished to try and step into Kōno's shoes, and shortly after his death, several of them, including Nakasone Yasuhiro and Mori Kiyoshi, made a tentative bid for power. They were rebuffed. The faction, instead, chose to elect a new faction leader: Shigemasa Seishi, a close confederate of Kōno. He proved to be unable to quell the dissidents. Next, an attempt was made at group leadership. A board of directors composed of five men was elected and met once a week with a board of advisors, senior men in the faction who had been elected nine or ten times, to make the important decisions for the faction. These interim arrangements continued more than a year but in the end did not work out. Finally, in December 1966, the faction formally split, with Nakasone the leader of one group and Mori the leader of the other.

Since then, Nakasone has challenged the party president in his leadership, led his faction through a lower house election, and been able to attract strong financial backers who would like to see him in the prime minister's chair. Nakasone has demonstrated all the attributes of a faction leader, and his faction is slowly growing in membership. The Mori followers were not so fortunate. Mori was killed in an accident in 1968 and the faction reverted to group leadership, this time under Matsuda Takechiyo and Sonoda Sunao. These men were chosen because they had served in the Diet longer than all the other Mori followers, Matsuda having been elected eleven times, and Sonoda nine times. Diet experience is an important criterion for leadership, but not important enough to insure the cohesion of the faction. Newsmen suggest that the Mori faction is presently in the process of dissolution.[17]

The response of the Ōno and Kōno factions is the most common pattern when the problem of succession arises. Lieutenants lead men out to form new factions of their own. If these lieutenants can establish credentials as a possible future

[17] *Asahi Shimbun*, July 19, 1968, p. 18.

prime minister, the new factions may be expected to stick together and probably increase in size. If the lieutenants can not establish these credentials, then attrition sets in, and gradually the followers drift off into other factions. The instance of the Ikeda faction is unique. This is the first time a faction has transferred leadership and kept the faction intact. Up until the present, the faction leader rather than the faction was important. The faction was the extension of one man's will to be prime minister. Perhaps we are now entering a stage where the faction rather than the faction leader will be important. Perhaps the factions are in the process of becoming self-perpetuating entities capable of choosing new leaders from within the structure, but it is too early to be sure.

The need for political funds contributed to the development of the factions. Before the war, land, particularly farm land, was held by a small minority. It is estimated that "nearly three-fourths of the farm population was dependent partially or wholly on rented land."[18] The tenancy system has been condemned as unjust, cruel, and degrading, but it produced a form of paternalism that made it at least tolerable to the tenants. Though the landowner had great economic powers, he also had social responsibilities. He was expected to look after the welfare of his villagers. After the war, the American occupation forces stripped the landowner of his economic powers by putting ownership of the land in the hands of the farmers themselves, but the Occupation did not institute a system to compensate for the social services the landlord supplied to the village. With the removal of the landowner, the villager turned to his Dietman.

The village makes great demands. The elders want to purchase fire-fighting equipment. The village schools want either a piano or an organ; nowadays, it is more likely to be a swimming pool. Well-stuffed envelopes are expected at each festival, wedding, and funeral. The shopkeeper expects a wreath when he opens a new store. Somebody must pay for

[18] Hugh Borton, *Japan's Modern Century* (New York: Ronald Press, 1955), p. 214.

26

the outings of the boy scouts. When the ladies of the village decide to visit the hot springs, somebody must hire a bus. For these and all other expenses, the Dietman is expected to pay handsomely. Before the war, the wealthy landowner could supply all these services without inordinate strain on his purse. Most of the postwar politicians cannot. Since the villager is inclined to give his support to the politician who does the most for him, there is vigorous competition among the politicians over who can supply the most largesse for the community.

There is virtually no limit on the amount of money that can be spent serving the community. Shōriki Matsutarō, a Dietman and owner of the *Yomiuri Shimbun*, a leading national daily, has built a splendiferous newspaper plant with some of the world's most modern and expensive reproduction equipment in the small city of Takaoka in Toyama prefecture, his election district, simply to provide his electorate with a newspaper. The plant is reputed to be losing money, but the farmers of Toyama get, by wire, the front pages of the Tokyo edition of the *Yomiuri*, and Shōriki keeps winning elections.

Katō Ryōgorō spoke out bluntly on money, people, and the factions on his retirement after fifty years in Japanese politics, including service as the speaker of the lower house. When asked what was wrong with Japanese politics, he answered, "First of all, the electorate is at fault." Warming to his subject, he continued,

> They *force* the politicians to spend money on them. For instance, any time anything happens, they immediately demand a wreath. . . . When they come to Tokyo from the provinces, they demand a box lunch. . . . What's more, they act as if these demands were a natural right. They lead the politicians around by the nose. But I can't waste any sympathy on the Dietmen. As soon as they run out of money, they go crying to their faction leader. This is what makes the factions strong.[19]

[19] *Sankei Shimbun*, evening edition, November 11, 1963, p. 1. See also *Yomiuri Shimbun*, October 10, 1963, p. 14.

27

Doing favors requires a staff. Nakasone Yasuhiro, one of the successors to leadership of the former Kōno faction, maintains a standing staff of thirteen men located strategically in three offices, and his staff is by no means regarded as large. Tanaka Kakuei, who prides himself on a modern office, keeps more than twenty secretaries employed in serving his electoral district, and had many more to help in other tasks when he served as secretary general of the party. At the other end of the scale are the young Dietmen who burn a small candle. I asked Tanikawa Kazuo, a thirty-six year old Dietman who has been elected three times from Hiroshima, how large his staff was. He said, "I have three offices, eight fulltime secretaries, and I don't know how many part-time drivers and the like. Last year, I didn't have so many people. But I was beginning to have troubles in my election district. Since I hired these men, things have taken a turn for the better. I no longer have any doubts about the next election."[20]

The *Yomiuri Shimbun* has investigated the finances of two young Dietmen, one from Aichi prefecture and one from Hokkaidō, who are trying to make do on an absolute minimum.[21] The *Yomiuri* estimated that the Dietman from Aichi spent about $1,400 a month and the Dietman from Hokkaidō about $2,150 a month. The income these two Dietmen receive from the government is about $700 a month, half the expenses of the Aichi politician and a third of the expenses of the Hokkaidō politician. The party has recently started to supplement this income. Twice a year, in late December and in mid-July, the traditional gift-giving time in Japan, the secretary general has given token sums to each of the conservative politicians. But it does not cover the gap. The *Yomiuri* asked the Aichi politician what he did to obtain the rest of the money. He answered, "The only thing I can do is go and get it from my faction leader."[22]

20 Tanikawa Kazuo, interview, July 25, 1966.
21 Yomiuri Shimbun Seiji-bu [Yomiuri Political Section], *Seitō* [Political Parties] (Tokyo: Yomiuri Shimbun Sha, 1966), pp. 62-65.
22 *Ibid.*, p. 65.

THE FACTIONS

These funds for cultivating the politicians' electoral garden are a drop in the bucket compared to what they need to run an election campaign. There are legal limits to the amount of money that can be spent in an election, but the law is out of date and it is an open secret that elections cost many times the limit. The politicians are hesitant to talk openly about the real costs of an election, but the *Asahi Shimbun* quotes a knowledgeable politician as saying, "In lower house elections, the cost per candidate averages perhaps 15,000,000 yen [$41,000]. But there are men who spend 30,000,000 yen [$83,000]."[23] The *Sankei Shimbun* has published the election expenses of an unnamed conservative politician who spent approximately 20,000,000 yen [$55,000] in the 1963 general elections.[24] The *Mainichi Shimbun* has recently made the statement: "There are many legislators who need election war chests of 40,000,000 to 50,000,000 yen [$111,000-139,000]."[25] There is great variation in these figures. Different explanations can be given, but the scholar Nakamura Kikuo, who has himself stood for election and lost, comes closest to the mark when he writes, "I have doubts whether the candidates know themselves how much money they spend in an election."[26]

No matter how much money an election may really cost, the candidate, if the *Sankei Shimbun* is correct, can only hope to receive 4,000,000 yen [$11,000] from the party.[27] The rest of the money he must gather on his own.

Nakamura Kikuo lists six sources that the politicians tap in their search for funds.[28] He mentions former schoolmates, friends and relations, business firms (particularly concerns in which the politician serves as an executive or an advisor), and the politician's personal estate. He says that the poli-

23 *Asahi Shimbun*, August 4, 1964, p. 2.
24 *Sankei Shimbun*, January 1, 1965, p. 5.
25 *Mainichi Shimbun*, May 10, 1966, p. 2.
26 Nakamura Kikuo, *Gendai Seiji no Jittai* [The True Conditions of Present Day Politics] (Tokyo: Yūshindō, 1965), p. 330.
27 *Sankei Shimbun*, January 1, 1965, p. 5.
28 Nakamura, *Gendai Seiji no Jittai*, p. 326.

29

ticians are sometimes forced into the hands of the loan sharks. He also mentions the factions, and notes that most Dietmen have recourse to them.

The factions perform three services in helping the politician gather political funds. First, the faction leader himself will give funds directly to his follower. Second, the faction leader will arrange for the candidate to meet influential members of the business community. Third, membership in the faction will permit the politician to tap other members of the faction for funds, though this is frowned on in some of the factions.

Political funds received from the factions fall into two main categories: the funds needed for the daily expenses of the politician and the funds needed for running an election campaign. The first are usually distributed twice a year in mid-July and in late December. The faction leader may supplement these funds from time to time. He is expected to play the role of a lord of the manor, and most try to live up to expectations. When a faction member is going overseas, building a new home, or needs extra money for some other reason, often the faction leader will help him with a contribution.

Election funds are distributed shortly before an election, although the faction leader may have given small sums earlier to members of the faction who are running for the first time. No general rule can be drawn about the way in which the faction leader gives election funds to the candidates. In one faction, funds are distributed according to the number of times the candidate has won an election. By this system, the younger members of the faction receive more money than the old-timers who have won many elections and have less need of the money. A more common practice is for each faction member to receive a basic sum to be supplemented later by the faction leader if the member is having trouble. Or each faction member works out his election funds with the faction leader; men with firm districts get less than those with shaky districts. Tanikawa Kazuo spoke for at least some of the politicians when he said, "The politicians don't like going to the faction leader and pestering him for money. They would

30

rather go it alone. But neither do they like losing an election. Somehow, between these two dislikes a balance is struck." He paused, then added, "If possible, a politician likes to give money to the faction. It increases his prestige."[29]

The amount of money it takes to run a faction remains the subject of constant controversy. None of the faction leaders has chosen to speak on the subject, and other politicians have said little to dispel the mystery. They agree that the amount differs between factions, that there are rich factions and poor factions, and that the fortunes of the factions vary from year to year. The political section of the *Yomiuri Shimbun* has recently published an estimate:

It is well known that each of the factions collects funds independently. The amount differs between factions. Even the small factions, if the expenses for running a headquarters and for funds distributed to the faction members twice a year are included, need from $83,000 to $139,000. When it comes to the larger factions which have more than fifty Dietmen, regular expenses run between $278,000 and $545,000. For elections, it is common knowledge that even the leader of a middle-sized faction must collect $545,000. A grand total of all the money collected by the factions, would seem to be about twice what the party itself needs.[30]

These figures are admittedly imprecise and raise more questions than they answer. But for the average city worker, whose average monthly income is $150.00, these figures add up to a lot of money.[31]

Competition for appointment to posts in the party, cabinet, and Diet also has fostered the growth of the factions. The sharpest competition among the conservative politicians is for a seat in the cabinet. Shortly after Prime Minister Satō

[29] Tanikawa Kazuo, interview, July 25, 1966.
[30] Yomiuri, *Seitō*, p. 126.
[31] Japan. *Kokkai Tōkei Teiyō* [Statistical Abstract of Japan] (Tokyo: National Diet Library, 1965), p. 280. The figure is for the year 1963.

shuffled his cabinet in August 1966, the newspaper reporters interviewed Arafune Seijūrō, the new minister of transportation, and asked why he had campaigned so ardently for a seat in the cabinet. Arafune tossed off a few political bromides, and then blurted out, "If you don't get to be a minister, your election district goes to pot."[32]

Arafune pays great attention to his election district. He is regarded throughout the party as a strong campaigner. He has won eight elections, and in the last four, he received the greatest number of votes of any candidate in his election district. He has nothing to worry about. But Arafune is expressing a sentiment held by all the politicians. A seat in the cabinet gives increased strength at the polls. The statistics support this belief. In Table 3, I have listed the members of the cabinet who were in office at the time of the 1963 general elections, calculated the percentage of the total votes they won in their electoral districts, and compared this percentage with

TABLE 3. COMPARISON OF THE PERCENTAGE OF VOTES WON BY MEMBERS OF THE CABINET SERVING AT THE TIME OF THE 1963 GENERAL ELECTIONS WITH PERCENTAGE OF VOTES WON BY THESE MEN IN 1960

Name	Percentage of votes in the 1960 elections	Percentage of votes in the 1963 elections	Percentage change
Akagi Munenori	18.1	23.8	5.7
Yamamura Shinjirō	17.7	32.9	15.2
Fukuda Tokuyasu	16.3	17.3	1.0
Tanaka Kakuei	23.6	28.6	5.0
Fukuda Hajime	18.1	20.4	2.3
Kōno Ichirō	16.0	20.7	4.7
Hayakawa Takashi	24.1	27.8	3.7
Ōhashi Takeo	19.3	17.9	−1.4
Nadao Hirokichi	24.5	28.3	3.8
Satō Eisaku	21.1	26.0	4.9
Ōhira Masayoshi	27.3	27.8	0.5
Ayabe Kentarō	20.6	22.4	1.8
Kaya Okinori	26.7	25.7	−1.0

SOURCE: Calculated from statistics of Jichishō [Home Ministry].

[32] *Asahi Shimbun*, August 3, 1966, p. 2.

similar calculations made for the 1960 general elections when these men were not in the cabinet.

Politics are rarely consistent; as the table shows, there were a few ministers whose percentage of the vote decreased, but special circumstances can be adduced to explain each case. But the general principle is clear. A post in the cabinet means an increase of votes. Aside from percentages, each of the ministers, with one exception, received the greatest number of votes of any of the candidates in his district.[33] This is always an exhilarating experience for any politician.

Arafune did not wait long after his appointment as transportation minister to demonstrate how the post can be used to make friends at home. With the publication of the new national railways schedule in September, it became apparent that four fast express trains had been ordered to stop daily in Fukaya, a small city that heretofore had been passed by. Fukaya is located in one corner of Arafune's election district. The railway authorities were more than slightly embarrassed and explained the situation "as if they had something stuck between their back molars." Even Arafune was a little defensive. "One more station is not going to make that much difference," he said to newsmen. A city official in Fukaya was more outspoken in giving the local view. "We had been petitioning the railway authorities for quite some time. But thanks to the appointment of our native son to the post of transportation minister, our hopes were suddenly realized. We must express our gratitude."[34]

Appointment to a ministerial post is also supposed to offer the opportunity for fund raising. The *Yomiuri Shimbun* political section, for example, alleges that "through the use of the powers of government offices . . . substantial political funds can be gathered."[35] I do not know whether these charges

[33] Ōhira Masayoshi did not occupy the top spot in his election district. The heavy responsibilities and travel demanded of the foreign minister did not permit him to return to his election district as often as he should have.

[34] *Asahi Shimbun,* September 4, 1966, p. 15.

[35] Yomiuri, *Seitō,* p. 27.

33

are true, but no sooner had the Fukaya stew been set on the political burner to bubble than Arafune became involved in another incident that showed how these rumors can arise. A socialist rose in the upper house and asked whether it was true that after a series of conferences between Arafune and the leaders of maritime transport, private railways, and industries connected with the national railways, one of Arafune's secretaries had visited these businessmen and solicited their membership in a club supporting Arafune. It had monthly dues of several hundred dollars. Several of the businessmen, the socialist said he had heard, found this too brazen and had complained to party headquarters. Arafune answered that "unknown to him, members of his organization had approached these businessmen. . . . But," the *Asahi Shimbun* reported, "people had warned him that this might invite misunderstanding and the party had brought his attention to the matter, too." Arafune had therefore asked for the withdrawal of the new members from his organization and had returned their membership fees. "I have decided that I am going to dissolve the support organization clearly and soon."[36]

Barely two weeks had passed before Arafune was again under attack, this time for taking two textile businessmen with him when he visited South Korea to attend a Japanese-South Korean ministerial conference. This proved to be too much for the government. After 72 days in office, Arafune was obliged to submit his resignation to the prime minister.[37] Although the conservative politicians may have found Arafune's conduct reprehensible, his constituents did not. In the January 1967 general elections, the voters of the third district of Saitama prefecture returned Arafune to the Diet with more votes than he had ever received before.[38]

36 *Asahi Shimbun*, September 28, 1966, p. 1.
37 *Asahi Shimbun*, October 12, 1966, p. 1.
38 Japan. Jichishō Senkyo Kyoku, *Shugiin Giin Sōsenkyo, Saikō Saibansho Saibankan Kokumin Shinsa: Kekka Shirabe* [Survey of Results of the General Elections of the House of Representatives and People's Judgment of the Legal Officers of the Supreme Court] (Tokyo: Jichishō Senkyo Kyoku, 1967), p. 218.

Another reason why Dietmen want to become ministers is that none of the top positions in the party are open to them until they have had ministerial experience. Finally, a minister is generally regarded as standing at the pinnacle of Japanese society; many men desire the post for prestige or as a climax to their careers. For all these reasons, competition for a seat in the cabinet is vigorous. Although cabinets change frequently, only eighteen men can be appointed at one time. To secure one of these seats of glory, the politician must have the backing of the faction.

Besides pursuing cabinet posts, the senior politicians compete for chairmanships of the standing committees in the lower house and for the seven committees in the party. The middle level politicians fight to become division chiefs in the policy affairs research council. The younger politicians squabble over appointment as parliamentary vice ministers. Altogether, there are better than 200 posts in the party and government to which appointments must be made every year. The factions make lists of posts desired by each of the men in the faction and stand ready to defend the members' interests when the appointments are made.

The election system for the lower house provides another element conducive to the growth of the factions. Since this system will be analyzed in detail in a later chapter, here we need only mention that in the elections for the lower house, several candidates are elected from the same electoral district. There is vigorous competition among them, although they may come from the same party. Since the party must treat all its candidates impartially, the candidates turn to the factions for support. The faction not only assists its Diet members in the elections, but also actively searches out and supports new candidates; more members means more strength for the faction, and particularly more votes in the party presidential election. A faction, however, rarely accepts a new candidate from an election district in which it already has a member. They would be fighting one another and the new candidate might defeat the old at the polls. A political critic

35

explains this connection between the elections and the factions in the *Asahi Journal*:

It's not too much to say that entering a faction is an essential condition for becoming a politician [Dietman]. The fellow who wants to become a politician looks around his election district. He does not approach any of the factions that already have Dietmen elected from his district. He finds it awkward to belong to the same faction of a Dietman whom he will have to fight to get his share of the conservative vote. The faction leader is also studying the election districts throughout the nation. He wants to expand his political strength by adding new men to his faction. In the election districts where he does not have a man he is always scouting for a new candidate who has a chance of winning. When he finds one, he gives him money, helps him out. The interests of the faction leader and the new candidate coincide. This is often the way ties are formed between them.[39]

For example, Morishita Motoharu decided to run from the district of Tokushima in the 1963 elections. He found himself faced with candidates from the Miki, Kawashima, Kishi, and Ikeda factions. He promptly approached the Kōno faction. Since they felt that he had a chance of winning, they welcomed him into their ranks and gave him their help. Morishita fulfilled their expectations. He campaigned vigorously and won handsomely.

How do the factions help the candidates in the elections? As mentioned above, the factions can and do provide political funds. But the backing of a faction need not involve the actual handing over of money to be financially beneficial. In each region there are always many politicians aspiring to a seat in the Diet. So many fail that they are not taken too seriously by the electorate. But recognition of a candidate by a faction

---

[39] Henshūbu [Editorial Staff], "Sōsenkyo no Naka no Habatsu Kōsō" [The Factional Fight in the General Elections], *Asahi Jānaru*, Vol. 9, no. 6 (February 10, 1967), p. 21.

elevates him to the status of a major contender. Mori Kiyoshi explains: "Many people say that Japanese politics require a great deal of money. The problem is not that serious. If the candidate is able to demonstrate that he has a good chance of winning at the polls, he will find that contributors naturally come to him."[40] Even if the faction did nothing more than recognize the candidate, this in itself would help the new candidate collect funds.

The second great service that the faction provides the candidate is to campaign on his behalf. Dietman Kobayashi Takeji says, "It is said that the factions are bad, but under the present system you have to have them. When you ask somebody to campaign for you in the elections, you go to men with whom you have a special relationship within the party. There is no other way."[41] Every summer after the Diet session is over, the faction members who are well known to the public—usually, the faction leader and the members of the faction who are or have recently been ministers—team up with lesser-known members of the faction and tour the election districts. Five or so Dietmen storming through the countryside generate a great deal of excitement among the electorate. The meetings which they hold, usually billed as reports on the Diet session, prove extremely helpful to the candidates. Although this sort of campaigning flourishes in the summer, it goes on throughout the year.

Most of the factions supplement barnstorming with publication. They issue from time to time pamphlets and brochures to be used by the faction members in their election districts. The old Kōno faction, and presently the Nakasone branch of it, have gone one step further than the other factions in helping their candidates by holding a faction convention every year in one of the major cities, usually Tokyo. Each of the faction's candidates brings to this convention twenty young

40 Mori Kiyoshi, interview, July 6, 1966.

41 Senkyo Seido Shingikai, *Dai-niji Senkyo Seido Shingikai Giji Sokki-roku* [Transcript of the Proceedings of the Second Election System Deliberation Commission] (Tokyo, 1963), p. 231.

members from his electoral district, making a total of about a thousand people. For three days, they have seminars, rallies, and speeches. One of the secretaries to Nakasone says, "These conventions really help the candidates. The young men feel that they have really gotten into big-time politics. When they go back to their electoral districts, they pour on the heat in working for the candidates."[42]

The third major service that the factions provide their candidates is that they work to secure the party nomination for them. Shortly before an election, an election policy committee will meet and decide which of the candidates the party will endorse. Each of the factions will fight to have its men receive this endorsement. The candidates are many and the endorsements few. If the candidate does not have the backing of one of the factions he stands little chance of being endorsed.

Not all the faction-backed candidates are endorsed by the party. And if the candidate fails to obtain the party endorsement, the faction will no longer campaign openly on his behalf. All members of the party are obliged to support party candidates, and none of the faction leaders wishes to furnish the other factions with an excuse for dragging him before the party discipline committee. But failure to obtain endorsement is not fatal to a candidate's chances. First, endorsements are given just before an election and the hard work of building a support organization has been underway for some time. Secondly, although the faction members may not make speeches on behalf of a candidate who has not been endorsed, they will continue to render him support covertly. The new candidate rarely considers the lack of party endorsement sufficient reason to withdraw from the election. He will usually stand and run as an independent. If he wins, he will join the party after the election.

When notification of the general election is given, each of the factions sets up a campaign headquarters in one of the hotels clustered in the center of Tokyo. From there, pop sing-

42 Kobayashi Katsumi, interview, September 15, 1966.

ers, popular novelists, baseball players, and movie stars are dispatched to the regions to help the faction's candidates. Literature is prepared and distributed. Candidates come to plead for more funds. Whispered conversations compete with jangling phones. In short, the factions act like full-fledged, independent political parties.

Elections have come to affect the strength of the factions just as much as they do that of the party. Initially, the factions depended on recruiting Dietmen as members. There is still some movement by the Dietmen from one faction to another, but in the main the loyalties between the faction and its members remain firm. Nowadays, new faction members must be gained through the electoral process.

Kōno Ichirō was not the first man to use the elections to increase the size of his faction, but he has been the most successful to date. In the 1963 elections, he put forward 22 new men to run. Of these, six men did not obtain the party endorsement and were forced to run as independents. Three of them won. In all, fourteen of Kōno's candidates were elected. Kōno's faction before the elections had 31 members. In one election he was able to increase his numerical strength by roughly a half.[43] This was a major victory. Even the prime minister, who is regarded as the strongest politician in the country, was only able to get six new men from his faction elected. Within the party, Kōno was harshly criticized for his actions. But in the 1967 elections, other faction leaders chose to emulate him.

There are also psychological reasons for the factions. One is to satisfy the need for identity. A Dietman's secretary explained to me the Japanese politician's need to belong during a walk around one of the still ponds in the beautiful green gardens of Meiji Shrine. We were feeding the gold, black, and white mottled carp, who swam majestically to the surface, grabbed the bread crusts in a flash of broken water, and then sank slowly, their scales glimmering out in the water's depth. "In Japanese politics, there are a few men like these carp.

[43] *Ibid.*

They pay no heed to what others are doing, cruise slowly around by themselves, attract attention by standing alone. But most Japanese politicians are like *that!*" He pointed to a school of light brown minnows zigzagging through the shallows. "Japanese politicians like to move in a group, and the more in the group the better."[44]

Matsuda Takechiyo, a conservative doyen with eleven elections under his belt, can easily be identified as one of the carp. Among his confreres, he is known as the "homeless Texan," since he spent twelve years wandering and studying throughout the United States.

> The most important thing for a politician is talk. Before the war, the Dietmen were always in the corridors or committee rooms of the Diet. That was where they were supposed to be. If the president of a company wanted to see them, he had to come around to the back door of the Diet building, locate a page, and send him in search of the Dietmen. Sometimes they made connections, sometimes they did not. But the important point is that the Dietman regarded being in the Diet as his first job. So he had plenty of opportunity to talk with his fellow Dietmen.
>
> Nowadays, it is all different. Each Dietman has an office, usually several of them. He has a cluster of secretaries who spend all their time making appointments for him. The government has even given him an apartment. Today, there are too many places for the politicians to go. There is no natural meeting place. As a result, they never get together.
>
> Another point. In the old days, the young Dietmen used to spend all their time getting prepared for speeches in the Diet. They learned politics by serving as assistant whips under the older politicians. Nowadays, they have no chance to speak, because debate has gone out of style in the Diet. They have no way of learning their trade

[44] Kobayashi Katsumi, interview, August 15, 1966.

because the old whip system has fallen apart. They have no forum for their ideas. They get no important assignments because they have no political experience. They have nothing to do.

Nothing to do and no place to be. It's no wonder they drift to the factions.[45]

The conservatives slip into the factions as into an old shoe. The scholar Nakamura writes, "Japan has a modern constitution and an advanced political system. But we are ensnarled in the old, pre-modern factions. . . ."[46] Nakamura is not historically accurate. The factions to which he refers are new, dating from 1957, while the basic organs of the party, as we shall see in later chapters, have been in existence since the turn of the century. But Nakamura is talking sociology. And in these terms, the party is new and the factions are old.

Japan has spent more than a century trying to catch up with the modern world. To be judged old-fashioned is the political death sentence. The party has resolutely put aside all that is tinged with the past and concentrates on burnishing a modern image. But the Dietman feels a little uncomfortable in its glare; he talks new but thinks old, and continues to look to his faction for both comfort and support.

The factions were not made for public exposure, although in truth, they receive more attention than the party itself. They have adopted the social values, customs, and relationships of an older Japan. The newsmen, when they write about the factions, frequently draw on examples in *sumō*, Japanese wrestling, or the *han*, the feudal clans, to make their points. This vocabulary is particularly apt in describing the factions. The old concepts of loyalty, hierarchy, and duty hold sway in them. And the Dietman (or any other Japanese) feels very comfortable when he steps into this world.

But it is not only comfort that attracts the Dietmen to the factions. They are the focus of Japanese politics. A cabinet

[45] Matsuda Takechiyo, interview, May 23, 1966.
[46] Nakamura Kikuo, *Shindan—Nihon no Seiji Taishitsu* [The Japanese Body Politic—A Diagnosis] (Tokyo: Ronsō-shā, 1961), p. 12.

shuffle approaches its climax and the Dietmen, even those who stand no chance of appointment, gather at the factional headquarters to consider means of putting pressure on the prime minister and to await his appointments. The party conference is convened to elect a new party president, but the factions will have made their final decisions in the faction meeting the night before. No secretary general will make an important decision until the factions' opinions are heard. Any Japanese politician who wishes to participate fully in Japanese politics—and there are few in the lower house who do not—will naturally gravitate to the factions. This desire to be in on all the political drama may be as strong a reason as any of the concrete economic and political benefits to explain the importance of the factions.

The factions were thus created in response to psychological hungers and the needs of politicians. These hungers and needs are common to all the factions. Are all the factions therefore the same or are their differences between them?

Part of the answer to this question can be drawn from statistics. Table 4 demonstrates that the age level differs between factions. 44% of the party members are over sixty and 23% of its members are under 49 years of age. In Nakasone's faction, however, 52% of its members are below 49. And in Murakami's faction 40% of its members are below 49. These can generally be regarded as the factions of the young men. Other factions have a higher percentage of men over sixty years of age than the party does. These factions are: Matsumura (75%), Fujiyama (69%), Kawashima (65%) and Ishii (64%). Matsumura himself is the grand old master at 85 years of age.

Table 5 shows differences between the factions in national legislative experience. 56% of the party members have been elected more than six times. 69% of the members of the Fujiyama faction and all four members of the Matsumura faction have been elected more than six times. Thus these two factions are the richest in legislative experience, although they are both on the decline. No new members came to the Fuji-

TABLE 4. PROFILE OF FACTIONS ACCORDING TO AGE

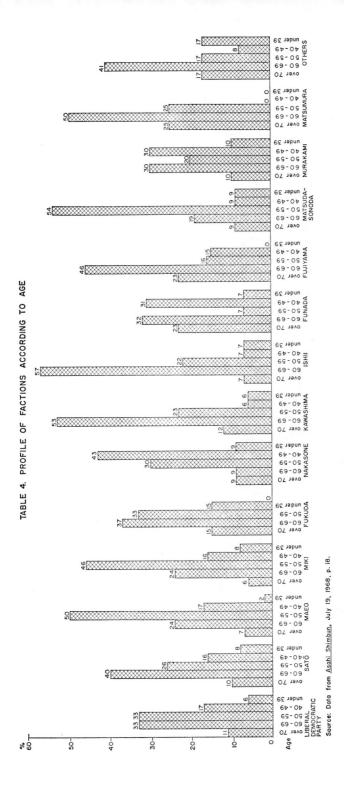

Source: Data from Asahi Shimbun, July 19, 1968, p. 18.

TABLE 5. PROFILE OF FACTIONS ACCORDING TO NATIONAL LEGISLATIVE EXPERIENCE

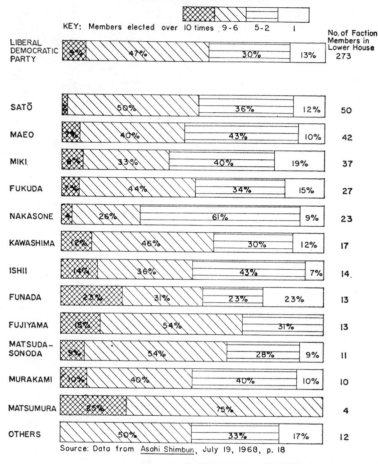

KEY: Members elected over 10 times . 9-6   5-2   1

No. of Faction Members in Lower House

Faction	Members elected over 10 times	9-6	5-2	1	No. of Faction Members in Lower House
LIBERAL DEMOCRATIC PARTY		47%	30%	13%	273
SATŌ		50%	36%	12%	50
MAEO		40%	43%	10%	42
MIKI		33%	40%	19%	37
FUKUDA		44%	34%	15%	27
NAKASONE		26%	61%	9%	23
KAWASHIMA		46%	30%	12%	17
ISHII	14%	36%	43%	7%	14.
FUNADA	23%	31%	23%	23%	13
FUJIYAMA	15%	54%	31%		13
MATSUDA-SONODA	9%	54%	28%	9%	11
MURAKAMI	10%	40%	40%	10%	10
MATSUMURA	25%	75%			4
OTHERS		50%	33%	17%	12

Source: Data from Asahi Shimbun, July 19, 1968, p. 18

yama faction after the 1967 elections. No new members have ever joined the Matsumura faction through elections. On the other hand, some factions have relatively little legislative experience. 23% of Funada's faction and 19% of Miki's faction have been elected only once in comparison with the

44

overall party average of 18%. Miki and Funada are regarded as the front runners to succeed Prime Minister Satō. Clearly they are adding new members for the coming battle in the party presidential elections. The members of Nakasone's faction are still relatively new to the Diet: 70% have been elected less than five times while throughout the party only 43% of the members fall into this category.

Table 6 compares the factions according to the occupations

TABLE 6. PROFILE OF FACTIONS ACCORDING TO PREVIOUS OCCUPATIONS OF ITS LOWER HOUSE MEMBERS

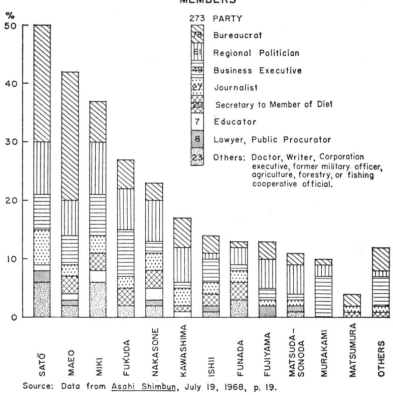

Source: Data from <u>Asahi Shimbun</u>, July 19, 1968, p. 19.

of its members before they were elected to the lower house. Some factions have a high percentage of former bureaucrats. 40% of the Satō faction and 52% of the Maeo faction have been bureaucrats, while only 28% of the party members in general have been bureaucrats. 45% of the Matsua-Sonoda faction have been active in prefectural politics, compared with a party average of 22%. 70% of the Murakami faction are drawn from business in comparison with a party average of 18%.

Nobody argues over these figures. The question is, are they politically significant? Answers vary. One of the running debates in the political world is whether the factions can be placed in an ideological spectrum. "Look carefully," says Sakata Michita, a conservative Dietman, "and you will see that there are political differences among the factions."[47] "The factions are not built solely on interests," says Kurogane Yasumi, another conservative Dietman; "they are also gatherings of people with similar patterns of thinking."[48] The press generally accords the Matsumura faction the furthest left position and the Fukuda faction the furthest right position in the factional line-up, but no one is really sure just where those two positions are. There is also general consensus that each of the factions has a unique flavor, and that many times this flavor is imparted by the faction leader himself. Ikeda Hayato was a bureaucrat from the Finance Ministry, and his faction, now the Maeo faction, has many former finance bureaucrats within it. It can be expected to have strong views on finance and economic policy. Kōno Ichirō served many times as agricultural minister and his faction paid great attention to agricultural policy. Ōno Bamboku was a product of the prewar parties. He stressed the personal relationship in politics. "If you're interested in policy and argument," said Kōno Ichirō at the banquet celebrating the creation of the Ōno faction, "then you're welcome to join my faction. If you're interested in enjoying the arts of the

[47] Sakata Michita, interview, May 18, 1966.
[48] Kurogane Yasumi, interview, August 23, 1966.

geisha and drinking sake, then you're better off gathering around Ōno."[49] But these predilections of the factions are not pervasive, definite, or comprehensive enough to be called ideologies. Part of the reason for the confusion in the factions' positions can be found in the election system. There have been four elections (in 1958, 1960, 1963, and 1967) since the formation of the conservative party and the emergence of the factions. Prior to the first election, the Dietmen were free to form any sort of grouping they wished, whether it be by age, region, electoral class, or ideology. But in 1958, the factions faced their first election and the imperatives of the election had to be met.

First of all, a faction cannot tolerate two of its members coming from the same electoral district, since they would by necessity be fighting one another, disrupting whatever inner harmony there was within the faction, as well as using factional funds at cross purposes. There are exceptions. In the Satō faction both Tsubokawa Shinzō and Ueki Kōshirō come from Fukui. In the Kawashima faction, Ogasa Kōshō and Akita Daisuke come from Tokushima. In the Maeo faction, Tosaka Jujiro and Niwa Kyōshirō come from the third district of Ibaragi. But as a general rule, faction members come from different electoral districts.

Factions have also had to induct new members through the elections or else face gradual attrition. There have been cases where a faction leader has started from scratch, selected a person whom he wished to make a Diet member, found an election district, secured the party nomination, and pushed the candidate through the campaign to victory. But the usual pattern is for the faction to look over the electoral districts in which it is not represented and then back one of the promising candidates there. Likewise, a promising candidate will naturally ask for help from the factions which are not already present in the election district from which he chooses

49 Watanabe Tsuneo, *Habatsu* [Factions] (2nd edn., Tokyo: Kōbundo, 1963), p. 54.

47

to run. Under this scheme of things, ideology, beyond a general avowal of democracy and parliamentary rule and an explicit rejection of Marxism, has had to take a back seat.

Some factions have been more aggressive than others in searching out and supporting new candidates. The Kōno faction mentioned above is an example. A faction leader preparing to make a bid for the prime minister's job is often very eager to add more followers to his stable, and the more actively he searches out new candidates the less he can be concerned with ideological affinity. The most active factions, then, have the least political ideology.

The failure of the factions to develop a political philosophy has recently resulted in the development of other informal policy groups. Issues that preoccupy the conservatives are policy towards Asia (particularly China), defense, neutralism, and internal security. The conservatives have split into two groups, and debate between them over these issues is vigorous. One of the groups is called the Asia Study Group; its members are drawn chiefly from the Satō, Kishi-Fukuda, and Kawashima factions. The other group is called the Afro-Asia Study Group; its membership centers on the Miki-Matsumura and former Kōno factions. But the factional lines are not clear. There are members of the former Kōno faction in the A-study group and members of the Satō faction in the AA-study group.[50] The groups are supra-factional. The press and the politicians claim that the factions are undergoing a "reorganization." Whether these policy-oriented groups are to be the factions of the future remains to be seen. Such groups have not as yet taken over any of the other functions of the "old line" factions.

I have so far only spoken of the lower house. There is an even more complicated factional system in the upper house. Each councillor not only has membership in one of the factions of the lower house but also belongs to another faction unique to the upper house. Generally, factional allegiance

[50] Yomiuri, *Seitō*, pp. 86-89.

is weaker among the councillors than it is among the representatives.

The reasons for the lack of strong factional allegiance can be found first in the nature of the upper house. Constitutionally, the House of Councillors is considerably the weaker of the two houses. When the House of Representatives is dissolved, the House of Councillors is closed. The cabinet may convoke the House of Councillors in the case of a national emergency, but any measures the councillors enact are null and void unless agreed to by the House of Representatives within ten days after the next Diet session opens.[51] Although the House of Councillors can reject or modify a lower house bill, the original bill becomes law if passed again in the House of Representatives by a majority of two-thirds of the members present.[52] The budget must first be submitted to the lower house and in the event the House of Councillors do not agree, "the decision of the House of Representatives shall be the decision of the Diet."[53] The same power of ultimate decision is given to the lower house in the election of the prime minister,[54] and in the conclusion of treaties.[55] Factions are built on the struggle for power and the seat of power is the lower house.

Since the upper house does not share equal power in the legislative process, election to its chambers has in many ways become the postwar equivalent of the prewar system of conferring titles of nobility. Some have caustically called it a retirement system for distinguished elders from all fields of endeavor. While it is difficult to accept this judgment completely, it is true that many of the councillors have made their name in fields other than politics. Finance and business have sent company presidents and bankers, the cultural world has sent authors and scholars, labor has sent union leaders,

51 Japan. "Nippon Koku Kempō" [Japanese National Constitution] in *Roppō Zensho* [Compendium of Laws] (Tokyo: Iwanami, 1960). Art. 54. Hereafter cited as Japan, *Constitution*.
52 *Ibid.*, Art. 59.
53 *Ibid.*, Art. 60.   54 *Ibid.*, Art. 67.   55 *Ibid.*, Art. 61.

and agriculture has sent heads of cooperatives to its chambers. Many of these men see no need of acquiring further fame and recognition through participation in the daily ruckus of Japanese politics. They are content to leave this role to the younger and more vigorous politicians of the lower house. The councillors believe themselves to be above party. Their interest is a dispassionate concern for the nation. This mood is antithetical to factional allegiance.

Perhaps an even stronger reason for the councillors' weak factional allegiances is the nature of the election system. Upper house elections are different from lower house elections. In the House of Councillors, one hundred of the candidates (two-fifths of the house) are from a national constituency,[56] that is, the candidates are elected from the nation at large. Candidates who are well-known publicly or candidates who have an organization with a large membership backing them, usually win in the national constituency. These candidates have relatively less need for political funds that the factions provide.

The remaining 150 candidates run in electoral districts that coincide with the prefecture.[57] All of the large factions have their sympathizers in the prefectural assemblies, and it is these politicians who get out the votes at election time. If an upper house candidate is to win, he must not alienate any of these prefectural politicians. The upper house candidate in the prefectural district will therefore play down his factional ties.

Elections to the upper house do not occur as frequently as elections to the lower house; the term of office for the councillors is six years, with half the members being elected every three years.[58] The councillor is not under the unrelenting pressure of the lower house member to stand on the hustings at a moment's notice. When the councillor does stand for elections, he needs funds, which may come in part from

---

[56] Japan. "Kōshoku Senkyo Hō" [Public Offices Election Law] in *Roppō Zensho* [Compendium of Laws] (Tokyo: Iwanami, 1960). Art. 4, par. 2. [57] *Ibid.* [58] Japan, *Constitution*, Art. 46.

the faction leader. But much can happen to a faction and its power during his six-year term. Prudence dictates that the councillor adopt a historical perspective; his allegiance to one faction need not be unswerving. These are all good reasons why the councillors have maintained their independence. But there are also strong forces pushing the factions towards them, and the greatest of these is the party presidential election: the councillors control about one-third of the votes.

There has always been some degree of informal organization in the upper house. There was, for example, the Green Breeze Society formed by the famous writer Yamamoto Yūzō, which, while conservative in outlook, did not identify with any national party. There have also been informal clusters of politicians that can more properly be thought of as friendship clubs. The councillors have also associated with the powerful lower house politicians, but the association has never been close. It was not until after the second presidential election, in 1956, that factional recruiting started in earnest in the upper house.

In the 1956 party presidential elections, Kishi Nobusuke lost to Ishibashi Tanzan by seven ballots. Kishi was determined to recoup his defeat in the next election. Realizing the important role that the councillors could play in the elections, he enlisted the support of Matsuno Tsuruhei, then speaker of the upper house. Around Matsuno there was an informal group of followers and confidantes. Using this group as a nucleus, Matsuno set about building a faction in the upper house. This faction came to be known as the Seishin Club and its members were councillors who had previously been associated with the factions of Kishi and his brother, Satō Eisaku.

Action bred counteraction. The other faction leaders were not willing to give Kishi a free hand in organizing the upper house. Strategy was plotted, councillors enlisted, alliances made, and in due course, the Mizuho Club was brought into existence. This club was composed of the councillors associated with three other lower house factions: the Ōno, the Kōno, and the Fujiyama factions.

The formation of these two factions divided the upper house into opposing camps. It was inevitable that some of the councillors did not wish to be associated with either of these two factions, yet felt the need for some sort of organization if they were to maintain their voice in the affairs of the upper house. A third faction was born. This group was called the Konwa Society. It was composed of the councillors associated with the remaining three lower house factions: the Ikeda, Ishii, and Miki factions.

These three upper house factions control the appointments of members of the House of Councillors to the positions in the cabinet, the party, and the upper house. Some of the skirmishes between the factions for posts can become quite vigorous, but it seems to be generally agreed that the competition among the councillors is not so fierce as it is among the representatives, due in part to the more limited number of conservative councillors. "Most councillors can anticipate appointment to important posts in their sphere of activity not too many years after their first election, and appointment to a cabinet post after their second election," says Nabeshima Naotsugu, a conservative councillor.[59] This lack of competition for posts has not strengthened factional loyalty.

The upper house factions are led collectively, probably because the candidates for the prime minister traditionally come from the lower house. The Konwa Society has five or six men who watch out for its interests. The Mizuho Club has selected one or two councillors from each of the lower house factions with which they are associated. The Seishin Club has a single leader, but there are lieutenants with whom he consults. One result of this arrangement is that it does not breed the strong personal loyalties and dedication which some of the lower house members have for their factional leader.

Prime Minister Kishi's plan, in a sense, has failed. While

[59] Nabeshima Naotsugu, interview, February 3, 1966.

almost all the conservative councillors have been enrolled on the faction rosters, they have not become the fierce samurai they were supposed to be. Some councillors with aplomb forget to attend the gatherings of the lower house factions but attend the meetings of two of the upper house factions. The Japanese political world will undoubtedly see many changes in the years ahead, but the tepid attitude of the councillors towards the factions will in all likelihood remain the same.

The attitude of all the Dietmen toward the factions is ambivalent. For many years there has been a movement among them to "modernize" the party. The movement has meant various things to various politicians. But almost all the politicians will agree that abolition of the factions lies at the heart of it.

Each prime minister, after he has assumed office, has denounced the factions. "All my efforts will go into the abolition of the factions," said Ishibashi Tanzan. "Abolition of the factions is the voice of heaven," said Kishi Nobusuke. "Modernization of the party is my greatest responsibility," said Ikeda Hayato.[60] The present prime minister, Satō Eisaku, was only following a long tradition when he announced, "I start with myself," and dissolved the Thursday Club, his faction.[61] Various reform commissions have from time to time been created in the party and they too, have harshly criticised the factions. In 1963, after a year-long study of the party machinery, a group of better than a hundred conservative politicians headed by Miki Takeo concluded, "However inconsequential our studies have been, there is one thing which we strongly urge must be realized by all means and at all costs. That is the abolition of the factions."[62] In 1965, Tanaka Kakuei, then the secretary general of the party, issued another reform report, whose opening sentence read, "The essential condition for the Liberal Dem-

60 *Asahi Shimbun*, August 1, 1964, p. 2.

61 *Yomiuri Shimbun*, January 6, 1966, p. 2.

62 Jiyūminshutō, *Soshiki Chōsakai Tōshin* [Report of the Organization Investigation Commission] (Tokyo: Jiyūminshutō, January, 1964), p. 3. Hereafter called the *Miki Report*.

ocratic party to emerge and grow in both name and fact as a modern political party responsible for the nation's policies, is the abolition of the factions."[63]

All this criticism has not been without effect. Various reforms have been initiated and heralded as a further step in the modernization of the party. But they have done little more than nibble at the edges of the faction's authority. If the politicians really wanted the factions done away with, they would have long ago ceased to exist. Perhaps the reason for this equivocal attitude is that for every argument that can be summoned against the factions, there is a rebuttal.

One argument used against the factions is that they divert money to themselves that should be going into the party coffers. They use this money not to fight the opposition parties but to fight other conservatives. There is much substance to the argument, but one high party official offered the following observation:

> In reality, because the factions gather money separately from the party headquarters, we are able to maintain the strength of the Liberal Democratic party. If the factions were suddenly to stop gathering money, there would be a comparative increase in the funds going to the party. But it is certain that the total funds available to the conservatives would drop by one-half and the party's strength would gradually deteriorate.[64]

A second argument against the factions is that appointments to important posts in the party and cabinet are based primarily on factional balance. "When a new cabinet is being formed or a cabinet reshuffle is being carried out, the various factions in the Liberal Democratic party desperately strive to get members into the cabinet. . . . Whether the person would make a responsible cabinet minister is considered a

63 Jiyūminshutō, *Tōkindaika ni kansuru Kanjichō Shian* [Proposal of the Secretary General Concerning the Modernization of the Party] (n.p., September 25, 1965), p. 5.
64 *Yomiuri Shimbun*, January 11, 1966, p. 2.

matter of only secondary importance, [and] it is only natural that 'shoddy goods' should appear," explains one columnist.[65] In a later chapter we shall see that this charge is only partly true. But assuming for the moment that it is true, no other basis for choosing a cabinet has yet been advanced. The newspapers and the politicians talk about selecting "the right man for the right spot," but this is more a prayer than a principle and involves subjective judgments on which no two politicians will agree. If cabinets formed before the emergence of the factions are any precedent, Japan without the factions might be faced with (1) cabinets whose members rarely change, (2) cabinets chosen on the basis of age and seniority in the party, or (3) cabinets chosen to advance the private political interests of the prime minister. None of these criteria fulfills the ideal of the proper man for the proper slot. We will argue in a later chapter that the present system, while far from ideal, provides not only a check on the prime minister but also gives him the freedom to pick the right man by adjudicating competing claims of the factions.

A third charge against the factions is that "the greatest factor weakening the leadership of the party president is the existence of the factions. The party president is elected by the factions and therefore is dominated by them. He cannot exhibit independent leadership."[66] Kōno Kenzō, vice speaker of the upper house, argues the other side of the case. "The conservatives are the party perennially in power. If the factions weren't in existence, we would be under the dictatorship of the prime minister. The factions are a check on his unilateral actions."[67]

A fourth charge against the factions deals not with the strength but the quality of the prime minister. Under the present system, the prime minister is invariably a faction leader, but the qualities necessary to become a faction leader are not necessarily the qualities that are desired in a prime

[65] *Asahi Shimbun*, October 13, 1966, p. 1.
[66] *Miki Report*, p. 91.
[67] Kōno Kenzō, interview, January 25, 1966.

55

minister. Change the presidential election system, reformers urge, and do away with the factions. The *Yomiuri Shimbun* argues:

> As the method of selecting the party leader changes, the type of party leader will change, and finally, the type of person hoping to become the party leader will change. . . . What will be required of this new leadership will not be the talent for gathering money or maneuvering in the back room, but rather will be a philosophy and a policy, articulateness and wholesomeness, decision and dignity, prescience and insight into foreign and domestic affairs —all the attributes of a modern politician.[68]

The *Yomiuri* is correct in saying that changes in the electoral system will produce a different type of leader. But just what the changes should be no one has agreed upon. And whether the changes will produce the type of leader the *Yomiuri* wants is open to still further doubt. One could also argue the case the other way around. The factions didn't produce the leaders. The leaders produced the factions.

All these arguments, both pro and con, are interesting but beside the point. The factions are not going to be done away with by edict. They are an integral part of conservative politics. They fulfill the functions which the party does not. They are the responses of working politicians to a set of political conditions and their abolition would depend on a change in these conditions.

Factional politics have been successful because they have taken place in a closed political system. The party to date has been a parliamentary party. Its structure at best has only extended to the prefectural level. The men wielding the levers of power can be counted in the hundreds. Now there are signs that the party is gradually becoming popularly based. There is still a long road ahead, and progress is slow. The politicians find the present system comfortable and predictable and they are not going to change it quickly for a system that is un-

[68] *Yomiuri Shimbun*, January 30, 1966, p. 2.

certain and untried. But politicians, by the nature of their trade, try to give the people what they want.

Perhaps the factions can follow the lead of the party and become popularly based. The move of the former Kōno faction to hold a yearly convention for the young men who assist the faction's Dietmen in the elections can be interpreted as a move in this direction. But this is an extraordinarily expensive proposition. It is more probable that, as the Japanese people come to identify with the party, the factions will gradually fall back, lose their importance, and be severely limited in their functions. The future of the factions depends on the people.

CHAPTER III

The Economic Community

THE entertainment districts of Akasaka and Shimbashi are the backdrop for many political talks, particularly between the economic community and the politicians.

Ishikawa Tatsuzō offers the following description of such meetings in his 1966 political bestseller, *Corona of Gold*:

> At dusk, the streets of the Akasaka district fill with a heavy sound like that of an incoming tide. Lines of gleaming black limousines quietly flow through the streets, pause, then silently move on again. Passengers, middle-aged and elderly, alight and step through the gates of their favorite restaurants. Brightly colored shadows—flawlessly dressed geisha—are sucked in through the back entrances. Behind the enclosing high wooden fences, it is strangely quiet.
>
> This silence is what separates this place from the entertainment districts of the ordinary people. The strumming of the samisen is hardly ever heard. Instead of coming for entertainment, most customers have come for discreet discussions. Schemes buried in their breasts, masters of the alchemy of trickery, calculation, and barter, they quietly sip from their sake cups. Here is the back stage of Japanese politics, the kitchen for the Japanese economy. Here secret understandings are made, personal alliances are drawn. Japan is governed from Akasaka and Shimbashi—the districts of the willows and flowers.[1]

The economic community is an integral part of conservative politics. It has a powerful voice in the direction of conserva-

[1] Ishikawa Tatsuzō, *Kinkanshoku* [The Corona of Gold] (Tokyo: Shin-chō-sha, 1966), pp. 25-26.

tive affairs. The actual or potential power of a politician has often been described to me in terms of the number of times he meets with the businessmen each week. The *Asahi Shimbun* alleges that the prime minister can be found in meetings with members of the economic community "practically every night."[2] The *Mainichi Shimbun* gives the reason why:

In present-day Japan, it is impossible to sit in the chair of the prime minister without the support of the economic circles. The reason is that vast sums of money are needed in politics. To win the presidential election within the Liberal Democratic party, the faction leaders must distribute huge sums of money regularly in order to attract to their side a majority of the politicians, who are convinced that money is everything. Money has become, in effect, political power. In order to collect these sums of money, there is no recourse but to rely on economic circles.[3]

Historically, the economic community has been close to the government and the conservative parties, though not always in such a commanding position. During the Meiji era, the government took the lead in the industrialization of Japan and the businessmen listened carefully to what the officials said and did what they were told. But the industrialization process was to generate its own political power. The Russo-Japanese War of 1905, which tested Japan's economic strength as well as its military ardor, marked the emergence of the economic community as a force in Japanese politics. At the time, "the economic community was conceived to be only the men of finance."[4] But with the further development of industry, the stature of the manufacturers grew. After World War I, when the parties were beginning to come to

2 *Asahi Shimbun*, November 2, 1966, p. 1.
3 *Mainichi Shimbun*, December 16, 1966, p. 15.
4 *Nihon Kōgyō Kurabu Jūgonen Shi* [A History of the First Fifteen Years of the Japan Industrial Club] quoted in Suzuki Yukio, *Seiji o Ugokasu Keieisha* [Business Executives Who Move Politics] (Tokyo: Nihon Keizai Shimbun-sha, 1965), p. 30.

power, Japan's economy was dominated by the *zaibatsu*. The most powerful of these houses, the Mitsui and the Mitsubishi, formed close associations with the two leading political parties. The Mitsui stood behind the Friends of Constitutional Government Association and the Mitsubishi stood behind the Constitutional Democratic party.

This was an age of classic capitalism and it exhibited both the worst and best facets of the system. On the plus side of the ledger, the two houses of Mitsui and Mitsubishi wielded such overwhelming influence that there was little need for scrambling after special concessions. The reins of power were held by a very small group of men and these men upheld a strict political morality among themselves. On the debit side of the ledger, the government was clearly oligarchic: although universal male suffrage was granted in 1925, little was done to give the average Japanese a larger share in political society.

With the end of World War II, American occupation authorities fragmented holdings of the *zaibatsu* and purged their top officials. To fill the gap in leadership, "presidents and directors of the small companies on the fringes of the *zaibatsu* found themselves elevated to high positions in the business hierarchy. War had ravaged industry and dried up the sources of capital. Inflation and food shortages caused the labor movement to become both radical and violent. These new managers had all they could do to handle the affairs of the day."[5] But as the years passed, business gradually restored its close connections with the political world. Today, there is a strong trend towards the further consolidation of Japanese business. But no one group controls the Japanese economy. The first question, then, is what constitutes the economic community as a force in postwar Japanese politics? It is those men who gather or contribute funds to the political world, or are able to influence the making of national decisions, or both. There are four groups of such men, which overlap considerably in membership.

[5] *Ibid.*, p. 31.

The first group comprises leaders of basic industries and large financial institutions of Japan. Examples of the industries are steel, gas, and electric power, and examples of the men who represent them are Inayama Yoshihiro, the president of Yawata Iron and Steel Company, Kikawada Kazutaka, the president of Tokyo Electric Power Company, and Anzai Masao, the president of Shōwa Denkō Company. The financial institutions are chiefly banks, led by such men as Iwasa Yoshizane, president of the Fuji Bank, Satō Kiichirō, chairman of the board of the Mitsui Bank, and Tajitsu Wataru, the president of the Mitsubishi Bank.

The second group is composed of the representatives of the four major economic organizations: the Federation of Economic Organizations, the Japan Chamber of Commerce, the Japan Committee for Economic Development, and the Japan Federation of Employers' Organizations.

The Federation of Economic Organizations is clearly the representative of big business. All major companies and institutions have seats and the occupant is usually the president of the company. The Japan Chamber of Commerce has a much broader membership. It regards itself as a spokesman for small and medium-size businesses as well as for the larger companies. The Japan Committee for Economic Development is unique. Formed immediately after the war to cope with the problems of Japan's economic recovery, it is composed of like-thinking and, in their words, "progressive businessmen banded together without a regard for rank of industry." The Japan Federation of Employers' Organizations concerns itself chiefly with labor relations. When Japanese labor became organized nationally after the war, this organization was set up to counter it.

The third group within the economic community is made up of owners of concerns. Men who fall into this group range from Matsushita Kōnosuke of the Matsushita Electrical Industries, Idemitsu Sazō of the Idemitsu Oil Company, and Ishibashi Shōjirō of the Bridgestone Tire Company, to Nagata Masaichi of Daiei Motion Pictures and Osano Kenji of

61

International Motors. The fourth group includes the representatives of industrial federations and the leaders of small and medium-sized enterprises. Examples of the federations are the Sake Brewers' Federation, Life Insurance Federation and Ōsaka Taxi Association. Examples of the leaders are easy enough to cite, but their names are unimportant. Their strength comes from their numbers. There are about 700,000 companies carried on the tax rolls of the Finance Ministry.[6] Even if only a fraction of them make political contributions (and these contributions may be small), they still may well constitute the bedrock of financial support for the conservative party.

Men in the first two groups, the representatives of the first-line companies and the officers in the economic federation, constitute the mainstream of the economic community, and it is to them that the politicians pay the most attention. "At present, economics and politics are one. But in order to maintain an intimate connection between them, a channel is needed. The mainstream of the economic community fulfils this role. . . ."[7] This mainstream of the economic community has several characteristics which should be noted.

First of all, most of these men have their offices in Tokyo. "There are some businessmen in Ōsaka who commute regularly to Tokyo, says Ōwada Toshio, an economic reporter for the *Sankei Shimbun*.[8] "Hotta Shōzō of the Sumitomo Bank is an example and he should be regarded as a leader. You shouldn't overlook Ishida Taizō of Toyota Motors who comes from Nagoya. But as a general rule, the economic community and its leaders are based in Tokyo." The business of influencing a government is hard work, requiring constant presence in the capital.

The second characteristic of the men in the mainstream of the economic community is that they are managers and

---

[6] *Asahi Shimbun*, December 15, 1966, p. 15.

[7] Fukumoto Kunio, "Kansai Zaikai no Shisō to Kōdō" [Thought and Activities of Kansai Business Community], *Chūō Kōron* (April 1964), p. 65.

[8] Ōwada Toshio, interview, November 22, 1966.

administrators. One reason is that the largest concerns of Japan can no longer afford the luxury of private ownership. Most of them have gone public. The true capitalists, the owners of industry, occupy a distinctly secondary place. They are generally first-generation capitalists. They have started their business from scratch, and the main brunt of their energy goes into the development of their company. They appear to have little time for politics. "Honda is a good example," says Arakawa Hiroshi, a former editorial writer on the *Sankei Shimbun*.[9] "He holds a respected international position in the world of motors, particularly motorcycles. All his energies go into his company, which he built from nothing. He has little to do with the politicians."

A third characteristic is that entrepreneurial ability, size of industry, or rank within the industry do not necessarily determine the degree of influence a man has in the economic community. It is true that Ishizaka Taizō, the president of the Federation of Economic Organizations, made his reputation bolstering the flagging fortunes of the Tōshiba Industries and resolving a serious labor dispute in which this company was involved. But the second in command, Uemura Kōgorō, is a former bureaucrat and has never managed a major industry. Kosaka Tokusaburō, the spokesman for the Japan Federation of Employers' Organizations, is the president of only a middle-sized chemical concern.

A fourth characteristic is that none of the leaders in the economic community, despite their deep involvement in the politics of Japan, are likely to become legislators. Indeed, one man, Fujii Heigo, a vice-president of Yawata Iron and Steel Company and a vice-chairman on the Japan Committee for Economic Development, has followed the opposite course, serving as a member of the upper house before becoming a businessman. Although Diet members may have had business experience, there is a tradition in Japan that top businessmen do not run for a seat in the lower house. Yamashita Seiichi, the managing director of the Japan Committee

9 Arakawa Hiroshi, interview, November 22, 1966.

for Economic Development, explains one of the reasons for the tradition: "By the time a businessman has risen high enough in his company to be in a position to run for office, he is usually pretty old. He doesn't want to start all over again as a freshman Dietman."[10] Exceptions can be found. Fujiyama Aiichirō, a member of the lower house and a faction leader in the conservative party, was once a businessman. But other than undertaking an occasional economic mission at the government's request, in general the leaders of the economic community do not seek high office, either appointive or elective, in the government.

How does the economic community get its views across to the political world?

First, all the big economic federations have large and competent research staffs who prepare formal position papers on aspects of the economy or, indeed, on any matter of interest to them, which they submit formally to the prime minister. A second avenue is through the ministries. Around each ministry have been created deliberation councils—half-private, half-public bodies which consider new policies. The members of the economic community always have seats reserved for them on these organs. A third route is through the party leaders and the party committees. The party has a policy affairs research council which considers policies for the party. The members of the economic community appear before its divisions and commissions to give their views. Members of the economic community are also in regular contact with the top members of the party. There is, for example, the Third Thursday Society, a group composed of the top members of the Japan Committee for Economic Development and the three top members of the party, which meet, as its title states, on the third Thursday of every month to confer. These are the formal routes of communication.

The members of the economic community are also exceptionally conscious of the press. If they have something to say, it invariably finds its way into the newspapers. The eco-

[10] Yamashita Seiichi, interview, November 22, 1966.

nomic pages, of course, they dominate with ease, but it is not at all unusual to find their views on the front pages. The economic recommendations of the federations many times receive detailed treatment in the newspapers. There are also economic magazines that explain their interests. Moreover, federation leaders appear frequently on public affairs and panel shows on television. Their public relations sense extends even to the field of music: they are the sponsors of a music group, the Min'on, which arranges and sponsors musical concerts throughout the nation so that this field will not be dominated by the left.

There are also informal channels of communication. Around each minister and important member of the party, the members of the economic community have formed clubs. Each meets with its politician at least once a month, sometimes more often. The members of the economic community maintain that these gatherings are social. "There is almost no serious talk between the leaders of industry and the politicians there. These clubs go no farther than being occasions for a political leader and his financial sponsors to get to know each other better."[11]

One of these clubs, which is currently attracting a great deal of attention because it is built around the prime minister, is the Chōei Society. Anzai Hiroshi, the vice president of the Tokyo Gas Company, describes the group in these words, "Since Mr. Satō was not too well known among the business community, the Chōei Society, was formed around him about three years ago. We selected one member from each of the first-line companies and put the club together. We gather and chat with Mr. Satō about once a month, usually from six to about seven in the evening. At least forty members are always present and we talk freely about current problems. . . . Mr. Satō actively seeks out the opinions of the veterans of the group . . . but the atmosphere is light and informal."[12] This

11 *Asahi Shimbun*, evening edition, November 2, 1966, p. 1.

12 "Satō Eisaku-shi o Meguru Jimmyaku" [Men Surrounding Mr. Satō Eisaku], *Top Research*, Special Spring Issue, 1966, pp. 23-24.

club is unusual in that its membership is large and composed almost exclusively of company presidents, with a sprinkling of bank directors. Usually, the membership of such a club is much smaller and may not be so prestigious. But the mood of the Chōei Society seems to be similar to that of other clubs —an informal gathering with free-wheeling conversation.

At one time, Prime Minister Satō Eisaku was meeting regularly with more than twenty of these groups, which gave him effective liaison with about 280 top executives.[13] This is exceptional, even for a prime minister. Prime Minister Kishi, who also believed in maintaining a wide range of contacts with the economic community, was not able to maintain this pace. Prime Minister Ikeda followed the principle of having much more intimate contact with a smaller group of industrialists and financiers.

The members of the economic community are also in effective liaison with the factions and their leaders, as well as with the politicians who occupy important posts in the government and the party. Most of the factions have ancillary organizations by which the members of the economic community and the members of the faction are brought together on a regular basis to exchange views. For example, the former Ikeda faction has two groups, the Kōchikai and the Suehiro Society. The Kōchikai meets regularly for study sessions, usually once a week, to listen to formal lectures on problems facing the nation by various experts drawn from the bureaucracy and business. All members of the faction as well as a sizeable number of bureaucrats and businessmen attend. The people in attendance may well number in the hundreds. The Suehiro Society is a much more limited group. Here the leaders of the faction meet with a handful of members of the economic community, a little more than forty in all. The old Kōno organization had the same type of organization. Its two clubs were the Azabudai Club, the general meeting of the members of the faction and the economic community, and the Sankin

13 Suzuki, *Keieisha*, pp. 121-128.

Society, a group of about forty businessmen. The latter group met once a month, usually on the third Friday. It was headed by Nagata Masaichi of Daiei Motion Pictures, Hagiwara Kichitarō of Hokkaido Mining and Shipping, and Kawai Yoshinari of the Komatsu Manufacturing Company. These three industrialists were instrumental in talking Kōno out of launching a new conservative party in 1960.[14]

There are also occasions when the politicians and the members of the economic community get together to form a group to deal with a subject of common interest. There is, for example, the Japan-Republic of China Cooperation Committee. The press refers to this organization as "the Taiwan lobby," which is certainly a misnomer. Among its members from the political side are Yoshida Shigeru and Kishi Nobusuke, both former prime ministers; Fukuda Takeo, the present secretary general of the party; Funada Naka, a former speaker of the lower house; and Ishii Mitsujirō, the present speaker of the lower house. From the economic community are Adachi Tadashi, the president of the Japan Chamber of Commerce, and Ishizaka Taizō, the president of the Federation of Economic Organizations. These men do not put pressure on the center of government; they are the center of government. "The committee was formed in 1956 and is composed of twelve members from the political and economic community. From time to time, it visits Taiwan and works for, among other things, the continuation of economic aid to the Republic of China."[15]

Finally, it is not an uncommon practice for the major companies to place politicians on the payroll as advisors or consultants. Most of the politicians and members of the economic community went to the same schools, and this tie is utilized for the exchange of ideas. Marriage and family ties are also important. For example, Anzai Masao, the president of

[14] *Asahi Shimbun*, August 19, 1960, p. 2.
[15] *Ibid.*, September 17, 1966, p. 2.

67

Shōwa Denkō Company, is connected through family ties to five conservative politicians.[16]

Out of this myriad of opportunities for contact, a torrent of talk gushes through the political world; it is difficult to tell who is saying what to whom and whether the advice is being followed. I asked a news executive for the Japan Broadcasting Corporation how he copes with this ceaseless dialogue. His answer was:

Each prime minister has his key political brains and economic advisors and their views must always be regarded with special care. But generally, I just listen first to the reporters running after the politicians and then to the reporters covering the business community. When they tell me different things, I relax. But when both groups of reporters start telling me the same thing, I pay close attention. Something is about to happen.[17]

Why does the economic community maintain such close association with the political world? What are its interests and motives?

The primary concern of the economic community (aside from making a profit) is to maintain and develop a modern capitalist system. All reporters, businessmen, and politicians are unanimous in declaring this to be the community's ultimate function, although each man formulates the statement a little differently. Ōwada Toshio, a reporter on the *Sankei Shimbun*, puts it this way: "The aim of the economic community is to establish long-term economic stability. Anything connected with this goal they take an interest in."[18] Suzuki Yukio, an editorial writer on the *Nihon Keizai Shimbun*, explains this interest more fully:

16 Yashiro, Kenzō, "Seizaikai no Jimmyaku o Saguru" [Probing the Human Sources of the Political and Economic Community], *Ekonomisuto*, Vol. 42, no. 15 (April 10, 1964), p. 66.
17 Ogata Akira, interview, April 1, 1965.
18 Ōwada Toshio, interview, November 22, 1966.

In order to maintain the existing system and protect the general interests of capital, the economic community seeks benefits by supplying political funds. . . . They oppose the labor unions and the revisionist forces through a common front of management organizations . . . and by daily P.R. efforts in the mass media. From time to time, they conciliate (and occasionally instigate) fights in the conservative political world and mediate differences among various industries, between industries and finance, between industries and the bureaucracy. In short, their task is to exercise 'environmental control' to protect the general interests of capital.[19]

Arakawa Hiroshi, a former editorial writer for the *Sankei Shimbun*, gives a concrete example: "The big topic in the economic community today is taking the restrictions off the free movement of capital into the country. All the leaders of the economic community are urging this policy on the government. This move will open Japan to the entry of some of the large concerns of the West and I don't suppose there is any business leader who doesn't worry that his industry will be hurt. But they have put aside their individual worries and are trying to work for the benefit of the nation. They realize that Japanese business must be able to stand without artificial supports in the international economy if it is to continue to progress."[20] The principal spokesmen for this over-all goal are the leaders of the economic federations.

The second goal of the economic community—and in this case, it is the industrial federations that are the most interested and the most outspoken—is to secure favorable treatment for their particular segment of the economy. The Taxi Federation opposes a rise in the tax on propane gas, a fuel to which they all switched after the taxes on gasoline became too high. The Automobile Manufacturers' Association fights a rise in the age qualification for driving licenses. The chemi-

[19] Suzuki, *Keieisha*, p. 28.
[20] Arakawa Hiroshi, interview, November 22, 1965.

69

cal manufacturers fight with the agricultural cooperatives over the price of fertilizer. The banks oppose changes in conditions for taxing depositors' funds. The Sake Brewers' Federation wants to buy rice at a favorable price. The trucking industry wants to avoid putting speed recording devices on its vehicles. Everybody wants special considerations on the taxes his industry pays.

In this role, the economic community is no more than a pressure group and many times not only are industries pitted against industries, but companies against companies with the same industry. Two American companies, Grumman and Lockheed, formed special relationships with separate Japanese trade companies to sell military hardware to Japan. The fight over which fighter plane to adopt for Japan's defense reached epic proportions. The steel industry in 1965 found that it had overproduced. The government tried to cut back by reducing the production quotas of the various steel companies. Sumitomo, which had just finished building a new plant, found these new quotas discriminatory. The squabble lasted for several months. A similar case took place in the spinning industry; Nisshimbō found quotas unsatisfactory.

In all such disputes, the industry first tries to resolve the dispute by itself. Indeed, one of the major tasks of the top leaders of the economic community is to find acceptable compromises. But almost inevitably the politicians and the bureaucrats find themselves embroiled. The bureaucrats have the power to license and to regulate. The politicians have the power of political decision. "It's like a game of paper, scissors, and rock," says Kōno Kenzō, a vice speaker of the upper house, "The businessmen have influence over the politicians, the politicians control the bureaucracy, and the bureaucrats keep the businessmen in line. It's a natural system of checks and balances. It's also a rough game, but that's politics all over."[21]

Individual companies have a third motive in maintaining a close relation with the political world: to secure special

[21] Kōno Kenzō, interview, January 25, 1966.

concessions. The *Asahi Shimbun* quotes an unnamed source within the construction industry who explains what this means for that particular industry:

> In the case of most public construction, talks within the industry decide whose turn it is to get the contract. However, on occasion, there are cases when the agency controlling the bidding lets it be known indirectly to leaders in the industry that the contract should go to such and such a company. We men in the business call this the 'voice of heaven' or the 'august command.' When the agency controlling the bidding itself breaks the rules for competitive bidding it is pretty clear that the agency has had heavy pressure put on it by a powerful politician. Even though we complain among ourselves that such and such a company really shelled out the money, we follow the august command and allow the bid to go to such and such a company. On the surface, of course, it appears that that company won the contract with the most favorable bid.[22]

All this is, of course, highly illegal. The spokesmen for the economic community maintain that this sort of hanky-panky is the exception; the press and other critics maintain that it happens all too frequently. It is hard to judge who is correct.

Competition also furnishes a motive. Competition at all levels of the Japanese economic world is hot and furious. When a company learns that its competitor is actively seeking out contacts in the political world, it many times believes that it too must make a similar effort, lest it be left out in the cold. All elements of the economic community fulminate against "excessive competition" and the listener suspects that they mean competition for the help of the political world as well.

Finally, the prestige of the individual officers of the major companies constitutes a motive. There is hardly an industry

[22] *Asahi Shimbun*, evening edition, November 1, 1966, p. 1.

in Japan that has sufficient capital. Most operate under a debt burden that would be intolerable in other countries. The Japanese executive is not measured by his ability to create new industrial techniques, to expand sales, or to develop new markets. Rather, he is judged by his talent to borrow money and manage his debt. In brief, his standing in the business community will be determined by his reputation with the nation's financial institutions. A businessman's close association with the political world will assist him in dealing with the banks, since they, in turn, are increasingly subject to political control.

From the politicians' point of view, the reason they pay such careful attention to the voice of the economic community is that the community is the principal source of political funds. The next question we pose is how, then, are political contributions made to the political community?

Generally, financial contributions flow the same way that opinion does: to the parties and to the factions and individual politicians. The most orthodox route is through the People's Association, a group of paid fund raisers who work in the actual party headquarters in Tokyo and in each of the prefectural federations. This association is a clearing house for funds from the various industries given in the association's name to the party. Most business concerns contribute to this organization on a regular basis. Funds that are collected this way cover about 70% of the daily expenses of the party.[23] The association also makes further assessments upon its members at times when the party is in special need of funds. In 1963 and 1966, for example, special contributions were solicited for the general elections. In 1964, a drive was made for funds to cover the public relations costs to counteract a scare campaign of the socialists and communists against the entry of an American nuclear-powered submarine into a Japanese port. In 1965, funds were gathered to publicize the benefits to be gained from re-establishing relations with South

[23] *Asahi Shimbun*, September 29, 1966, p. 2.

Korea. Some industries, however, prefer to give their money directly to the party, usually through its secretary general.

But the People's Association is not the only recipient of funds. Members of the economic community also give to the factions and individual politicians. The *Asahi Shimbun* explains why:

> Contributions made to the People's Association are absolutely colorless. The People's Association has a firm policy in the case of funds given to the Liberal Democratic party, not to reveal either the donor or the amount that he gave. The contributor, no matter how much money he puts out, cannot expect a favor in return. Most of the large corporations only give enough to the People's Association to maintain a formal relationship. A greater proportion of their funds goes to the individual politicians and the factions.[24]

Because members of the economic community make financial gifts to the various factions, speculation has arisen that the economic community can be divided along factional lines. A review of the reports delivered to the Home Ministry for 1965 shows that the Beer Federation gave both to the party and to the Ikeda faction, but to no other faction. Similarly, the Ōsaka Taxi Association gave to the party and the Miki faction. Mitsui Trading Company gave to the party and to the old Kōno faction, but the largest share of its political contributions went to the Kawashima faction. On the other hand, the Mitsui Group, Idemitsu Oil Company, and Itō Chū Trading Company, the Marubeni-Iida Trading Company, and the Matsushita Electrical Industry all distributed their funds to all the factions fairly equally.[25] One critic notes:

> The financial relationships between the first-line companies and the factions within the Liberal Democratic party are entangled with such complicated matters as

[24] *Ibid.*
[25] From figures obtained from Home Ministry reports.

73

the financial condition of the company, the personal relations of the company president, and the election district in which the company's major plant is located. Yet two patterns can be seen. In one case, funds are concentrated on a single designated faction. In the other case, funds are distributed to all factions, though there may be differences in the amount.[26]

However the money may flow, most members of the economic community do not openly favor one faction. For example, they will not limit their attendance to one of the faction meetings, but will in most instances attend several of them. "The top members of the economic community do not want to be identified with a specific faction," says Ōwada Toshio. "Their interests are much broader."[27]

Moreover, some of the large companies have institutionalized their political contributions. In such companies, the total amount to be given to the political world is decided at a meeting of the board of directors; meetings at a lower level decide how the funds should be distributed. Most of the first-line companies have a vice president and staff who collect data on the parties, maintain liaison with the politicians, and keep abreast of policy considerations. The factions, of course, are considered in these deliberations. The *Mainichi Shimbun* cites the following case: "In one first-line company a large chart is kept on which are listed the amounts of money to be given each faction each month. When the faction representative appears, this amount is handed over. When the factions ask for more than their monthly allotment, the directors of the company must make a decision."[28] What one company gives, another company soon finds out about; all reach a rough understanding on the amounts to be given to the political world.

26 Ōyama Ryōichi, "Saikyō Pawā Eriito—Zaikai" [The Economic Community—The Strongest Power Elite], *Ekonomisuto*, Vol. 42, no. 15 (April 10, 1964), p. 48.
27 Ōwada Toshio, interview, November 22, 1966.
28 *Mainichi Shimbun*, December 20, 1966, p. 15.

Giving funds to the individual politicians has also been criticized. The charge is frequently heard that these funds are mainly directed towards concession-hunting and bolstering the prestige of a company officer rather than furthering the general position of capital. We need only note here that this is not the only motive. Many businessmen talk highmindedly among themselves about "bringing up the politicians."[29] When they spot a promising politician, they like to insure that financial problems will not prevent him from winning at the polls or rising in the party. This sort of "scholarship" cannot be given through the party. Other businessmen talk about their long association with some of the senior politicians. Many times, they went to school together and have risen stride by stride in their separate worlds. Certainly a contribution to an old friend is not inappropriate, they argue. For the recipient politician, these funds have a dual significance. Not only do they help him defray his expenses but they also give him standing in the political world. "One of the standards by which a politician is judged is his ability to gather funds. It may well be the major standard. High aspirations, ability, articulateness, integrity are all said to be secondary or tertiary qualifications," says the *Asahi Shimbun*.[30] Another critic seconds this view: "It may well be that the only criterion used to decide a politician's ability is his capacity to gather funds."[31] Needless to say, the political community has come under strong attack for this attitude.

But few censure the business community for forming a close association with the politicians. Most responsible critics acknowledge that industry, banking, and commerce are a major concern of an industrialized state and that their interests must be recognized. Nor is the businessman indicted for making political contributions. Politics costs money, and the money must come from somewhere. But money and politics are flammable tinder. There are cases where the relationship

29 *Asahi Shimbun*, November 22, 1965, p. 2.
30 *Ibid.*, October 4, 1966, p. 1.
31 Togawa Isamu, *Seiji Shikin* [Political Funds] (Tokyo: Uchida Rōkakuho, 1961), p. 165.

between the politician and the businessman has been ignited by special interest—to the detriment of both the economic community and the political world. Kobayashi Ataru, a former banker and an influential figure within the economic community, has angrily criticized politician and businessman alike:

> We must sit up and give serious thought to dissolving the distrust the people have . . . towards capitalism itself. At the same time, the politicians should not be so greedy for money. We'll take care to supply the necessary funds through legitimate channels. The politician should use the money where he believes it to be appropriate without being conscious of who gave it to him. Politics are dirty because the politicians think that strings are attached to the money. They ought to forget who gave them the money. And the businessmen constantly reminding the politicians where they got the money is also wrong. Individual political contributions ought to be done away with.[32]

Kobayashi is not alone in his views. Prime Minister Satō Eisaku has spoken publicly in the same tone to the same theme. "Political funds are a problem. . . . In particular, I think that the collection of political funds by individuals ought to be restricted. A system ought to be created whereby funds are centered on the parties."[33] Men of good will and high moral purpose in both the political world and the economic community have expended great energies in trying to build an institutional framework that would insure adequate political funds, yet make them impervious to private manipulation. "It is true that the political and economic worlds have repeatedly put considerable effort into rationalizing political contributions. But it must be said that much remains to be done."[34]

[32] Suzuki, *Keieisha*, p. 70.
[33] *Sankei Shimbun*, evening edition, December 5, 1966, p. 1.
[34] Togawa, *Seiji Shikin*, p. 185.

THE ECONOMIC COMMUNITY

When party politics were reborn in the postwar world, there were virtually no checks on political funds. Companies had to report some contributions to the tax office and the politicians had to record some election expenses. Stimulus to reform came with the exposure of several financial scandals. Considerable research was done on American and English legislation, and in July, 1948, with the unanimous consent of both parties, Japan passed a political fund regulation law. Its main provision was that all political contributions must be reported to the government and made public twice a year. The law has been strengthened and revised several times but the general consensus is, as one political reporter airily comments, "It has more holes than a wicker basket."[35]

So public legislation was not the panacea it was held out to be. The next impetus towards reform came in 1955. One move was initiated by the politicians and another by the economic community.

When the Liberal Democratic party was created, the politicians decided to use the party law as a means of regulating political funds. They wrote provisions that set up a budget system for party expenditures and made these expenditures subject to the approval of the party conference, which met once a year.[36] Party finances became partially known to the public for the first time. The idea was exciting, but the implementation was weak. The budgets that have been presented to the party conference have been vague and never debated.

Anticipating general elections, two leaders of the economic community, Ishikawa Ichirō, then president of the Federation of Economic Organizations, and Fujiyama Aiichirō, then president of the chamber of commerce, decided in January, 1955 to try to pool contributions of the economic community. They created an ad hoc organization known as the

35 *Asahi Shimbun*, October 29, 1966, p. 4.
36 Jiyūminshutō, "Tōsoku" [Party Law] in *Wagatō no Kihon Hōshin* [Basic Policies of Our Party] (Tokyo: Jiyūminshutō Kōkoku Iinkai, 1966). Art. 96.

77

Economic Reconstruction Conference which was to serve as the central repository for voluntary contributions from the various companies and federations. Uemura Kōgorō was chosen as chairman, since he had no strong political coloration and no ties with any industry. The division of funds was made by committee and they were given in the conference's name.

Initially, the conference met with mixed success. Although its stated goal was the collection of three hundred million yen, it received only one hundred million yen. But other members of the business community found the concept stimulating. A second conference was started in Nagoya, and a third conference was begun among the small-sized and medium-sized enterprises. The businessmen decided to put the conference on a permanent basis. As time passed, the organization grew stronger and eventually proved to be one of the major sources of funds for the parties. Home Ministry reports show that from its inception in 1955 to 1960, it gave 25 hundred million yen and in addition, in the election of December, 1960, it was able to muster the all-time high of 800 million yen, of which 770 million went to the conservative party.[37]

But this election led to the demise of the organization. Businessmen had steadily been complaining about the rising costs of elections. Rising costs were acceptable if benefits accrued, they explained, but the conservatives had not been able to hold their own. Something was obviously wrong. A second complaint centered around the factions. One of the by-products of pooling contributions was supposed to be their elimination. Instead of fading away, the factions had become more prominent and more insistent in demanding funds from the individual businessman, the companies, and the industrial federations. Finally, the businessmen criticized the politicians for relying solely on the economic community for contributions and not trying to tap all sources.

The politicians also had their complaints. Channeling all

[37] Togawa, *Seiji Shikin*, p. 176.

funds through a single source, they said, made it appear that the politicians were the errand boys of the economic community. The leaders of the conference had become identified with Prime Minister Kishi, and many politicians suspected that the conference had become his personal fund-raising vehicle. Rather than indulge in further recrimination, the politicians and the businessmen decided by mutual consent to dissolve the organization.[38]

Dissolution left the financial ball in the politicians' court. A committee was appointed within the party to study the matter. Responding to the charge that the conservative politicians were the puppets of the business community, the committee decided to expand the party's base for fund-raising and appeal directly to the electorate. To prevent contributions from becoming the kitty of one faction, they recommended establishing a financial overseers' committee of five men, a figure they had picked up in their study of the financial arrangements of the English conservative party. Prime Minister Ikeda accepted their first recommendation, but suggested that the overseers' committee be expanded, and that these additional men also gather funds. The revised plan was accepted by the rest of the party. Forty men gathered and, splitting into groups of two and three, began canvassing the steel, coal, electric power, shipbuilding, maritime products, and spinning industries. There were some initial problems when some of the politicians began accusing each other of squirreling away some of the contributions for their own faction, but this accusation was dispelled by giving the committee factional balance.[39] Today, the financial committee has twelve members, headed by a chairman from the prime minister's faction. The politicians differ over the effectiveness of the committee.

The other recommendation of the committee—that financial appeals should be made directly to the electorate—seemed to have been forgotten in the early 1960's. But it

[38] Kosaka Zentarō, interview, May 25, 1966.
[39] Togawa, *Seiji Shikin*, p. 181.

was not long before the politicians returned to this theme. The dissolution of the Economic Reconstruction Conference and the establishment of the finance committee had done nothing but break up large contributions into small contributions, they argued. The source of the funds was still the economic community. Furthermore, although factional balance was maintained, politicians rather than disinterested businessmen were collecting the money, and the dangers of mismanagement were increased.

This thinking culminated in the launching of the People's Association in August, 1961. "This association," the founders declared, "is a body dedicated to building a bright and rich Japan and to fostering the growth of a modern conservative party built on the base of freedom and democracy."[40] Provision was made for individual and corporate membership. Although similar in many ways to the Economic Reconstruction Conference, it was different in three respects. First, the Economic Reconstruction Conference formally proclaimed its independence and contributed to all political parties; the People's Association was clearly a child of the Liberal Democratic party. The Economic Reconstruction Conference made no provision for registration or regular contributions; the People's Association provided for membership and monthly assessments. Finally, the Economic Reconstruction Conference was directed toward the business community; the People's Association hoped to enroll both the business community and the man in the street.

The dreams of basing the financial structure upon the general party membership did not materialize. As the secretary general's report of 1965 laboriously explained, "In principle, party funds should be generated among members of the party. From this point of view, there are still many unsatisfactory points in the present condition of the party. Among the regular party members, the number of contributors does not

---

[40] People's Association pamphlet quoted in *ibid.*, p. 182.

exceed ten percent."[41] Soga Yoshiharu, a member of the party's bureaucracy, explains: "Today, there are branch offices of the People's Association established in each of the prefectures. They gather funds, which they send to Tokyo. But with the exception of a few places like Tokyo and Ōsaka, these funds even fail to meet the expenses of the regional party chapters."[42]

Nevertheless, the People's Association has not been a complete failure. The economic community rallied to its support. The politicians continue to hope for a popularly based party with dues-paying members. But as of now, they are obliged to rely on the economic community for sustenance.

[41] Jiyūminshutō, *Tokindaika ni Kansuru Kanjichō Shian* [Proposal of the Secretary General Concerning the Modernization of the Party] (n.p., September 25, 1965), p. 67.
[42] Soga Yoshiharu, interview, October 19, 1966.

CHAPTER IV

The Party, The Prefectures, and The People

"AT THE time the party was formed," recalls Adachi Kōichi, one of the party bureaucrats, "if we used the word 'organization,' the party bigwigs would yell at us to stop imitating the communists."[1]

If this was the attitude in 1955, one can well imagine what attention the conservatives gave to organization before the war. True, both prewar parties, The Friends of Constitutional Government Association and the Constitutional Democratic party, had party branch offices in each prefectural capital, but only in rare instances could party organs be found in the other cities, towns, or villages. "Generally, the party branches were nothing more than liaison offices for the prefectural assemblymen and other local political leaders."[2]

In prewar Japan, the conservative politician did not really need party branches in the countryside. Japanese villages were communal. "The existence of the individual was not recognized except as an integral part of the community."[3] When villages voted, they usually voted as a unit. Within each of the villages, there was a leading family, usually a large landowner, who made the decisions for the village.[4] The task of the politician, then, was to win the support of the leading families. Since many of the politicians were the sons of one of the leading families in the district, and since these leading

[1] Quoted in Matsushita Keiichi, *Gendai Nihon no Seijiteki Kōsei* [Political Structure of Contemporary Japan] (Tokyo: Tokyo University Press, 1962), p. 149.

[2] *Asahi Shimbun*, August 26, 1962, p. 2.

[3] Fukutake Tadashi, "The Communal Character and Democratic Development of Farming Villages," *Journal of Social and Political Ideas in Japan*, Vol. 2, no. 3 (December 1964), p. 83.

[4] Miyamoto Ken'ichi, "Kusa no Ne Hoshushugi [Grassroots Conservatism]," in *Machi no Seiji, Mura no Seiji* [Town Politics, Village Politics] (Tokyo: Keisō Shobō, 1965), p. 341.

families were intertwined through marriage and other ties, the prewar politician could rely on his family to gather the vote. He needed no other organization. Kurogane Yasumi, a conservative Dietman whose father was a political leader before the war, says, "In the old days, the *jiban* [a politician's political domain] was most clearly defined and firm. There was no room at all for another politician to try to develop it for his own purposes."[5]

When the conservative parties merged in 1955, they adopted, despite opposition, plans for building a national organization as the framework for a popularly based party. "Not much was done right away," recalls Okamoto Masao, the chief of the party's Central Academy of Politics. "People were still accustomed to thinking in terms of the two conservative parties in existence before the merger. But by 1957, after Kishi Nobusuke became prime minister, things began to get underway."[6]

Each passing year has seen increased efforts to organize. Today, the National Organization Committee is one of the largest, in terms of staff, of the seven committees in the party. The party has launched an ambitious program of recruiting young men from the universities, giving them six months political training at the Central Academy of Politics, a school established by the party, and sending them into the regions as organizers. There are at present sixty of these organizers and the party intends to increase their number. Since 1960, the party has also paid the fees for high school graduates (between the ages of 25 and 30 years old) to take a two-year extension course in agriculture, followed by a stint at the Central Academy of Politics, with the understanding that these men will return to work in organizing the farm communities. The party's intent is to have one of these men in each village in Japan; 1,852 men have already completed the course.[7] The party has not been stingy in financing organiza-

5 *Asahi Shimbun*, August 26, 1962, p. 2.
6 Okamoto Masao, interview, October 19, 1966.
7 *Mainichi Shimbun*, May 4, 1966, p. 2.

tion. "I can't give you the exact figures," says Okamoto Masao, "but better than 10% of the total party budget is spent on organization."[8]

Prefectural federations have been established in all 46 prefectures, with headquarters in the prefectural capitals and branches—about 500 in all—spread throughout the countryside. Each prefectural federation is a microcosm of the party central headquarters. It has a federation chief, who corresponds to the party president, a secretary general, an executive council, a policy affairs research council, an organization committee and most of the other organs of the party headquarters in Tokyo. There is even a small party bureaucracy in each of the prefectures, ranging from three men in Tottori prefecture to twelve men in Hokkaido.[9]

The party has organized functionally as well as regionally. The national organization committee is broken down into ten bureaus: general affairs; agriculture, forestry and fisheries; commerce and industry; labor; peoples' livelihood; education; youth; women; speakers'; and research.[10] In almost all the prefectural federations, there is an equivalent subdivision. Particular attention is given to women and youth. Each has its own auxiliary organization within the party and two of the four seats given to each prefectural federation in the party conference, "the supreme organ of the party," are reserved for them.[11] If an occupation group is regionally based, it is attached to a prefectural federation. If the occupation group is nation-wide—postal workers are a case in point —it is attached directly to the national party headquarters. To groups and associations wary of being too closely identified with politics, the party is prepared to give a special designation called "friendly associations." "What a friendly association means in practice is that the leaders of the group are

[8] Okamoto Masao, interview, October 19, 1966.

[9] *Ibid.*

[10] Jiyūminshutō, "Tōsoku" [Party Law], in *Wagatō no Kihon Hōshin* [Basic Policies of Our Party] (Tokyo: Jiyūminshutō Kōkoku Iinkai, 1966), Art. 17.

[11] *Ibid.*, Art. 26.

84

clearly supporters of the party and they work on our behalf among their members," says Soga Yoshiharu, party bureaucrat concerned with organization.[12] There are more than six hundred groups which fall into this category.

On paper, this all reads quite well, but is the organization drive living up to expectations? Soga Yoshiharu says, "Every prefecture is different. Yamanashi and Shizuoka prefectures are our greatest successes. We have been able to do pretty well in Gumma, Hokkaido, and Chiba prefectures. Overall, we ought to be doing better."[13] Others are far harsher in their judgments. The scholar, Yoshimura Tadashi, writes, "The branches exist in name only. The prefectural federations are made up of a very small group—prefectural assemblymen, their families, and men with special connections. The general electorate has not joined."[14]

Yoshimura cites in evidence the case of Ibaraki prefecture. There are only 5,000 party members in a population of 2,047,000 and only 10% of these party members pay dues which amount to 200 yen (about $0.55) a year.[15] My own investigations in Chiba prefecture show the same pattern. In a population of 2,700,000, there are only 17,000 party members, 10,000 of which belong to the youth and ladies' auxiliaries. About 6% pay party dues. In October 1966, Japan had a population of 98,270,000.[16] In the same month, party headquarters stated dues-paying party members numbered 300,000.[17] The conclusion was drawn most descriptively by a party worker in Hiroshima. "The Liberal Democratic party is a ghost. It has no feet."[18]

Why is the Liberal Democratic party having such an uphill fight in organizing? One explanation centers on the quality of

12 Soga Yoshiharu, interview, October 19, 1966.
13 *Ibid.*
14 Yoshimura Tadashi, *Nihon Seiji no Shindan* [A Diagnosis of Japanese Politics] (Tokyo: Shinshin Shobō, 1964), p. 136.
15 *Ibid.*
16 *Asahi Evening News*, October 25, 1966, p. 1.
17 Okamoto Masao, interview, October 19, 1966.
18 *Asahi Shimbun*, August 5, 1964, p. 2.

regional leadership. Mori Kiyoshi, a former head of the National Organization Committee, speaks bluntly, "So long as we have old men leading the organization, local politics are not going to grow."[19] Soga Yoshiharu says, "The leaders in the regions don't understand the significance of party organization. They don't realize its importance."[20] A businessman in Kagoshima, the southernmost city of Japan, speaks of the leaders of the Kagoshima prefectural federation. "All those fellows do is ask you if you won't join the party, or fall out for a demonstration supporting a treaty, or give you sermons on 'new conservatism' or 'progress through stability.' They live in their own world. I've got to take care of myself."[21]

The young men in the party are particularly restive. Gotō Ichirō, a professor at Waseda University, observes, "The young like principles. The party has no platform which appeals to the young. There is a great deal of talk of the 'new conservatism' but there is very little 'ism' in it. I constantly hear the young men of the districts complaining that the Liberal Democratic party has no principles on which to stand and fight the opposition."[22] A young party worker says bitterly, "The leadership only wants you to join the party to win elections. There is no interest in daily party activities. I'm not going along with them."[23]

The party elders are frightened by this idealism in the young. They respond by excluding the young from the party councils. An example can be found in the by-elections for the upper house held in Hiroshima in January 1966. Two candidates were fighting for the party endorsement; one was backed by the farm organizations, the other, Nakatsui Makoto, was the speaker of the prefectural assembly. Because of his strength in the assembly, Nakatsui won the party endorsement handily, forcing the other candidate to run as an independent. One young party member commented, "The

19 *Ibid.*, February 17, 1966, p. 2.
20 Soga Yoshiharu, interview, October 19, 1966.
21 *Mainichi Shimbun*, May 3, 1966, p. 2.
22 Gotō Ichirō, interview, October 24, 1966.
23 *Asahi Shimbun*, August 5, 1964, p. 2.

young men were enthusiastic over the independent candidate. But now we and the women are not going to do anything. . . . I feel very strongly that the party nomination is not something that the bosses should decide on high and then push off on us. The opinion of the people of the prefecture should be sounded out. Recommendations should come from below."[24]

The same sentiment can be heard in Ōsaka. Nakayama Masaaki, the head of the youth section there, says, "The elders in the party, the city assemblymen and the regional assemblymen, appear to be afraid that if we form a youth section, the young men's vote will go to young assemblymen. At the party conference, they are willing to embrace the slogan, 'hope in the young,' but in reality, they are using all their energies to prevent young candidates from running for office."[25] Gotō Ichirō speaks in the same vein. "The party is willing to give two of the four seats in the prefectural delegation to the party conference to the youth and women. But each prefecture has only one vote and this vote is in the hands of the party elders. Thought should be given to allowing the others to have a voice in the party decisions."[26]

If the powers of the youth and women have not been harnessed, neither have the energies of the Dietmen always been given for the benefit of the party. The Hiroshima by-elections in January 1966 again offer a case in point. At least two Dietmen found it to their interests to do as little as possible to help Nakatsui, the speaker of the prefectural assembly. They were thinking of their own elections. The independent candidate was backed by the farm organizations and if they spoke out against him, the farm organizations might turn against them. "That's what they are frightened of," said Tominaga Sachio, the head of the prefectural party secretariat.[27]

But the major reason that the party has failed to grow is

24 *Ibid.*, February 15, 1966, p. 1.
25 *Yomiuri Shimbun*, January 13, 1966, p. 2.
26 Gotō Ichirō, interview, October 24, 1966.
27 *Asahi Shimbun*, February 15, 1966, p. 1.

HOW THE CONSERVATIVES RULE JAPAN

that each Dietman, particularly the members of the lower house, has his own individual support organization. The *kōenkai*, as this organization is called, occupies the center of the Dietmen's attention. Things which benefit the *kōenkai* receive their support. Things which do not benefit the *kōenkai* are left undone. Prime Minister Satō Eisaku says, "We have not yet been able to form a party organization. . . . If you ask why we are in this present state with no organization, the answer is that the *kōenkai* rather than the party is the important body in the election districts. . . . No matter how hard the party labors, it can't seem to build itself up as it wishes to."[28]

The *kōenkai* is a new institution which appeared only after the war. When the Occupation purged the old political leaders, their political monopoly in the countryside was broken. Land reforms removed the economic underpinning for the dominance by leading local families. The introduction of diversified farming and new agricultural techniques, coupled with the flow of population to the cities, disrupted ancient custom. The high fluidity of conservative politics—sixteen political parties were to appear and disappear in the first decade after the war—meant that no single party was able to fill the organizational gap. Each candidate was left to his own resources. These and other reasons can be adduced to explain the emergence of the *kōenkai*. But whatever the reasons were, "by 1952, most of the Dietmen had created *kōenkai* for themselves."[29]

For an institution that occupies such a central position in Japanese politics, the *kōenkai* has received very little critical examination. A party worker in Kyūshū states that the *kōenkai* in his region range from an absolute minimum of 30,000 members to 50,000 members.[30] Tanaka Kakuei, the

[28] Senkyo Seido Shingikai, *Dai-sanji Senkyo Seido Shingikai Giji Sokkiroku* [Transcript of the Proceedings of the Third Election System Deliberation Commission] (Tokyo: n.p., 1964), p. 177.
[29] Okamoto Masao, interview, October 19, 1966.
[30] *Mainichi Shimbun*, May 3, 1966, p. 2.

88

former secretary general, boasts that there are ten million people organized in *kōenkai* throughout the country.[31] Nakamura Eiichi, the head of the election section in the home ministry, believes that most of the *kōenkai* are organized along similar lines, but cautions that this belief comes from casual observation, not careful investigation.[32] Neither the press nor the scholars has given the *kōenkai* the scrutiny they deserve. Without a body of research to draw upon, I am unable to generalize. I present here the structure of one *kōenkai*— that of Nakasone Yasuhiro—which I have investigated myself.[33] I make no claim that it is representative. It is, however, one of the oldest, is highly developed in structure, and it gathers the vote.

The Kantō plain is spread out like a huge fan with Tokyo at the pivot. About a hundred kilometers due north is the outer edge of the fan where the mountains begin. This is Gumma prefecture. Gumma is divided into three election districts and it is the third election district in which we shall be interested. In the southern part of this district is the city of Takasaki, a former castle town, which used to guard the northern approaches to Tokyo. Takasaki contains over one quarter the population of the electoral district. Also in the south, there are other small cities: Tomioka, Fujioka, and Annaka. The region is a patchwork of factories and farms with industry growing more important each year and drawing more and more people into the district. To the north there are steep mountains. There is one small city, Shibukawa, in the north, but outside of its environs, lumbering and small scale farming are the principal occupations. There are some hot springs where resorts will be found. The population

---

[31] *Ibid.*

[32] Nakamura Eiichi, interview, August 8, 1966.

[33] A group of Waseda scholars have investigated the political conditions in and surrounding Takasaki. Their investigations include a description of the Nakasone organization. See Waseda Daigaku Shakaikagaku Kenkyūjo, "Tōhyō Kōdō no Kenkyū" [A Study of Voting Behavior], *Shakai Kagaku Tōkyū*, Vol. 4, nos. 1 and 2 (March, 1959). Note particularly the section by Uchida Mitsuru, pp. 151-175.

is sparse. Gumma 3 is the district from which Nakasone has won nine elections.

Nakasone did not originally intend to become a politician. He had graduated from Tokyo University and entered the bureaucracy of the Home Ministry. In 1946, worried about the communist drift of the nation in the aftermath of the war, he decided to resign from the Home Ministry, return to his native city of Takasaki where his family owned a large lumbering concern, and stand for election. He was twenty-eight years old at the time.[34]

Upon his return to Takasaki, Nakasone surrounded himself with other young men who shared the same political ideals. Together they formed the Blue Cloud School. When election time came, these young men went throughout the countryside to speak on Nakasone's behalf. Nakasone's family, despite their opposition to the second son becoming a politician instead of a respected bureaucrat, lent their good name. Nakasone loaded a white bicycle in the back of a charcoal-burning truck. Where the truck couldn't go, the bicycle could. Nakasone spoke in each village and hamlet. The family's reputation, the legend of the white bicycle, and the efforts of the Blue Cloud School became the basis of Nakasone's first election victory.

The idea of a group of young men speaking directly to the people appealed to Nakasone's idealistic instincts, and the school's obvious success in bringing in the vote made Nakasone determined to build the Blue Cloud School into a permanent organization to work for him at the polls. This was a decision of considerable significance. As we have mentioned earlier, the usual formula for electoral success was for the politician to reach some understanding with the leading village or district families and allow them to gather the vote. "Nakasone was one of the first politicians to build a political organization based directly on the people," says Ōta Takeo,

[34] Nakasone Yasuhiro, *et al., Warera Taishōkko* [We Children of the Taishō Era] (Tokyo: Tokuma Shoten, 1961), p. 35.

one of Nakasone's secretaries, "and the other politicians have imitated him because of his success."[35]

Nakasone's *kōenkai* has grown considerably since he first established it twenty years ago. Let us turn first to its formal structure.

At the peak of Nakasone's organization sits a single man, Satō Kanehide, who has the title of All-Federation Chief (*rengō kaichō*). Satō has been in this position since the inception of the organization and he is one of a small group which shares Nakasone's inner confidences on election strategy. He is close to the Nakasone family, having worked for many years in the lumber concern, and finally, with the blessings of the family, branched out and started his own lumber business. He has looked after Nakasone since he was a boy. Attached to the All-Federation Chief is a secretariat composed of four men who have the title of "secretaries" to Nakasone. This secretariat is headed by Satō Harushige, who has also been with Nakasone for twenty years. He and the secretaries are responsible for all the administration of the *kōenkai*. There is no family connection between the two Satōs.

The headquarters is located across a busy street from the lumber yard in Takasaki. On one side of Nakasone's modest private home, there is a low Japanese-style building which houses the secretaries in a jumble of desks, telephones, tubular steel chairs, and overstuffed sofas. On the other side of Nakasone's home, there is a large two-storied building which, on its ground floor, has offices and small conference rooms as well as a large mat-covered room which can hold about fifty people. There is a formal auditorium with a small stage on the second floor. Except for the mat-covered room, the building looks like a small-town high school built in the United States circa 1930. This is all the physical equipment of the *kōenkai*.

Nakasone has divided the third electoral district of Gumma into seven federations (*gun-shi rengōkai*). For the most part, the federations follow the boundaries of the counties which

[35] Ōta Takeo, interview, August 6, 1966.

91

existed shortly after the war. Since Takasaki has so many voters, it is organized as a separate federation. Each federation has a chief, one of whom is presently serving in the prefectural assembly, but "all of whom are of the caliber of prefectural assemblymen."[36]

Beneath the counties are the villages, towns, and cities, and in Nakasone's organization, beneath the federations are the support groups (kōenkai).[37] There are about 130 of them throughout the various municipalities. Takasaki is divided along school district boundaries, each of the school districts being regarded as a support group. Each support group has a leader, and about thirty percent of these are city or town assemblymen.

Each of the support groups is divided into four or five sections (shibu). The sections correspond to large aza, a subdivision of the Japanese village. Beneath the sections are liaison men (renrakuin) who are responsible for keeping in touch with the Nakasone supporters in the smallest Japanese political unit, the small aza, a subdivision of the large aza. "The support group leaders, the section chiefs, and the liaison men are selected on the basis of political influence, occupation, and degree of political enthusiasm. After consultation with the All-Federation Chief, each organ selects its own leader," explains Onozato Hiroshi, another secretary.[38] In practice, most of the leaders on the lower levels turn out to be farmers.

When Nakasone first put his support organization together, he thought in terms of attracting the interest and vote of the

[36] Ibid.

[37] There is great confusion over the word, kōenkai; it is used quite freely by the Japanese politicians to refer to different groups. In Nakasone's case, kōenkai is used to refer to the groups to be found on the third echelon, in the towns, villages, and cities. I have translated kōenkai here as support group. Nakasone also uses the word, kōenkai, to refer to the complete organization in the electoral district. In this case, I have transliterated the word or used the translation, support organization. Finally, the word kōenkai is used by the politicians to refer to their financial backers. Usually they will modify it to make their meaning clear but not always. I have tried to avoid the use of the word kōenkai in this sense.

[38] Onozato Hiroshi, interview, August 7, 1966.

senior male of each household. With his allegiance in hand, the rest of the family could be expected to follow suit. But the family system in Japan has slowly been changing. The master of the household can no longer expect the rest of the family to follow his instructions, particularly in political matters. Each member of the family must be solicited, one by one.

Nakasone has been obliged to set up a series of parallel organizations. For married women, there is the Ayame Club, formed in 1956. (Ayame is a type of iris.) While it follows in general the same organization format as the men's group, it is entirely separate. This organization differs from the male support organization in that it collects dues, sufficient to defer the costs of running the society. The Ayame Club is extremely active and is headed by Nakasone's sister-in-law. It publishes its own newspaper four times a year.

In 1962, a new society was formed for the young men under thirty, called the Comradery of Youths. The reasons for its formation were that many of the young men felt intimidated by, or at least not in agreement with, their elders. There was also the fear on the part of Nakasone that the senior support organization was growing old and not enough attention was being paid to the new generation. This young society is still being built. It is expected that some day it will follow the same structure as the senior support organization, but at the present time there are gaps in its structure. The young men's society is not regarded as completely independent of the parent organization, but rather a loosely connected subsidiary organ. This connection is maintained so that young men will naturally enter into the senior organization and supply it with fresh blood.

In 1965, Nakasone created another society for young unmarried women. It is called the Sumire Club. (Sumire is a type of violet.) At the time of the present writing, the society is just beginning to get organized.

Four different societies, six levels of command—the structure is complex. I asked Ōta Takeo if it was difficult to man-

age. He shrugged his shoulders. I asked him if it was worth the effort. He looked at me incredulously. "Even if there were elections tomorrow and we had done nothing to prepare for them, 65,000 people would fall out and vote for Nakasone."[39]
What are the interests which hold the *kōenkai* together?

First of all is service. Nakasone—more specifically, the secretaries in Takasaki and Tokyo—must perform an infinite number of services. Generally, these services can be broken down into three categories: intercession with the government, support for community activities, and personal assistance for the constituents.

Nakasone is called upon by the towns and villages to assist them in obtaining funds from the government for the construction of new facilities or the repair of existing facilities. Examples are the paving of a road, the building of a bridge, the laying of water pipes and a sewage system, the construction of a new high school gymnasium or train station, or the installation of an intra-village communications system; the last is particularly desired in areas to which phone lines have not yet been laid. Nakasone's role is to put pressure on the appropriate government offices in Tokyo. One of the boasts of the secretaries is that they have a high batting average with the Construction Ministry. (Nakasone was a member of the Kōno faction and Kōno served as construction minister on two occasions.) Each of these projects in the countryside stands as concrete testimony of the effectiveness of Nakasone as a member of the Diet. The secretaries are not at all hesitant about pointing these landmarks out.

Nakasone is also expected to intervene in schemes which the government proposes but which his constituents oppose. For example, the Construction Ministry has declared its intention to build the Yamba Dam across the Agatsuma River. A considerable controversy rages in Naganohara, since part

---

[39] Ōta Takeo, interview, August 6, 1966. In the January 1967 elections, six candidates split 338,861 votes in Gumma 3. Yamaguchi Tsuruo, a Socialist party candidate, was able to win with 50,747 votes. Nakasone received 72,731 votes. *Asahi Shimbun*, January 31, 1967, p. 7. The election system will be explained in the next chapter.

of the town will be flooded out. The opposition expects Nakasone to represent its interests. Nakasone is expected to lend his name and give financial assistance to the functions of the communities. For example, the Junior Chamber of Commerce in Tomioka plans to build an auditorium. Since the government will not put forward the funds, the Jaycees are going to try to raise the money through subscription by putting on several stage shows. It is up to Nakasone to recruit the entertainers in Tokyo. Charity drives must not only be endorsed, but the secretaries and other leaders of the *kōenkai* must help raise funds. Nakasone is also expected to take part in each village celebration, funeral, and wedding. He sends a wreath for the opening of a new store and for funerals. Money is given for festivals and weddings. If necessary, a secretary is dispatched to represent Nakasone.

The demands placed on Nakasone by individual citizens for personal services is without limit. He is called upon to represent his constituents in tax disputes with the government and to assist them in securing pensions. He serves as the intermediary in gathering capital to establish a new business or to refinance an old concern. He serves as a lawyer in automobile accident cases. He is obliged to assist in getting the constituent's children into school and getting new graduates a job in some business firm.

To be sure, Nakasone provides these services for his constituents whether they are members of his *kōenkai* or not. "But when the people ask for things," says Ōta Takeo, "we encourage them to work through the local branch of the *kōenkai* instead of coming directly to us. If the local leader is on his toes, he can usually persuade them to join the *kōenkai*."[40]

But Nakasone maintains that service is not everything. "My *kōenkai* is a group of people who share common political ideals," he insists.[41] It must be granted that he is dili-

[40] *Ibid.*
[41] Nakasone Yasuhiro, interview, October 31, 1966.

gent in developing a political philosophy among his followers. In January of each year, he delivers a "state of the union address" before 4,000 or so of his followers in Takasaki. In March, the members of the Comradery of Youths are specially inducted into the army—usually for two days and a night. The purpose is to instill a sense of order and discipline, heighten the sense of duty to the nation, and give experience in group living. In July, representatives of the *kōenkai* hold a general meeting lasting several days for serious discussions of defense, the economy, foreign affairs, and agriculture. In August and September, when the Diet is out of session, Nakasone makes an extensive lecture tour of his district. For his first twelve years as a Dietman, Nakasone made it a point to return to his constituency every weekend, but since 1959, these visits have become less frequent.

All this attention has had its effect. I have taken no surveys, but in wandering through Nakasone's district and talking to his supporters, I found them to be well informed on his views and in agreement with them. But Nakasone is an extremely persuasive speaker and the message he delivers is highly nationalistic and one with which any right-thinking Japanese would agree. I am not convinced that it is political ideals, rather than charisma, that is the basis of the relationship. I think Onozato Hiroshi struck close to the mark when he said, "If Nakasone were to go communist, I don't know what would happen. But otherwise, Nakasone's supporters will follow him wherever he may lead."[42] I will return to this question of personality later in the chapter.

For the local politicians, the appeal of the *kōenkai* comes from its numbers. If the *kōenkai* delivers the vote for Nakasone in general elections, it can also deliver the vote for the local politicians in the local elections. This support is particularly meaningful in the case of Nakasone's organization. Again hearkening back to political ideals, Ōta Takeo said,

[42] Onozato Hiroshi, interview, August 7, 1966.

The basic consideration in the selection of leaders in the organization was that they share the same political ideals as Nakasone. No attempt was made to graft on to the organization political bosses who already had power in the villages. I don't know about the other conservative politicians, but at the present time, the political influence of the leaders of the Nakasone organization comes from the organization itself and not from the outside.[43]

The various branches spend a great deal of their energies debating whom to support in the local elections. While the final decision will rest with Satō Kanehide or with Nakasone himself, they will usually go along with the recommendations of the subsidiary organs.

The *kōenkai* serves a social and cultural role in the community. This role is particularly apparent in the case of the Ayame Club. Its activities are almost entirely social. It sponsors folk dances, travel, sewing classes, and cooking schools. Nakasone chose to open his lead article in the January 1965 issue of the Ayame Club newspaper with congratulations to the Imperial family for the birth of another prince, combining nationalism and family affairs.[44] The men's organizations also carry out a "cultural program." Various experts and authorities—usually bureaucrats from the prefectural government, but occasionally a "man of culture" from Tokyo—speak before the support groups. Despite the advent of television, Japanese villages are lonely and isolated. The *kōenkai* can serve as the focal point for all community activities.

Finally, the *kōenkai* has come to be the fundamental political organ in the countryside. The party organs rarely extend down further than the prefectural capital. Even if a party branch is found in the outlying areas, it is usually part of some Dietman's *kōenkai*. "Party branches exist, but usually in name only. Look behind the party signboard and you

---

[43] Ōta Takeo, interview, August 6, 1966.
[44] *Ayame Kaiho*, January 1, 1966, p. 1.

usually find someone's *kōenkai*,"[45] says Soga Yoshiharu. If the farmer, shopkeeper, or inn owner wishes to play a part in politics, he must join a *kōenkai*.

Nakasone is not the only politician who has a *kōenkai* in the third electoral district of Gumma. Fukuda Takeo, who is presently serving as the secretary general of the party, and Obuchi Keizō, a young Dietman who has won two elections, also run from the same district, and they, too, have *kōenkai*. The organization of all three *kōenkai* is the same. Each has its federations, its support groups, its branches, and its liaison men. Each has its auxiliaries for the young men, the wives, the young ladies. The difference between them lies in the *jiban*, the areas in which their supporters are clustered. Nakasone and Fukuda have horizontal *jiban*, while Obuchi has a vertical *jiban*.

Localism is still a powerful force in Japanese politics. Most politicians are natives of the district from which they run for office. In the third district, Obuchi was born in Nakanojō, Agatsuma County; Fukuda was born in the town of Gumma, Gumma County; and Nakasone was born in the city of Takasaki.

The traditional method by which a conservative politician puts together enough votes to win a Diet seat is to work intensively on his birthplace and a few other specially selected areas. We have earlier discussed the communal aspects of the Japanese village. Social pressures can still be mustered to push the great majority of the inhabitants of a village into voting for a given candidate. The politician aims at gathering a great number of votes from a small number of villages. This is a traditional or vertical *jiban*.

Despite his youth, Obuchi has followed tradition. He inherited his *jiban* from his father, Obuchi Mitsuhei, a former Dietman; his father built the *jiban* shortly after the war. Obuchi's main strength lies in the north, in the county of Agatsuma. In the part of Nakanojō where he was born,

Obuchi received 1,014 of the 1,355 votes cast (74%).[46] Throughout Nakanojō he received 64.9% of the vote. And in other small northern villages, Obuchi received from 43% to 73% of the vote. Throughout the north, Obuchi got better than half the vote even though there were five other candidates. On the other hand, Obuchi did poorly in the south and in the cities (except for Shibukawa, a northern city). Obuchi was only able to pick up 6,784 votes out of a total of 94,387 votes (7.2%) in Takasaki and 4.2% of the vote in the town of Gumma. Obuchi, then, gets a lot of votes from a few places. His *jiban* is vertical.

Nakasone is just the opposite. He gathers his vote fairly equally throughout the entire electoral district. Although his birthplace is Takasaki, he only received 26.4% of the vote there; the sense of community is fast disappearing in the large cities. In the entire third district, Nakasone received 21.7% of the total vote. Yet his second-strongest area, the county of Kanra, gave him only 31.8% of its vote. Nakasone's *jiban* is not without its traditional aspects. He draws a fairly heavy percentage (26.5%) of the vote in the small city of Annaka, since it is the birthplace of his mother. But Nakasone's *jiban* is regarded as modern or horizontal.

Fukuda stands in between Nakasone and Obuchi. In the town of his birth, Gumma, he received 63.8% of the vote and the county of Gumma gave him 48.5% of its vote. Other than this area, Fukuda gathers the vote pretty equally from all parts of the electoral district.

The above percentages show most clearly which type of *jiban* the three candidates have. But they do not show the actual number of votes needed to win an election. Although the town of Gumma gave 63.8% of its vote to Fukuda, it has only 2.5% of the registered voters. In the graphs of Table 7, I have tried to show how the *jiban* looks when the number of votes is incorporated into the calculations.

46 All the figures used in this section on the *jiban* are calculated from statistics furnished in Gumma Ken. Senkyo Kanri Iinkai, *Senkyo no Kiroku* [Election Proceedings], January 29, 1967.

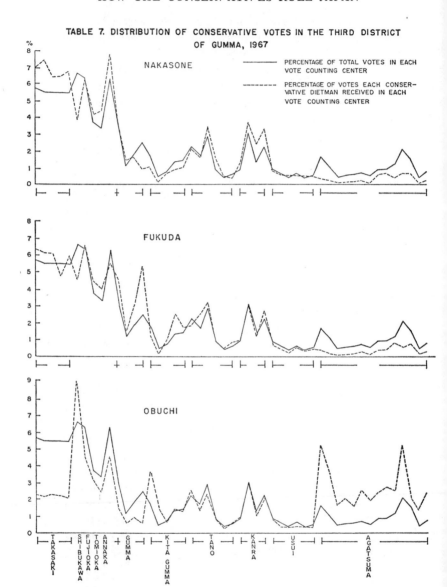

TABLE 7. DISTRIBUTION OF CONSERVATIVE VOTES IN THE THIRD DISTRICT OF GUMMA, 1967

Source: Gumma-Ken. Senkyo Kanri Iinkai. Senkyo no Kiroku (Election Proceedings), January 29, 1967

100

The smaller the political unit, the more clearly the *jiban* can be seen. In the 1967 elections, there were 49 vote-counting centers in the third electoral district. Since these centers are established for convenience, the actual number of votes delivered to each center differs. I have therefore divided the total number of votes in the electoral district by the number of votes in each of these centers, and plotted this percentage on the graphs. This (solid) line is the same for all three graphs. I have arranged the cities on the graphs in the order used by the Gumma authorities. Takasaki, the largest city, is first. It accounts for the first five points on the chart since it has five vote-counting centers. The next four points are the four major cities, Shibukawa in the north and Annaka, Fujioka, and Tomioka in the south. Each has one vote-counting center, except for Tomioka, which has two. The counties, of which there are six, come next. Each of them has a varying number of vote-counting centers.

Next, I took the votes which each of the candidates received in each of the vote-counting centers, compared it to the total vote of each of the candidates, and plotted the percentage on the three graphs (dotted line). If each of the candidates received his vote equally throughout the electoral district, the two lines on each chart would be identical. If one of the candidates received a disproportionately large or small share of the vote in the vote-counting district, the lines diverge. The more nearly the two lines coincide, the more horizontal the *jiban*. The greater the divergence, the more vertical the *jiban*.

The results are pretty much as we have described above. First, Nakasone's case. He showed strength in the five centers of Takasaki, the county of Kanra and neighboring city of Tomioka, and Annaka. With the possible exception of Annaka, there are no great disparities. The two lines parallel each other. We can reaffirm the statement that Nakasone has a horizontal *jiban*.

Next, Fukuda's case. Three of the towns in the county of Gumma contribute more than their share of the vote to

101

Fukuda. The highest peak, of course, is his birthplace, the town of Gumma. Shintō, which is officially part of Kita Gumma County, but which adjoins the town of Gumma, shows great voting enthusiasm for Fukuda, but the number of votes it contributes is not too high. Other than these places, Fukuda's vote line hews closely to the standard. He also has a horizontal *jiban*.

Last, Obuchi's case. The northern city of Shibukawa, a traditional Obuchi stronghold, gives 9% of his total vote. Adjoining Shibukawa to the north are the two villages of Komochi and Onogami (the first two points in Kita Gumma), where Obuchi picks up a heavy cluster of votes. The rest of his strength is concentrated in the thirteen villages of Agatsuma. The highest peak is his birthplace, Nakanojō. Obuchi has a vertical *jiban*.

What are the strengths and weaknesses of the *kōenkai?*

At first glance, they would appear to be admirable political institutions. They reach down to the base of society, they serve as a transmission belt for ideas and desires traveling both up and down, they operate year in and year out, not just at election time, and they are intimately involved with all aspects of the people's life. Yet they are the target of criticism.

A complaint offered by some, though not all, Dietmen is that they take too much energy and money. A Dietman's secretary in Kagawa prefecture says, "Every day, forty or fifty people come here to ask for something or to talk something over. The things we can take care of here, we take care of here. But some of the problems are too big for us. Every morning, I call Tokyo and try to get solutions from the teacher [Dietman]. It's hard for the teacher and it's hard for us. Thanks to the system, we don't even get Sunday off."[47] For a Dietman who would rather deal with the greater affairs of state, the complaints are understandable. But these services would probably have to be given even though there were no *kōenkai*. "If you don't like running errands for your con-

[47] *Mainichi Shimbun*, May 10, 1966, p. 2.

stituents," says Yamamoto Katsuichi, "then you had better give up being a Dietman."[48]

The charge that the *kōenkai* cost too much money deserves to be taken more seriously. Most *kōenkai* are built on a vertical *jiban* like Obuchi's. "Nakasone's *kōenkai* is rare," declares Miyake Hisayuki, a reporter on the *Mainichi Shimbun*; "Most of them center on the Dietman's birthplace and a few other pockets in the district."[49] "There is not a great deal of difference between the way the vote is gathered now and the way it was gathered in the past," says Tanaka Tatsuo, who learned prewar politics from his father Tanaka Giichi, the prime minister from 1927 to 1929, and who is now a Dietman in his own right.[50] But the social structure of Japan is changing. Masumi Junnosuke, a scholar who has studied the various types of *jiban*, states, "The traditional organizational network is dissolving. It is becoming impossible for the candidate to concentrate on special areas to gather the vote. The tendency is emerging whereby the vote must be gathered over a much wider area."[51] The widespread organization needed for this sort of endeavor costs money. Nakasone claims that his organization is not particularly expensive. Perhaps not. But all the other Dietmen will not be as fortunate as he.

A further criticism centers on the relationship of the Dietman and his *kōenkai*. Nakasone claims his *kōenkai* is built on the relationship of shared political ideals. But not all *kōenkai* have this basis. Consider the following description of a *kōenkai* meeting:

> The scene is a small sea-coast village . . . in Aichi Prefecture. Better than a hundred men and women are gathered in the auditorium of the elementary school. . . . They are clapping their hands and singing.

48 Yamamoto Katsuichi, interview, October 24, 1966.
49 Miyake Hisayuki, interview, October 1, 1966.
50 Tanaka Tatsuo, interview, November 17, 1965.
51 Masumi Junnosuke, "Sen-Kyūhyaku-Gojū-Gonen no Seiji Taisei" [The Political Structure of 1955], *Shisō* (June 1964), p. 55.

"Toughened by the winds of Mount Ibuki,
Blossoms the flower of peace of a united Asia.
This is the road which Kuno Chūji follows.
Firmly treading the red carpets of the Diet,
The man Kuno Chūji proceeds in triumph."

Finally, bathed in loud applause, Dietman Kuno Chūji climbs the podium and begins to talk. "My friends, politics is not a matter for the head. Let us put aside difficult things like policy debate. Let's be friendly! Let's sing and dance! Let's enjoy ourselves!" Once again the chorus starts, "Firmly treading the red carpets. . . ." Kuno Chūji has won seven elections and is regarded as a candidate for the next cabinet. He has held "songfests" four times in each of 150 places for a grand total of 600 meetings at which he has "sung and danced" with the 100,000 members of his kōenkai in the past six months.[52]

Kuno Chūji is not alone in stressing the personal aspects of the kōenkai. If the songs of the Dietmen are an accurate measure, better than seventy legislators are following the same path. The critics insist that the kōenkai is not a political organ but a social club, if not a personal cortege. Nakasone notes, "Even though nobody is prevented from joining, a kōenkai soon takes on the flavor of a private society and becomes exclusive and inner-directed. This atmosphere ill befits a public political organ."[53] Moreover, once a citizen enters a kōenkai, he rarely leaves. "Nobody has resigned from my kōenkai," explains Nakasone. "I guess if I did something wrong, they might. But short of that, the members will stay loyal."[54] Personal allegiance has a clear priority over political responsibility. In this atmosphere there is little room for criticism of the Dietman's policies. There is only personal adulation. This environment, in which personality and conviviality

[52] *Mainichi Shimbun*, May 10, 1966, p. 2.
[53] Nakasone Yasuhiro, interview, October 31, 1966.
[54] *Ibid.*

are dominant, does little to heighten political consciousness and direct the citizen's attention to the higher affairs of state. The main thrust of criticism—at least by the Dietmen— is towards the duplication of effort. Each politician is obliged to create a *kōenkai*, which means there may be as many as five or six in the same election district. Why can't the *kōenkai* be incorporated into the party structure?

This idea has concerned the party leaders since it was broached in 1963 by Ishida Hirohide, then chairman of the national organization committee, and Miki Takeo, then chairman of the organizational research committee. Kuraishi Tadao is only the last in a long line of speakers when he announced shortly after his appointment as chairman of the national organization committee in 1966, that he was going to increase the party membership by three million within the span of a year. When the newsmen expressed doubts over the possibility of realizing these brave ambitions, Kuraishi answered, "I'm not blowing off hot air. If the party branches and the *kōenkai* of the Dietmen cooperate, and if the members of the *kōenkai* can be induced to join the party, we shall soon gather about 3,000,000 members. All that's needed is a little effort."[55]

Kuraishi's argument is impeccable. But the hitch lies in persuading the members of the *kōenkai* to join the party. On various membership drives, the Dietmen have enrolled members of their support organizations in the party, and have, indeed, paid their dues from their own pocket. But the members of the *kōenkai* regard this act as a formal gesture forced on them by Tokyo. They show no desire to be part of the party.

This lack of desire has many explanations. One is that the party does not do much for the candidates or the support organizations. I asked one of Nakasone's secretaries how much the party regional organization assisted him. He answered, "The party has a regional organizer based in Maebashi, the prefectural capital. He comes over here to Taka-

[55] *Asahi Shimbun*, August 16, 1966, p. 2.

saki on occasion, usually with an armful of party propaganda for us to distribute. Other than that, we don't see very much of him."[56] Another secretary who had overheard the conversation chimed in, "We distribute all of his propaganda for him—just as soon as we have stamped every copy with Nakasone's name."[57] I did not have the opportunity of hearing the regional organizer's views. But since he is alone in Gumma, his organizational efforts are limited.

Regional elections also inhibit the merger of the support organizations with the party structure. "This clearly becomes apparent in a contest over a single seat, such as the governor of a prefecture, the major of a city, or the leader of a regional organ."[58] Usually several candidates emerge from the conservative camp. The party is unable to limit the candidates to one. The winner will be the candidate from the strongest support organization. No local politician dares rely on the party to further his ambitions. His future will lie with the support organizations.

The *kōenkai* are also more effective than the party organs in helping the voter. A small businessman in Kagoshima said, "One of the side effects of last year's drop in the price of sweet potatoes was that my starch factory began to go broke. Men with connections with the Dietmen or with the farm cooperatives managed to keep their fingers in the honey pot. I was the only idiot. I went to the prefectural assemblymen. All they said was that lifting the import restrictions on sugar was bad. I didn't understand what they were talking about. I've got doubts whether they were even listening to what I said."[59]

Tanaka Kakuei, a former secretary general, boasts that his prefecture, Niigata, has the best party organization in the nation. Niigata is not a wealthy prefecture, and when the

56 Ōta Takeo, interview, August 6, 1966. The regional organizer is not acting unusually. He doesn't have any way of distributing his pamphlets except through the *kōenkai* of each conservative Dietman.

57 Kobayashi Katsumi, interview, August 6, 1966.

58 *Asahi Shimbun*, August 16, 1966, p. 2.

59 *Mainichi Shimbun*, May 3, 1966, p. 2.

heavy winter snows come, the menfolk depart for the east and south to find employment. The wives are left. Last year, the socialists began arranging for them to make artificial flowers in their homes to keep them occupied and to provide them with extra money. Word of this venture was not long in reaching the leaders of the prefectural federation. "All they did," complained members of Tanaka's *kōenkai*, "was to turn to us and tell us to take care of it."[60]

A major reason why the *kōenkai* cannot be drawn into the party structure lies in the popular attitudes toward the politicians and the parties. The *Asahi Shimbun* reports, "When a voter is urged to join the party because he supports a conservative candidate, he answers, 'I only support Mr. A. I don't have any desire to join the party.' This talk can be heard in any prefectural federation."[61] Two interpretations are offered. One is that the Japanese has no sense of party. He looks only at the politician's personality. The second explanation is that the citizen has thrown in the towel so far as the parties are concerned. "The great majority of the people do not expect anything from the parties. . . . At times, they appear to have forsaken them."[62]

There has been some statistical evidence gathered on a national basis which shows that the Japanese citizen is inclined to vote for the man rather than the party. Following each election, the Clean Elections Federation, a semi-public organization, has conducted a national survey of more than two thousand people. One of the questions they have asked is "Did you consider the party or the candidate's personality most seriously when you voted?" The results have been:

[60] *Asahi Shimbun*, February 15, 1966, p. 2. Although the prefectural federation did not do anything, Tanaka's *kōenkai* scurried about and found part-time work for the housewives.

[61] *Ibid.*, August 16, 1966, p. 2.

[62] Fujiwara Hirotatsu and Tomita Nobuo, "Kokumin Seiji Ishiki no Kichō to Henka no Taiyō [The Basis and Mode of Change of the Political Consciousness of the People]," *Seikei Ronsō*, Vol. 31, no. 6 (January 1964), p. 140.

TABLE 8. NATIONAL SURVEY TO DETERMINE THE BASIS FOR THE VOTE
IN 1958, 1960, 1963, AND 1967 ELECTIONS

Voting Basis	Percent of Vote			
	1967	1963	1960	1958
Voted on basis of party	37	31	33	32
Voted on basis of candidate's personality	47	51	43	45
Cannot make this sort of generalization	12	14	19	10
Unclear	4	4	5	13
Totals	100	100	100	100

SOURCE: Kōmei Senkyo Renmei, *Sōsenkyo no Jittai* [True Conditions of the General Elections] (Tokyo, 1958, 1960, 1963, 1967).

Breaking the 1967 figures down further, the survey showed that among the citizens who voted for a conservative party candidate, there is even a greater predilection toward the politician. 54% of these voters cast their ballot on the basis of the candidate's personality, 30% voted for the party, 13% refused to generalize, and 3% gave unclear answers.[63] These statistics push the reader to the conclusion that the man is all-important, that there is little sense of party in Japan.

But there is one informed group in Japan that has not reached this conclusion: the politicians. Although lower house members have always carried party colors, the other politicians—the councillors and the local politicians—had found it advantageous in the past to be independent. One of the trends of the postwar years has been the growing adherence of these politicians to the parties. In the first upper house election, in 1947, 43% of the councillors were independents. Today all but 5% are affiliated with a party.[64] Likewise, the governors, the prefectural assemblymen, even the mayors and the city, town, and village assemblymen are in-

[63] Kōmei Senkyo Renmei, *Sōsenkyo no Jittai* [True Conditions of the General Elections] (Tokyo, March 1967), p. 23.
[64] Yomiuri Shimbun Seiji-bu, *Seitō* [Political Parties], Yomiuri Shimbun-sha, 1966, p. 109.

creasingly wearing the party label.[65] It can be argued that this trend is a response to the growing sense of party among the populace. The claim that the people have given up on the parties goes too far. True, there are many misgivings concerning the parties. In 1963, Professors Tomita Nobuo and Fujiwara Hirotatsu asked the residents of Tokyo and a farm village in Ibaraki prefecture which of the political forces—parties, financial circles, labor unions, farm cooperatives, etc.—they disliked the most. 38.2% of the respondents answered, the parties.[66] On the other hand, the *Asahi Shimbun* has conducted national surveys at least once a year, and more often if the cabinet is under severe attack or facing a crisis, and they have found that there is a relatively stable degree of support offered the conservative party and that "this support is independent of the support offered a conservative cabinet."[67]

But the Japanese does not openly declare his support. The pollsters have great difficulties in getting people to express their political views, particularly regarding the parties.[68] One of the reasons for this reluctance lies with the newspapers. Not one of them has ever supported a registration drive for the parties. To the contrary, throughout the postwar period, they have been vicious in their attacks on the parties, particularly the conservative party. The *Asahi Shimbun*, for example, makes extraordinary efforts to insure precision and balance in its domestic reporting, yet it allows a columnist to say on the front page, "The conservative party is rotten through and through and is oozing pus."[69] As matters presently stand, for a Japanese to announce support openly for the parties is tantamount to publicly espousing corruption.

A tendency to look first to personality, a negative sense

---

65 *Asahi Shimbun*, November 27, 1965, p. 5.

66 Fujiwara and Tomita, "Seiji Ishiki," p. 98.

67 Ōnishi Yutaka, "Sūji de Miru Seitō Shiji no Suii" [Numerical Analysis of Changes in Party Support], *Asahi Jānaru* (September 5, 1965), p. 97. See Table 9.

68 *Ibid.*

69 *Asahi Shimbun*, October 14, 1966, p. 1.

TABLE 9. COMPARISON OF POPULAR SUPPORT OF THE CABINETS AND CONSERVATIVE PARTY

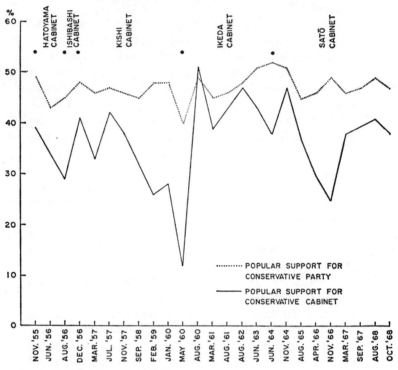

Source: Asahi Shimbun, July 19, 1968.

of party, and a hostile atmosphere conspire to keep the voter within the *kōenkai* and away from formal adherence to the party.

The final and perhaps most important reason why the *kōenkai* will not be amalgamated into the party structure lies in the elections. We turn to an examination of this system in the next chapter.

110

CHAPTER V

The Elections

"THERE is a fundamental difference between the members of the Diet and the apes," Ōno Bamboku, the late vice president of the Liberal Democratic party declaimed. "If an ape slips and falls out of a tree, he remains an ape. But let a member of the Diet lose an election and . . ."[1] Nothing occupies a politician more than the elections. Nothing influences a party more than the electoral system.

Japan has three electoral systems. One for the upper house, one for the lower house, and one for the regional offices: prefectural governor, prefectural assemblymen, the city, town, and village mayors, and the city, town, and village assemblymen. Each of these election systems has had its influence on the structure of the party. But the lower house is the focus of the nation's politics and its members dominate the party. Its election system has influenced the party the most. We shall therefore concentrate our attention on the lower house elections.

Elections are the tie between the government and the people. "The reason for the dissolution of the lower house is to discover further where public opinion rests through the newly elected Diet members," wrote Itō Hirobumi, the principal drafter of Japan's first constitution.[2] In theory at least, political parties, whose strength lie with the populace, should stand to benefit by elections. But in the years before the war, dissolution and new elections, or the threat of them, were often used as a method of weakening or cowing the parties. Under the first constitution, the emperor, acting on the advice of a small group of advisors, appointed the prime minis-

[1] *Asahi Shimbun*, August 18, 1964, p. 2.

[2] Itō Hirobumi, *Kempō Gikai* [Commentary on the Constitution] (15th ed. revised; Tokyo: Maruzen, 1935), p. 18.

ter[3] and many times he chose a bureaucrat, military officer, or sometimes the leader of a minority party. The new prime minister had to get his legislative program through the Diet, which was the stronghold of the parties. He therefore repeatedly threatened dissolution and general elections, which cost the parties a great deal of money and in which officialdom could interfere through police intimidation,[4] until he was able to build his own political party or secure the acquiescence of the existing parties to his rule. Katsura Tarō, who served as prime minister three times between 1901 and 1913, stated the strategy most clearly: "To smash the resistance of the parties, dissolve, and then dissolve again." Hayashi Senjūrō, the prime minister in 1937, openly repeated the same injunction, "Dissolve the Diet innumerable times, and the parties are forced to surrender."[5]

Today the parties need not fear the prime minister.[6] Although the new constitution does not restrict him in dissolving the House of Representatives other than to specify that elections must be held every four years,[7] it does make him responsible to the Diet, and thus ensures party supremacy. The emperor still has the formal power to dissolve the house and proclaim general elections, but he must act on "the advice and approval of the cabinet,"[8] the majority of whose members must be chosen from the Diet by the prime minis-

3 Japan. "Teikoku Kempō" [Imperial Constitution] in *Roppō Zensho* [Compendium of Laws] (5th rev. ed., Tokyo: Iwanami, 1934), Art. 10.

4 *Asahi Shimbun*, August 30, 1962, p. 2.

5 Quoted in Watanabe Tsuneo, *Tōshu to Seitō* [Party Leaders and Political Parties] (Tokyo: Kōbundō, 1961), p. 188.

6 Watanabe notes, however, that Prime Minister Yoshida, in the elections shortly after the war, used general elections to build the strength of his followers within one of the conservative parties. We observed in the second chapter that the present factions use the elections to build their strength vis-à-vis other factions. Watanabe has made a detailed study of all the dissolutions in Japanese parliamentary history and has written an excellent analysis of the role of dissolution in Japanese politics. See *ibid.*, pp. 157-198.

7 Japan. "Nippon Koku Kempō" [Japanese National Constitution] in *Roppō Zensho* [Compendium of Laws] (Tokyo: Iwanami, 1960), Art. 45.

8 *Ibid.*, Art. 7, par. 3, 4.

ter,[9] who, in turn, "shall be designated from among the members of the Diet by a resolution of the Diet."[10] The charge can be made, however, that the election system itself, which was designed before the war, encourages division and thus weakens the parties. The most unusual provision of the present electoral law, and the one which gives rise to these charges, relates to the electoral districts. Japan has experimented with various electoral districts since she passed her first electoral law in 1890.[11] At first, she devised a "small" electoral district from which one candidate was elected by a single entry ballot. Next, she tried a "large" election district in which as many as thirteen candidates were elected. In 1925, Wakatsuki Reijirō, then home minister, tried to combine the strengths of the large and small election districts and created a "middle-sized" election district in which three, four, or five candidates were elected by a single entry ballot. After the war, Japan reverted to the large election district for one election, but in 1947 reestablished essentially the same middle-sized districts that she had before the war. By 1967, fifteen elections had been held under this system.

Wakatsuki drew upon two principles. The first was to divide the election seats equally among the population. The second was to hold on to existing political divisions as closely as possible. When the middle-sized districts were re-created in 1947, these same principles were followed. A prewar law established 466 seats in the lower house. This figure was divided into the total population to establish a representative-to-population ratio. Since 1871, Japan has had a system of prefectures throughout the nation. Wakatsuki in 1925, and his successors in 1947, decided to have the election districts follow these administrative divisions as closely as possible.

9 *Ibid.*, Art. 68.
10 *Ibid.*, Art. 67.
11 Senkyo Seido Nanajū-nen Kinenkai, *Senkyo-hō no Enkaku* [The History of the Elections Laws] (Tokyo: Daiichi Hōki Shuppan K.K., 1959). This volume lists all the changes in the Japanese electoral law since its inception.

The population figure for each legislative seat was divided into the figure for total population of the prefecture. In 1947, Fukui and Tottori prefectures were found to have populations sufficient for four legislative seats and they became four-man election districts. The prefectures of Yamanashi, Shiga, Nara, Shimane, Tokushima, Kōchi, and Saga had populations sufficient for five representatives and they became five-man election districts.

The rest of the prefectures had much larger populations. They were subdivided so that no electoral district would have more than five representatives. Aomori prefecture, for example, was found to have a population large enough for seven representatives. It was split into two election districts, one four-man district and one three-man district. Ōsaka, a large metropolis, was split into five electoral districts. Tokyo had seven electoral districts.

The 1947 system has remained fundamentally intact over the years. When the island of Amami Ōshima was returned to Japan by the United States in 1953, another legislative seat was added. In 1964, nineteen more legislative seats and five more electoral districts were added to adjust for migration of the population to the cities, making a total of 486 representatives in the lower house, from 122 electoral districts. These districts include 43 three-man districts, 39 four-man districts, and 40 five-man districts.

The system is not perfect. Two complaints are voiced. One is that the rural districts are over-represented. While the general ratio of representation is one to 200,040, the difference in the ratio between electoral districts may vary by 70,000. In the second district of Tochigi, Fujio Masayuki won a seat in the 1967 general elections with 34,901 votes. In the seventh district of Tokyo, Nakamura Kōichi lost with 96,620 votes.[12]

The reason for the unbalance is easy to explain but hard to correct. Immediately after the war, the economy was in a shambles. Overseas soldiers returned to their traditional

[12] Jichishō [Home Ministry] statistics.

114

homes in the countryside rather than to the factories in the city. It was at this juncture that the election system was re-established, and it reflected an abnormally large rural population. With the restoration of industrial strength, people streamed into the cities. For example, Tokyo's population has about doubled in the past fifteen years[13] and it is still growing. The electoral system is supposed to be adjusted every five years on the basis of a national census. But this legality poses political problems. It is easy enough to add seats for the cities, but almost impossible to take seats away from the countryside. The only solution, then, is to continue to expand the number of seats in the lower house. The politicians of all parties are generally agreed that the Diet is too large already.

The second complaint is that the minority political parties don't get all the legislative seats to which the popular vote entitles them. The following chart examines this charge in the light of the past six lower house elections. "Percent of vote" means the party's percentage of the total popular vote. "Percent of seats" means the ratio of the party's seats to the total number of seats in the lower house, expressed in a percentage. "Percent difference" is the result of subtracting one of these figures from the other. A plus sign means that the party received more legislative seats than popular votes. A minus figure means the popular votes were greater than the legislative seats.

The number of legislative seats does not reflect exactly the popular vote. In each election, the conservatives fared better than they should have and the opposition parties and independents got less than they deserved. Various reasons can be adduced. The communists, for example, view the elections as a way to heighten political consciousness rather than win legislative seats. They run candidates in every district, even though these candidates do not have the slightest chance of winning, and squander enough votes for five lower house

13 *Asahi Nenkan* [Asahi Yearbook] (Tokyo: Asahi Shimbun Company, 1966), p. 233.

115

TABLE 10. COMPARISON OF PERCENTAGE OF LEGISLATIVE SEATS TO THE PERCENTAGE OF THE TOTAL VOTE THE PARTIES RECEIVED IN THE LOWER HOUSE ELECTIONS, 1953-1967

	Conservative Parties			Renovationist Parties			Clean Government Party			Other		
	% of vote	% of seats	% difference	% of vote	% of seats	% difference	% of vote	% of seats	% difference	% of vote	% of seats	% difference
1953	65.7	66.5	+0.8	29.5	30.9	+1.4				4.8	2.6	−2.2
1955	63.2	63.6	+0.4	32.2	34.7	+2.5				4.6	1.7	−2.9
1958	57.8	61.5	+3.7	35.5	35.7	+0.2				6.7	2.8	−3.9
1960	57.6	63.5	+5.9	39.3	35.3	−4.0				3.2	1.3	−1.9
1963	54.7	60.6	+5.9	40.4	36.8	−3.6				4.9	2.6	−2.3
1967	48.8	57.0	+8.2	40.2	36.0	−4.2	5.4	5.1	−0.3	5.7	2.0	−3.7

Note: "Other" means regional parties and independents, most of whom affiliate with the conservatives after the election. In the 1953 elections, the conservative parties were the Liberal party and the Progressive party and the renovationist parties were the Left Wing Socialists, the Right Wing Socialists, and the Communists. In the 1955 elections, the conservative parties were the Liberal party and the Democratic party. The renovationist parties were the same as in the 1953 elections. In the 1958 elections, the conservative party was the Liberal Democratic party and the renovationist parties were the Socialist party and the Communist party. In the 1960, 1963 and 1967 elections, the conservative party was the Liberal Democratic party and the renovationist parties were the Socialist party, the Democratic Socialist party, and the Communist party. The Clean Government party ran in the lower house elections for the first time in 1967. It does not fall easily into either the conservative or renovationist category. Since it won 25 seats, it is a large party, and cannot be shrugged off by placing it in the "other" category.

SOURCE: Calculated from the statistics of Jichishō [Home Ministry].

seats. A second reason is that the conservative votes coalesce in one party, whereas the renovationist votes are split up among three. A third reason, which we shall explain later, is that independent votes are often conservative votes. The independent minuses should be deducted from the conservative plusses for a truer reading.

From time to time, members of the opposition mutter about the injustice, but not very loudly, because the injustice is not very great. Even though the electoral system does not result in perfect proportional representation, the percentage difference between the seats and the votes has never been great enough to frustrate the people's choice of the ruling party. Even though the farmer's vote is somewhat more valuable than his city cousin's vote, and the number of seats and votes do not always tally, the electoral system seems to reflect fairly accurately the will of the people.

So much for the electoral system. What about voting behavior? The first observation is that the vote is remarkably stable. The following table illustrates the turnout rate for the last six elections:

TURNOUT RATE OF ELIGIBLE VOTERS IN
LOWER HOUSE ELECTIONS BETWEEN 1953 AND 1967

Election	Male	Female	Average
1953	80.46	72.76	76.43
1955	78.35	70.44	74.22
1958	79.95	72.06	75.84
1960	79.79	74.42	76.99
1963	76.00	71.23	73.51
1967	72.36	70.02	71.14

SOURCE: Jichishō Senkyo Kyoku, *Shūgiin Giin Sōsenkyo Saiko Saibansho Saibankan Kokumin Shinsa: Kekka Shirabe* [Survey of the Results of the General Elections of the House of Representatives and the People's Judgment of the Legal Officers of the Supreme Court] (Jichisho Senkyō Kyoku, 1967), p. 6.

There is only about five percentage points difference between

117

the 1953 and 1967 elections and two percentage points difference between any two consecutive elections.

The second observation is that there are no violent swings from one side to the other in the elections. The Japanese electorate can be divided roughly into two groups: a majority, or at least a plurality, which supports the conservatives, and a minority that supports the renovationists. A glance at the percentage of the vote which each party received (Table 10) shows that one election differs from another only by a few points. Political loyalties are fairly constant. Even the 1960 elections did not show any great change in the electorate's political views, even though they followed on the heels of large-scale rioting in the major cities, protesting the renewal by the conservatives of a mutual security treaty with the United States. The conservatives lost only 0.2% of the popular vote they had received in 1958. Although over the years there has been a drift to the renovationist camp, the drift has been almost glacially slow, and probably based on changes in the economic structure.[14] Recent elections suggest it is not subject to projection at the same rate for the future.

Tsuchiya Shōzō, an election specialist, gives the accepted interpretation of what this stability means in terms of the parties:

> Nowadays, the sphere of influence of each party appears to be about settled in each region. It is difficult for the Liberal Democratic party to make inroads into the Socialist party's domain, or for the Socialist party to make inroads into the Liberal Democratic party's domain. Under the present middle-sized election district system, several candidates from the same party must

[14] The *Yomiuri Shimbun*, updating and further developing earlier research done by Ishida Hirohide, a former labor minister, has demonstrated that the decline of the conservative voting strength parallels with great fidelity the decline in numbers of workers in the primary (agriculture, fishing, and forestry) sector of the economy. Similarly, the growth in the renovationist parties' strength parallels almost exactly the growth in the number of workers in the secondary (manufacturing) sector of the economy. *Yomiuri Shimbun*, January 1, 1966, p. 2.

stand and fight in the same election district. Both the candidates and their campaign workers keep their hands off the domains of the opposition parties, where it is difficult to cut into the vote but aim at the domains of the candidates of the same party. These are the so-called election blood feuds and they can be observed in each district throughout the nation. Because of them, the election battles are becoming fiercer, are requiring increasing amounts of money, are giving rise to the development of factions within the parties, and are preventing party unity.[15]

Kobayashi Takeji, a conservative with more than ten years in the Diet, gives some idea of the intensity of these conflicts:

> The most trouble for us are the blood feuds. . . . Because of them, we don't fight the socialists. We are always too busy fighting among ourselves. Look at the men from the same electoral districts. They're terrible. They can't even talk pleasantly to each other in the Diet. That's because there is usually a serious war between them. And the people who work for them are worse. They're always fighting. If the candidates are caught being friendly in the election districts, neither of their support organizations will do anything for them at the next election. Everybody has had this terrible experience. The weak unity of the party is due to the election system.[16]

The election system may be fair to the electorate, but it is unfair to the parties.

I will describe some of these electoral fights later in the chapter, but first let me turn to the endorsement policy of

[15] Tsuchiya Shōzō, "Senkyo Seido no Kaisei Mondai ni tsuite" [Concerning the Reform Problem of the Electoral System]," *Shinseikei*, no. 190 (August 1, 1966), p. 10.
[16] Senkyo Seido Shingikai, *Dai-niji Senkyo Seido Shingikai Giji Sokkiroku* [Transcript of Proceedings of the Second Election System Deliberation Commission] (1963), pp. 230-231.

the Liberal Democratic party. An explanation of it will help make the election fights more comprehensible.

One way to limit the fighting among the conservatives is to limit the number of protagonists, and the conservative party tries to do this through its endorsement of candidates. Although success at the polls depends in large measure on the strength of a candidate's support organization, which he must build and support by himself, the endorsement of the party helps bring in the vote. First of all, endorsement means that the candidate is taken seriously in Tokyo, a factor that the politicians believe carries great weight with the electorate. Secondly, the candidate will receive money from the party and can use the services of the party's regional organization, such as they are. Thirdly, the candidate can call upon the support of other Dietmen to tour and speak in the district on his behalf.

There is a running argument over how many votes the party endorsement is worth. The *Nihon Keizai Shimbun* is on record as saying that it will bring ten to twenty thousand votes to the candidate.[17] Mori Kiyoshi, a former chairman of the party's national organization committee, uses the same figures.[18] Tanaka Kakuei, a former secretary general, believes a party-endorsed candidate has a 60% chance of winning.[19] Nobody knows just how valuable the party endorsement is, but all are agreed that it is a prize worth having.

The endorsement policy of the Liberal Democratic party was first enunciated in February 1958, shortly before the first general election the party faced after its inception in 1955. It has four major principles: endorsements recommended by the prefectural federations will be given careful consideration, no candidate under indictment for a criminal offense will be endorsed, preference will be given in the endorsements to incumbent Dietmen, and only candidates who have

[17] *Nihon Keizai Shimbun*, October 31, 1963, p. 5.
[18] Mori Kiyoshi, interview, July 6, 1966.
[19] Kokumin Seiji Kenkyūkai, "Kanjichō Shian to Tōkindaika" [The Secretary General's Proposal and the Modernization of the Party], Getsu-yōkai [Monday Club Report] (October 11, 1965), p. 3.

a chance of winning will be endorsed.[20] Each of these principles requires comment.

The principle of listening carefully to the recommendations of the prefectural federations is based on several considerations. One is that there are countless candidates begging for endorsement and the central headquarters can't keep track of them all. An official party history says, "The prefectural federations screened approximately 500 candidates for the 1958 elections. . . . The figure is about the same for the 1960 and 1963 elections."[21] Secondly, nobody knows the countryside better than local politicians who live there, and listening to them is prudent. Thirdly, the party is genuinely interested in broadening its base and one way to do this is to give the local politicians a greater stake in deciding party matters. Lastly, the brunt of the campaigning will fall on the shoulders of these politicians in the prefectural federations and it is good sense to listen to their opinions and not to put their noses out of joint.

One example of the importance of the views of a prefectural federation can be found in the third district of Fukushima in the 1967 elections. Here the party endorsed two new candidates: one supported by the prefectural federation and opposed by the prime minister; and the other supported by the prime minister but opposed by the prefectural federation. The prefectural federation's candidate received 56,077 votes and won. The prime minister's candidate lost with 23,066 votes.[22] Fujieda Sensuke, an election authority for the conservatives, estimates that the prefectural recommendations are accepted in about sixty percent of the cases.[23]

[20] Jiyūminshutō, *Jiyūminshutō Jūnen no Ayumi* [Ten Years of Progress with the Liberal Democratic Party] (Tokyo: Jiyūminshutō kōkoku Iinkai, 1966), pp. 266-267.

[21] *Ibid.*, p. 277.

[22] Japan. Jichishō Senkyo Kyoku, *Shūgiin Giin Sōsenkyo, Saikō-Saibansho Saibankan Kokumin Shinsa: Kekka Shirabe* [Survey of Results of the General Elections of the House of Representatives and People's Judgment of the Legal Officers of the Supreme Court] (Tokyo: Jichishō Senkyo Kyoku, 1967), p. 218. Hereafter, *Kekka Shirabe.*

[23] Fujieda Sensuke, interview, July 14, 1966.

But deciding party endorsements is important business and the central headquarters, more particularly the election policy committee, reserves the right to make the final decisions itself. The election policy committee is composed of the "president, the vice president, the secretary general, and twelve members nominated by the president."[24] It used to be that the presidential nominees were the faction leaders with a few other old-timers thrown in for balance, appearance, and prestige. Prime Minister Satō changed this practice. In an effort to further weaken the factions, he announced that position in the party organization rather than membership in a faction would be his criterion for selection. The chairmen of the party committees now have concurrent appointments to the election policy committee. But none of the politicians has been bold enough to predict that the factions will no longer have a role in the deciding of the endorsements.

The second principle, of not endorsing anyone who has violated the law, would seem on first glance to be sound politics. But this provision was adopted in the party only after long debate. Japan has some of the most stringent and detailed electoral laws of any nation.[25] Door-to-door campaigning is out,[26] no signature campaigns may be conducted,[27] the number and size of campaign posters is limited,[28] a candidate can have only one automobile and one set of loudspeakers.[29] The spirit of these laws is best epitomized in Article 140 of the public offices election law which states, "No person shall engage in acts tending to arouse enthusiasm . . . for the purposes of the election campaign," thus seemingly forbidding all effective political activity. The authors' intent, I am told, was to limit the amount of money that could be spent in a campaign by restricting the activities of the politicians. But

---

[24] Jiyūminshutō, "Tōsoku" [Party Law] in *Wagatō no Kihon Hōshin* [Basic Policies of Our Party] (Tokyo: Jiyūminshutō Kōkoku Iinkai, 1966), Art. 51.

[25] Japan. "Kōshoku Senkyo Hō" [Public Officers Election Law] in Roppō Zensho [Compendium of Laws] (Tokyo: Iwanami, 1960), pp. 44-164.

[26] *Ibid.*, Art. 138.   [27] *Ibid.*, par. 2.   [28] *Ibid.*, Arts. 143-147.
[29] *Ibid.*, Art. 141.

they prohibited practices and customs that had long been sanctioned by Japanese society. Great burdens are thus placed on the police, who are supposed to enforce the law, and the politicians, who are supposed to follow it. In truth, neither bears up very well.

The police manage to look the other way when most of the minor infractions of the law are committed. In the case of Article 140, for example, there has been only one arrest in the last four elections. But no matter how liberal the police may be, they cannot ignore charges of bribery and inducement with material interest. And some of Japan's most able politicians have been hung up on this provision. In the 1963 elections, a new record was set with 14,538 cases of bribery and inducement with material interest involving 31,210 people.[30] The 1967 elections were somewhat better; only 15,088 people were rounded up.[31]

Nakamura Kikuo, a scholar who has stood for elections himself, explains this high incidence of violation:

> Ask why there are so many cases of bribery in the elections and the answer is that many people look at the elections as festivals. In Japan, there are many festivals . . . which occur regularly throughout the year. . . . At each of these festivals, gifts of money are distributed, the celebrants gather in one of the buildings in the temple compound to feast and drink, the children carry portable shrines through the streets and are made happy by gifts of candy.
>
> Elections are the same. There is a steady stream of people into the candidate's election headquarters to eat and drink. They warm themselves around the braziers on the mats and excitedly gossip about past elections. Others show up promptly at meal time, talk a bit, eat, and then go home. Election headquarters are supposed to serve only light refreshments but that restriction is not always observed when one looks behind the scenes.

30 *Kekka Shirabe*, 1963, p. 155.   31 *Ibid.*, 1967, p. 172.

More stimulating refreshments are also served. The mood at the elections is no different from that during the festivals when people gather at the temple compounds to drink it up.[32]

In this passage Nakamura limits himself to describing election headquarters. But throughout the election district similar scenes are taking place under the sponsorship of the support organizations with funds provided by the candidates. "I don't want to shell out all that food and sake," a politician told me. "It's against the law and besides it costs me a lot of money. But hold a political rally without refreshments, and nobody shows up. Next thing you know, the voters are calling you a cheapskate and beginning to have doubts about your ability to look after the welfare of the district."

This atmosphere encourages more serious offenses than simply supplying food and drink. Sometimes election offenses are discovered which involve substantial sums of money. But the voters often repudiate the judgments of the courts and cause the party to have second thoughts about its present policy. In the 1960 elections, for example, Dietmen Ōkami Tsukasa, Fujiwara Setsuo, and Matsuda Tetsuzō had serious brushes with the law, and the party chose not to endorse them in the next elections. The three men stood as independents and took their case to the public. Fujiwara Setsuo and Ōkami Tsukasa lost, Fujiwara by a scant two thousand votes, Ōkami quite decisively. But Matsuda Tetsuzō forced the defeat of the party candidate endorsed in his place, and won with more votes than he received in the previous election.[33]

[32] Nakamura Kikuo, *Senkyosen* [The Election War] (Tokyo: Kōdansha, 1965), pp. 56-57.
[33] Matsuda Tetsuzō has a very solid and dependable following. He received almost an identical number of votes in the following elections:

1958	61,359
1960	61,446
1963	62,160
1967	62,914

Population changes rather than electoral violations proved his undoing. He lost in the 1967 elections.

124

The conservatives find themselves caught between the dictates of the law and the mores of the people. The politicians have chosen to stick with the people. The party has chosen to uphold the law. The people have refused to commit themselves but are apt to side with the politicians. It is an unhappy situation.

The third major principle that the party follows in awarding its endorsement is that incumbent Diet members shall be given priority. Since the present conservative party is a parliamentary group in which the Diet members sit on the inner councils and all others wait at the door, such a policy is perhaps unavoidable. But the election statistics attest to the validity of this course of action. There are three classes of candidates: men who have never occupied a Diet seat (new faces); men who occupied a seat when the Diet was dissolved for the elections (incumbents); and men who have occupied a Diet seat in the past but who, for one reason or another, are not members of the Diet when the elections are held (quondams). The party has endorsed candidates from all three classes. The following chart (Table 11) shows how they have fared in the four elections held since the party was formed.

Clearly the incumbents have demonstrated that their chances of success are greater than either the quondams or the new faces, and their chances are steadily rising. But the charge is made that this policy is short-sighted, that the party is digging a hole for itself. If only Dietmen are endorsed, the party will have no way of letting fresh blood into its veins and will, in due course, become moribund. This argument overlooks the factions, which keep the proceedings lively. We have seen in an earlier chapter that a candidate must create his own support organization. He will also have affiliated with one of the factions, and the faction members will have been actively assisting him in building this support organization. When the election policy committee meets to decide the endorsements, the faction leader fights to have his own men supported by the party. But failure to get the party endorse-

125

ment will not usually cause the faction leader to withdraw his support of the candidate nor the candidate to withdraw from the election. The candidate will form his own local political party, declare himself an independent, or announce he has the "semi-endorsement" of the Liberal Democratic party, and try his luck with the electorate. If he wins, he immediately affiliates with the Liberal Democratic party. From 1955 to 1967, 35 of the 141 new conservative Diet members entered the party by this route.

The last principle that the party follows is that winners must be chosen above all [*tōsen daiichi shugi*]. This would seem to be more of a prayer than a strategy, but it has several concrete applications.

First, the party will endorse no candidate until shortly before the elections. Mori Kiyoshi explains the reason: "There are many candidates in the countryside. The party has no way of knowing which one is going to turn out to be the strongest. If the party endorsed the candidates earlier, it might well find itself backing the wrong one."[34]

Secondly, the party strictly limits the number of its endorsements. Earlier, we have seen that three, four, or five men are elected from each electoral district. The party does not always endorse three men for a three-man district, four men for a four-man district, or five men for a five-man district. Rather it decides how many conservative candidates have a chance of winning in each electoral district and then endorses that number of candidates.

A few examples will make this point clear. The third electoral district of Tokyo is a four-man district. The renovationist parties have sufficient strength so that they are able consistently to elect two of their candidates to office. The conservative party limits itself to endorsing two candidates. The voters of the second district of Ishikawa have yet to elect their first renovationist candidate to office. It is a three-man

34 Mori Kiyoshi, interview, July 6, 1966.

TABLE 11. CHANCES OF ELECTION VICTORY, EXPRESSED IN PERCENTAGE, OF THREE TYPES OF CANDIDATES ENDORSED BY LIBERAL DEMOCRATIC PARTY FOR ELECTIONS TO THE HOUSE OF REPRESENTATIVES IN 1958, 1960, 1963, 1967

	New Faces	Incumbents	Quondams	Total
1958 Elections				
Total number of party endorsed candidates	52	287	74	413
Number of these candidates who won election	26	215	46	287
Percentage	50.0%	74.9%	60.2%	69.5%
1960 Elections				
Total number of party endorsed candidates	58	278	63	399
Number of these candidates who won election	29	226	41	296
Percentage	50.0%	81.3%	65.1%	74.2%
1963 Elections				
Total number of party endorsed candidates	48	270	41	359
Number of these candidates who won election	33	225	25	283
Percentage	68.7%	83.3%	60.9%	78.8%
1967 Elections				
Number of the endorsed candidates	48	268	25	341
Number of those who won election	27	234	16	277
Percentage	58.3%	87.3%	64.0%	81.2%

SOURCE: Jichishō [Home Ministry] statistics.

127

district and the conservative party endorses three men. The conservatives are weak in the first and sixth districts of Osaka. Although both of these districts send three men to the Diet, the conservatives only have enough strength to elect one man in each of these districts, and that is all they endorse.

Thirdly, the party uses this principle to justify the endorsement of new candidates. In each election, there are districts with a conservative incumbent who looks like a loser and a new face who looks like a winner. We have seen that tradition and statistics oblige the party to support the incumbent. The dilemma is whether the party should ignore the likely winner or endorse him, too, even though the party is doing what it set out not to do: endorsing too many candidates. The policy has varied under different prime ministers and secretary generals. But generally, the tendency is away from giving the endorsement to new faces.

The party has yet to find an appropriate principle to justify endorsing new men where it involves conflict with an incumbent. It is forced to rely on the factions to put forward independents. Even in cases where there is an opening for a new man—the incumbent has died or retired, or the opposition parties have weakened to the extent that a conservative can be elected—the party has found no way of stopping each faction from fighting to have its own candidate endorsed. In short, party endorsements may encourage clashes among the conservatives rather than dampening them.

Let us now look at the kinds of fights which may arise among the conservatives. As a standard for comparison, let us first turn to the election district of Arafune Seijūrō, the conservative politician of chapter 2, whose financial peccadilloes caused his resignation as transportation minister. Despite this incident and the newspapers' call for Arafune's defeat, he received more votes than he ever had before and the third district of Saitama remained a model of conservative peace. The 1967 election results were:

Saitama 3 (three-man district)[35]

LDP	Arafune Seijūrō	88,502	elected
LDP	Kamoda Sōichi	64,251	elected
JSP	Takada Tomiyuki	53,437	elected
Ind	Kurihara Fukuo	11,780	not elected
JCP	Saitō Kimiko	7,807	not elected

This district shows all the signs of stability. The number of candidates was limited. A wide gap existed between the winners and the losers. The two conservative candidates were unconcerned, because the independent Kurihara, in reality a conservative without the party endorsement, did not have enough votes to threaten them. The socialist Takada made no trouble since he had more than enough votes to stay comfortably in office. Neither the Socialist party nor the Liberal Democratic party felt obliged to endorse another candidate since there was no chance of either winning another seat. Arafune has been elected eight times, Kamoda has been elected four times, and the socialist Takada has been elected five times.

This pocket of tranquility is rare. In most of the electoral districts the conservatives are at each others' throats. One reason is that the party endorses too many candidates because the elections are not completely predictable and the party overestimates its chances. One district where the party has consistently endorsed too many candidates is the second district of Hiroshima, the home ground of former Prime Minister Ikeda Hayato.

The political predilections of the Hiroshima citizenry have changed little over the postwar years. The political divisions of the second district support one socialist and three con-

[35] LDP stands for Liberal Democratic party, JSP for Japan Socialist party, DSP for Democratic Socialist party, JCP for Japan Communist party, CGP for Clean Government party, and Ind for independent. The statistics for this and other examples are taken from *Kekka Shirabe*, 1960, 1963, 1967.

servative Dietmen. Trouble started in the 1958 elections when the Japan Socialist party became greedy and decided to run two candidates. The result was that these two candidates split the socialist vote and allowed Tanikawa Kazuo, a conservative who ran as an independent since he did not receive the party endorsement, to slip into office. For the first time, the four-man district had four conservatives representing it.

The socialists realized their mistake and in the 1960 elections put forward only one candidate. The district, predictably, chose three conservatives and one socialist to represent it. Tanikawa was squeezed out, but only by 3,000 votes.

This slight margin caused the conservatives to become greedy in turn. In the 1963 elections, the Liberal Democratic party not only endorsed the three conservative incumbents but Tanikawa as well. Tanikawa fought vigorously. Only Ikeda Hayato, the prime minister, received more votes in the district than he. But his fight was with the other conservatives, not with the socialist. Tanikawa won and the conservative Matsumoto lost.

Matsumoto was a proven vote-getter, as he had earlier won three elections. Since the party's endorsement of Tanikawa was in some measure responsible for Matsumoto's defeat, the party felt obliged to endorse him in the 1967 elections. Ikeda Hayato had died in 1965. Theoretically, this solved the party's problems; they could give Matsumoto Ikeda's endorsement and thus end up with three candidates. But the followers of Ikeda and Matsumoto had been fighting each other for many years. Even though the central party in Tokyo designated Matsumoto as the heir to the Ikeda votes, there was little chance that the Ikeda followers in Hiroshima would go along. The party was obliged to endorse a new candidate from the Ikeda organization, Masuoka, if it wanted to keep the Ikeda votes. The party again ended up with four candidates. The 1967 election results looked like this:

130

HIROSHIMA 2 (four-man district)

LDP	Masuoka Hiroyuki	61,235	elected
JSP	Hamada Mitsuto	55,752	elected
LDP	Tanikawa Kazuo	51,901	elected
LDP	Nakagawa Shunji	50,995	elected
LDP	Matsumoto Shunichi	49,616	not elected
Ind	Katō Yōzō	43,568	not elected
JCP	Harada Karuo	9,267	not elected

Masuoka took over the Ikeda organization with few defections. The socialist came in second with his usual fifty-some-odd thousand votes. It is with the next three candidates that we are particularly concerned. Tanikawa and Nakagawa won, and Matsumoto lost. But they were separated from each other by only about a thousand votes. There is nothing to suggest that the scramble for these thousand votes will prove any less vigorous in the next election than it was in this one.

Only occasionally does the party find itself embarrassed by endorsing too many candidates. A more usual pattern is for independents—conservatives who failed to get the party endorsement—to contest the elections. We have already seen two examples in Hiroshima: in the 1958 elections, Tanikawa tried it successfully; in the 1967 elections Katō Yōzō tried it and failed. Another example can be found in the second district of Saitama. This is a three-man district and is usually represented by two conservatives and a socialist. In the 1967 elections, Yamaguchi Toshio, a 26-year-old, decided that the time had come for him to take back the seat of his father Rokurōji, who had represented the district in the Diet until he died. Toshio asked for the party endorsement but was refused. The party supported the conservative incumbents Komiyama, a college professor, and Matsuyama, one of the few lady Dietmembers. The election results were:

SAITAMA 2 (three-man district)

| LDP | Komiyama Jūshirō | 74,172 | elected |
| Ind | Yamaguchi Toshio | 62,531 | elected |

131

JSP	Hiraoka Chūjirō	50,450	elected
LDP	Matsuyama Chieko	48,571	not elected
JSP	Shimizu Norimatsu	20,932	not elected
JCP	Yamahata Takeo	16,040	not elected
DSP	Hasegawa Tsutomu	15,624	not elected

The professor won, the lady lost, and the party learned anew that political loyalties neither die nor fade away in the countryside.

The elections which we have so far described have been highly injurious to the unity and discipline of the party but have not resulted in the loss of any legislative seats. There is another group of election patterns in which the conservatives chop each other to bits and the socialists walk away with the prize. I shall offer three examples with a caveat. The reader should be aware that I am predicting how an election might have come out if the conservatives had followed a different strategy. This is risky business. My conclusions will hold water statistically, but statistics and politics are two different matters.

Few people, however, will wish to argue that another conservative Dietman could not have been elected from the first district of Kagoshima in the 1967 elections. Kagoshima is the southernmost prefecture of the southernmost island of Japan. It is famous for two things: an active volcano and Saigō Takamori, a local samurai who got himself killed or killed himself leading an unsuccessful revolt against the government in 1877. Perhaps the influence of Saigō, the volcano, and the climate have given the people of Kagoshima the reputation of being hot-tempered, mule-headed, self-willed, and partial to quixotic causes. The election did little to change this image.

Four men are chosen from the first district. Ten candidates entered the race for these seats. Two were socialists. Seven were conservatives, four with party endorsement, three running as independents. The results of the election were:

KAGOSHIMA 1 (four-man district)

LDP	Kambayashiyama Eikichi	68,599	elected
LDP	Tokonami Tokuji	55,822	elected
JSP	Kawasaki Kanji	53,561	elected
JSP	Akaji Yūzō	50,910	elected
LDP	Uda Kunie	44,716	not elected
LDP	Kawakami Tameji	42,013	not elected
Ind	Kawano Katsuya	11,120	not elected
Ind	Nakamura Michiharu	9,879	not elected
Ind	Tōfuku Jun'ichi	6,506	not elected
JCP	Makinouchi Atsushi	4,097	not elected

Clearly, the conservatives had done two things wrong. First, they had endorsed one too many candidates. Secondly, they had failed to squeeze the other conservatives running as independents out of the race. If they had been able to take either one of those actions they probably would have won another seat.

A second type of election is where one of the conservative candidates takes too many of the votes and forces another conservative off the bottom of the lists. An example of this can be found in the third district of Niigata in the 1963 elections. Tanaka Kakuei is a former secretary general of the party and an extremely popular politician. Personality and political muscle conjoin to give him a lion's share of the vote, to the detriment of other conservatives in his district. The results of the 1963 elections were as follows:

NIIGATA 3 (five-man district)

LDP	Tanaka Kakuei	113,392	elected
LDP	Murayama Tatsuo	47,647	elected
JSP	Inamura Ryūichi	44,945	elected
JSP	Kobayashi Susumu	44,945	elected
LDP	Watari Shirō	44,331	elected
LDP	Ōno Ichirō	40,770	not elected
JSP	Miyake Shōichi	35,790	not elected
DSP	Katagiri Masami	15,497	not elected
JCP	Urasawa Yosaburō	7,644	not elected

It seems apparent that if Tanaka had directed some of his followers to vote for Ōno Ichirō, one of the socialists would have lost. Tomita Nobuo, an election specialist at Meiji University, cautions against such an easy conclusion.[36] Votes for Tanaka are not necessarily party votes, he argues. If Tanaka freed a group of his followers, their votes might go anywhere. But it would seem reasonable that with the strength of Tanaka's personality and handsome margin of excess votes, a way could have been found to put Ōno in the winner's column.

A more extraordinary example can be found in the third district of Kanagawa during the 1967 elections. This constituency was Kōno Ichirō's, the faction leader introduced in chapter 2. While Kōno Ichirō always picked up a goodly share of the vote for himself, he managed to leave enough votes so that other conservatives, particularly those from his own faction, could win, too. After the 1963 elections, for example, four of the five Dietmen were conservatives and three were from the Kōno faction. In 1965 Kōno Ichirō died and his son, Yōhei, decided to run in his stead. The 1967 elections promised to be even rougher than usual because the Clean Government party was running a candidate for the first time and expected to take a seat away from the conservatives. In the two branches of the old Kōno faction in particular and among the conservatives in general, doubt existed whether Yōhei had the stuff to win; many politicians freely predicted that Yōhei's seat would be the one that was lost. The results of the election were:

KANAGAWA 3 (five-man district)

LDP	Kōno Yōhei	106,827	elected
DSP	Kawamura Masaru	91,123	elected
JSP	Katō Mankichi	77,803	elected
JSP	Hirabayashi Takeshi	71,493	elected
CGP	Kohama Shinji	68,516	elected

[36] Tomita Nobuo, interview, October 12, 1966.

LDP	Andō Kaku	67,336	not elected
LDP	Kogane Yoshiteru	60,992	not elected
LDP	Kimura Gosuke	52,792	not elected
JCP	Uchino Takechiyo	22,834	not elected

The Clean Government party won its seat as expected. But Yōhei was not the sacrificial lamb. Old political loyalties among the prefectural people and the determination of a son to measure up to his father gave Yōhei a lion's share of the vote, more votes than his father ever got—in fact, too many votes. The other conservatives, all of them previous winners, lost.

The party can also suffer the loss of a seat when two of the conservatives get into a fight for the top position in the elections. Nakasone Yasuhiro and Fukuda Takeo have conducted one of these feuds in the third district of Gumma. This district, the reader will recall, is a four-man district. The socialists have enough votes so that one of the seats is tacitly earmarked for them. But the competition between Nakasone and Fukuda has become so fierce that in the 1955 and the 1960 elections, the socialists were able to garner two seats. The election results of 1960, the more disastrous of the two years for the conservatives, were as follows:

GUMMA 3 (four-man district)

LDP	Fukuda Takeo	92,099	elected
LDP	Nakasone Yasuhiro	76,274	elected
JSP	Kurihara Toshio	44,463	elected
JSP	Yamaguchi Tsuruo	39,398	elected
DSP	Numaga Kenji	29,313	not elected
LDP	Iyoku Yoshio	26,763	not elected

Granted that Iyoku Yoshio was a lack-luster candidate who was chosen from the prefectural assembly to run chiefly because he was closely connected with the powerful Obuchi family, and granted that Professor Tomita's warning also has pertinence in this situation, one may still suppose that a less competitive campaign between Fukuda and Nakasone might

135

have freed enough votes to have carried Iyoku through to victory.

Intramural fights among the conservatives are not always to the detriment of the party. An example where the party benefitted can be found in the fourth district of Niigata, the site of one of the bitterest fights in the 1963 elections. This district is a three-man district. For many years, it had been a pacified area with the vote neatly divided between the two conservatives, Tsukada Jūichirō, an eight-time winner, and Tanaka Shōji, a six-time winner; and the socialist Inomata Kōzō, a seven-time winner. Their vote over the years had been:

TANAKA SHŌJI	TSUKADA JŪICHIRŌ	INOMATA KŌZŌ
1953 — 79,777	1953 — 60,501	1953 — 52,945
1955 — 79,839	1955 — 58,956	1955 — 50,367
1958 — 75,530	1958 — 62,510	1958 — 58,545
1960 — 80,510	1960 — 53,542	1960 — 58,203

Other candidates had, of course, challenged these men. There was always a communist candidate who picked up between three and five thousand votes, another Socialist party candidate, and in 1960, a Democratic Socialist party candidate. These candidates never posed any threat to the suzerainty of the three old timers. The other candidates' vote and the total vote of the district was:

OTHER CANDIDATES	TOTAL VOTE
1953 — 28,876	1953 — 224,099
1955 — 41,903	1955 — 230,615
1958 — 39,207	1958 — 236,792
1960 — 21,135	1960 — 236,764

Tsukada Jūichirō decided after the 1960 elections that he had had enough of national politics and retired, subsequently to become the governor of Niigata. His retirement touched off a battle over who would succeed to his Diet seat. Tsukada pushed the candidacy of his son, Tōru. The Kōno faction

136

thought it saw an opening and urged the candidacy of Ōtake Tarō, a native of Niigata, a graduate of Tokyo University, a businessman, and a member of the prefectural assembly. The election policy committee, of course, endorsed Tanaka Shōji but balked at endorsing both Ōtake and the young Tsukada because of the strength of Inomata. The question was which of the two would get the endorsement, and it was resolved in favor of Ōtake, the candidate from the Kōno faction. This setback did not daunt the Tsukadas. Old Jūichirō pushed young Tōru forth as an independent and put his organization to work. The ferocity of the campaign frightened away all other minor candidates with the exception of the communist. On opening the ballot boxes, the results were:

NIIGATA 4 (three-man district)

LDP	Tanaka Shōji	62,187	elected
LDP	Ōtake Tarō	61,379	elected
Ind	Tsukada Tōru	60,450	elected
JSP	Inomata Kōzō	53,734	not elected
JCP	Terajima Taiji	5,249	not elected
	Total vote	243,359	

Inomata got his usual share of the vote, but the two new conservative candidates had been able to win through increasing the total vote, absorbing the vote going normally to the minor candidates, and whittling down Tanaka Shōji's support organization. The total vote set a new record for the district with 86.9% of the registered voters going to the polls. I investigated the voting turnout percentages to see if this set some sort of record for the nation in the 1963 elections. There were other districts with equal or higher percentage: the fifth district of Hyōgo (88.6%); the second district of Gifu (86.9%); and the third district of Nagano (87.4%).[37] In each of these districts there was a serious fight among the conservatives. Nothing apparently draws the voters like a good conservative blood-letting.

[37] *Kekka Shirabe*, 1963, pp. 56-59.

The conservative Dietmen have long been critical of the electoral state of affairs. Kawashima Shōjirō, the vice president of the party, says, "The elections show the party in its ugliest form. There is nothing that raises more distrust among the people."[38] While the conservatives recite a long litany of complaints, their attention seems to be primarily focused on two aspects: the party endorsements and the middle-sized election districts.

There is rarely a party meeting to discuss reform in which the question of party endorsements does not come up. In 1963, a reform commission headed by Miki Takeo, a former secretary general of the party, issued the following statement: "The endorsements have an important connection with the reliability of the party. Especially careful deliberations must be undertaken in deciding them. We must do away with the arbitrary decisions of a small group of the party leaders. We must study the qualities of and the conditions surrounding the candidates with impartiality."[39] In 1965, the new secretary general, Tanaka Kakuei, conducted the same sort of an exercise. In his reform proposals, he wrote:

In order to eliminate the evils of the factions, we must decide party endorsements for each of the elections with impartiality and fairness and based on the views of the heads of the various party organs. . . . After a review of existing policies, we must firmly establish principles for party endorsement. . . . We must strengthen the functions of the secretariat attached to the election policy committee. . . . We shall take measures to smooth over and unify differences of opinion between party headquarters and the regional organizations.[40]

38 *Asahi Shimbun*, September 14, 1964, p. 4.
39 Jiyūminshutō, *Soshiki Chōsakai Tōshin* [Report of the Organization Investigation Commission] (Tokyo: Jiyūminshutō, 1963), p. 76. Hereafter referred to as the *Miki Report*.
40 Jiyūminshutō, *Tōkindaika ni Kansuru Kanjichō Shian* [Proposal of the Secretary General Concerning Modernization of the Party] (September 25, 1965), pp. 7-9.

These are fine, brave, political words but the underlying concern of the party is clear. The party wants to automate a process that is now subject to the whims of the factions. The hope is that if such a process can be found, one more reason for the factions' existence is eliminated, and the unity of the party will be strengthened.

The various schemes and exhortations of the secretary generals may alleviate but will not solve the problem. After the impartial study is finished, all the recommendations heard, and especially careful deliberations concluded, someone or some group has to decide which candidate meets the criteria and gets the endorsement. Short of introducing a radical solution such as a primary system in which all the party members decide, the judgment of this group or person is going to be questioned. Factions aside, endorsements will continue as a point of contention.

The present principles the party uses in awarding its endorsements are adequate. They are based on reality and have weathered successive elections. If the party really wants to eliminate the role of the factions, then it should do what the factions are doing. It should offer its endorsements early and then work on the candidates' behalf.

The second major concern of the conservatives has been the electoral system itself. "Under the present electoral system, the fights between the candidates of the same party in the same electoral district are intense, the support organizations have become all-important, the weakening of the party organization is encouraged, and prodigious amounts of money are needed. We must devise a system under which the political parties will become the basis of the elections."[41] There has been no shortage of electoral systems proposed to correct the situation.

Most seriously considered is a proposal first put forward by Prime Minister Hatoyama in 1956, shortly after the party was formed. He suggested that one representative be elected from each district, a restoration of the "small" electoral sys-

[41] *Miki Report,* p. 91.

tem. Others have called it the one-man one-district system or the single member constituency. It is the simple majority single ballot system currently in effect in the United States, Great Britain, and the Dominions.

The opposition parties would stand to lose a goodly number of seats under this system and in order to sweeten the offering, most advocates suggest that the single member constituency be coupled with a system of proportional representation which would give a limited number of seats according to the percentage of the vote which each party received. Since no system which reduces the number of legislative seats stands any hope of adoption, the current suggestion is to increase the size of the lower house to five hundred seats, with four hundred Dietmen to be selected from the single member constituencies and one hundred Dietmen to be chosen by proportional representation. But the opposition parties have refused to take the bait. They want no part of a single member constituency with or without proportional representation.

If the out parties are united in their opposition, the conservatives are divided in their support. The party has split into three groups, one arguing vociferously for adoption, another adamantly opposing, with the rest choosing to sit on the fence. The dispute has gradually assumed the overtones of a factional fight, but "whether a Dietman supports or opposes the small election system can usually be determined after investigating conditions in his electoral district."[42] Estimates of the division of forces vary. But no matter what the precise strength of the various camps may be, the party would have great difficulties in pushing this reform through the Diet.

The advocates of the plan hold that its adoption would solve most of the difficulties which the electoral system has created in the party. The *Asahi Shimbun* has summarized their argument:

[42] *Asahi Shimbun,* February 14, 1966, p. 2.

If a single member constituency is created, the party itself will look after the campaign of each candidate and the factions will naturally disappear. . . . Elections based on money will be driven out, elections based on the party will be established firmly, and the nation's politics will be advanced greatly. . . .

To begin with, since there will be only one winner in each election district, each party will endorse only one candidate and the elections will become a fight between the parties. Elections will center on debate over policy, thus promoting the healthy growth of the parties. With policy becoming the principal issue, the currently prevalent appeals to private interest and bribery will lose their effectiveness. Since the election districts will become smaller, election expenses will become less and the elections will become cleaner.

Furthermore, if the small electoral district is adopted, two political parties will emerge and the political situation will become stabilized. This will contribute to the development of politics based on parliamentary democracy.

These are the principal arguments of the advocates of the small electoral system.[43]

The opponents of the small electoral system dispute whether these benefits will accrue to the party.[44] They note that the single member constituencies will be about the same size as the election districts for the prefectural assemblies. If the electoral districts become this small, they argue, the local politician who has been running errands for his neighbors will be favored over the men who have been running the

[43] *Asahi Shimbun*, September 14, 1964, p. 4.

[44] Yoshimura Tadashi is one of the most articulate opponents of the small electoral district. He has summarized most of the arguments used by the Dietmen and added a few more of his own. See Yoshimura Tadashi, "Shō-senkyoku-sei-ron no Munashisa" [The Emptiness of the Argument Concerning the Small Electoral System] in Rōyama Masamichi, *et al.*, *Shōsenkyokusei* [The Small Election District System] (Tokyo: Ushio Shuppan-sha, 1966), pp. 49-82.

country. The quality of the candidates will drop. "Cast a fine-meshed net and you catch little fish," says Kōno Kenzō, a former vice speaker of the upper house.[45] Since the local politicians will have a chance of winning in the national race, more rather than fewer men will compete for office. Thus there will be more rather than fewer fights between the conservatives. Party endorsement will become less meaningful since the candidates will run on highly local issues. The small size of the election districts means that the candidate will know virtually all the voters and will be expected to watch out for each of their interests and thus service will become more important than ever. Competition between candidates and service to the voter will conspire to make the elections more expensive. The close connection between the voters and the candidates suggests that bribery and appeal to self-interest will occur more readily than in the present elections, where there is a greater distance between the voters and the candidates. Nakasone has summarized the opposition's arguments, "There are many ways . . . of modernizing the party short of revising the electoral system. If the small electoral system is created, a politician will have to spend all his time cultivating his district. This will cost money, the politicians will become small-bore, and the level of the campaign will become degraded."[46]

So the argument goes. It is hard to dispute the contention of the reform advocates that the present electoral system is the cause of, or at least contributes to, the ills of the conservative party, that it causes division among the conservatives, and precludes cooperation in building a strong local base. Aoki Masashi, a Dietman who took particular interest in the electoral process, put this plaint clearly.

> The party organization committee dispatches a party worker to a prefecture with orders to organize, but he can't do anything. He goes to a village and tries to organ-

[45] Kōno Kenzō, interview, January 25, 1966.
[46] *Asahi Shimbun*, February 14, 1966, p. 2.

ize for the party but there are supporters for the various Dietmen in the village. They are already organized in groups around the Dietmen and they are shy about even producing their membership lists. Everything is based on the Dietmen. If you were able to put all these organizations together, you might be able to form a party organ. But they oppose each other. Under present conditions, it is impossible to organize for the party.[47]

This situation is, if anything, going to become worse. In the chapter on support organizations, we noted that there were two types of *jiban*, horizontal and vertical. Under the vertical organization, there were many cases where the candidates from the same electoral district could cooperate with each other since their supporters were clustered in different parts of the electoral districts. But these vertical organizations appear to be breaking down. Most *jibans* are turning into the horizontal type. These changes will further exacerbate the fights between the conservatives and hinder the building of a party with strong local roots.

It is also difficult to dispute the opponents who contend that the small election system will fail to produce elections based on the parties or strengthen party organization in the regions. Japan has had, in fact, one small election district for quite some time. This is the island of Amami Ōshima which sends one man to the lower house. Shimagami Zengorō, an election specialist for the socialists and the winner of seven elections himself, describes the conditions in this single member constituency:

Amami Ōshima is a one-man district. It's a race between the candidates of the Liberal Democratic party. Because the Socialist party is weak there, the first and the second positions go to the Liberal Democratic party. The Socialist party comes in third. The endorsed candi-

[47] Senkyo Seido Shingikai, *Dai-niji Senkyo Seido Shingikai Giji Sokkiroku* [Transcript of the Proceedings of the Second Election System Deliberation Council] (Tokyo: n.p., 1963), p. 229.

date and the unendorsed candidates of the Liberal Democratic party fight for the first and second position as if one vote will determine who wins. Conditions are pretty close to that in the farmlands. The Socialist party and the Liberal Democratic party don't fight. It's a fight between the endorsed and the unendorsed candidates of the Liberal Democratic party.[48]

Prediction on the basis of one district is risky, but Amami Ōshima seems to suggest that reform would cause little change from present conditions.

It is also valid to look at the examples of other nations. Maurice Duverger, the French political scientist, has studied the political systems of the West and he offers the following generalization: "The influence of party on candidatures varies in direct relation to the size of the constituencies. The larger the constituency, the greater the party influence: the smaller the constituency, the more restricted is the party intervention."[49] There is little to suggest that his observation is not applicable to Japan.

We have pointed out many of the weaknesses of the present electoral system. There are also strengths. Although the party we are dealing with has only been in existence for ten years, it was built upon other conservative parties which had been in power since the end of the war. This party should be exhibiting all the symptoms of a party that has ruled too long: a tendency towards oligarchy, a high proportion of aged politicians, satisfaction with the status quo, a penchant

[48] Senkyo Seido Shingikai, *Dai-ichiji Senkyo Seido Shingikai Kōmei Senkyo Suishin Undō ni kansuru Iinkai (Dai-san Iinkai) oyobi Senkyoku-betsu Teisū ni kansuru Iinkai (Dai-yon Iinkai) Giji Sokkiroku* [Transcript of the Proceedings of the Committee Concerned with the Movement Urging Clean Elections (No. 3 Committee) and the Committee Concerned with the Number of Seats in Each Election District (No. 4 Committee) of the First Election System Deliberation Commission] (Tokyo: n.p., 1961), pp. 399-400.

[49] Maurice Duverger, *Political Parties* (2nd English ed. rev.; New York: John Wiley and Sons, Inc., 1959), p. 357.

to take things easy, indifference to popular attitudes. But the election system has prevented political senescence.

First of all, the present electoral system keeps new blood circulating within the party. Earlier in the chapter, we pointed out that incumbent Dietmen stood the best chance in the elections. But this does not mean that the party is stagnant. The following chart compares the quondam and new faces with the total number of successful conservative candidates and shows that there is a relatively high turnover rate.

Turnover Rate of Conservative Dietmen in
Successive Lower House Elections 1958-1967

1958	25.1%	1963	20.8%
1960	27.0%	1967	15.5%

Source: Computed from Home Ministry statistics.

Although the conservative party has developed a seniority system—qualification for post and determination of rank are determined by the number of times the Dietmen have been successful at the polls—new Dietmen make their presence felt. New blood has a way of revitalizing the old organs.

Secondly, the present electoral system keeps the politicians in close touch with the people. Fear of another conservative stealing his voters keeps a politician firmly faced towards his constituency. When the Diet is not in session, the Dietmen are, of course, campaigning in the districts. But even when the Diet is in session, it is not unusual for many politicians to catch a train immediately after the close of the session Friday, make political rounds over the weekend, and return Monday morning in time for the afternoon session— and keep this schedule up week after week. Kurogane Yasumi says, "I make it a point to go back to my district every weekend."[50] Theoretically, Kurogane should not have to worry. Both his family and his wife's family have been active in politics for many years and Kurogane has been

[50] Kurogane Yasumi, interview, August 23, 1966.

elected six times and has served as chief cabinet secretary, a post with great public exposure. But high office and sustained public media attention is no assurance of success at the polls. For example, in the 1963 elections, former Prime Ministers Katayama Tetsu and Ishibashi Tanzan lost, and former Prime Minister Kishi came in fifth in a five-man district. The politicians claim that this incessant campaigning keeps them from doing their work in Tokyo. A Dietman's secretary notes that constant touring of the district makes the relationship between the politicians and the people more personal than political.[51] On the other hand, this constant attention to the public helps close the gap that has historically existed between the rulers and the ruled.

Thirdly, the present electoral system keeps the people involved and interested in the affairs of the nation. The voter has pretty well made up his mind about which of the two camps, renovationist or conservative, he is going to support. Without the fight between the conservatives, the elections would be altogether too predictable and dreary. The party may complain about the disarray of its political skirts. But the political fights draw the voters to the ballot boxes. There seems to be at least a ten percent difference in the turnout of voters between a stable district and a district where the conservatives are at each other's throats. Take the prefecture of Aomori in the 1963 elections, for example. In the first district, two conservative candidates were endorsed and elected. There were no independents around to cause trouble. Only 64.3% of the voters turned out. In the second district, however, there were five conservatives—three endorsed candidates and two independents—fighting for three legislative seats, and 74.7% of the voters turned out. The prefecture of Ishikawa is another case in point. In the first district, there were four candidates for three posts: two conservatives, one socialist, and one communist. The communist lost and the other candidates divided up the seats with a minimum of fuss and bother. The voting turnout was 68.1% In the second dis-

[51] Kobayashi Katsumi, letter, dated July 27, 1968.

trict, which is solid conservative territory, there was a donnybrook between three party-endorsed candidates and two so-called independents for three Diet seats. The voting turnout was 83.8%[52]

There are many factors which affect voting turnout, and perhaps I over-emphasize the fights. Moreover, these fights are not always conducted on the highest levels. Debate on policy and the destiny of the nation sometimes gets overlooked by the candidates, and their campaign workers who are busy with the mud buckets. But no voter can complain about being left out of politics, in an age when social isolation and political alienation are serious concerns.

We have given ample space to the views of the politicians concerning the elections. As a final point it may be well to inquire what the voters think about the system. In 1965, the government sponsored a wide-ranging survey and one of the questions asked was whether the elections should be centered on the parties. Only 11% of the electorate thought that this was a good idea.[53] Another question was whether there should be some basic reforms and only 18% responded favorably.[54] Drawing definite conclusions from public opinion polls is hazardous, but at least it appears at the moment that the voters like the elections pretty much the way they are. In this most basic of political decisions, they will probably continue to have their way.

[52] Jichishō [Home Ministry] statistics.

[53] Senkyo Seido Shingikai, *Senkyo no Jittai ni kansuru Seron Chōsa* [Public Opinion Survey Concerning the Actual State of the Elections] (August, 1965), p. 32.

[54] *Ibid.*, pp. 2, 34.

CHAPTER VI

Choosing the President

"Ikeda Hayato—242 votes!"

A cascade of applause and shouts bursts out. By a bare majority of four votes . . . Ikeda protected his right to the "seat of glory" for the third time.[1]

It was the moment of climax to the seventh party presidential election. Three contestants, Ikeda Hayato, Satō Eisaku, and Fujiyama Aiichirō, were fighting not only for the party presidency, but ultimately for the chair of the prime minister.

The voting started at 10:40 in the morning at the party conference held in the public hall in Bunkyo ward, [Tokyo]. . . . The order was first the representatives from the lower house, then the councillors from the upper house, and finally the prefectural delegates. The audience intently watched the movements of the electors, waiting for the moment when the results would be announced.

Satō occasionally patted the sweat off his forehead . . . Fujiyama stared intently at the hands of the ballot counters without moving a muscle. . . . Ikeda did nothing but switch his fan from time to time. . . .

As the counting proceeded, the eleven members of the presidential election committee stood up from their chairs and peered over to see which way the vote was going. At 11:20, the counting began to come to an end. Dietman Arafune, a member of the Kawashima faction, suddenly raised his left hand and gestured. A roar filled the hall.

Arafune returned to his seat. Once more, he stuck up

[1] *Mainichi Shimbun*, evening edition, July 10, 1964, p. 11.

148

two fingers on his left hand, then four fingers on his right
hand, finally two fingers on his left hand. It was a sign
that Ikeda had gotten 242 votes. The "owner" of the
chair of the party president was decided.
In the moment of defeat, Satō's eyebrows twitched.
But his features quickly returned to normal. He forced a
faint smile toward the clustered camera lights and flashbulbs. He motioned to the cameramen to sit down.
Tightlipped, Fujiyama stared at the ballot counters.
The preliminary fights behind the scenes for the party
presidency had been long . . . but the final performance
was a bare forty minutes. At 11:30, Takeyama Yūtarō,
the chairman of the presidential election committee, formally announced the results of the voting.
Ikeda, who had been elected for the third time, rose
and in his usual gravel voice, delivered his victory
statement. . . .
Immediately after the statement, Fujiyama and Satō
rose and together climbed the stage. They proffered the
handshake of congratulations. . . . Fujiyama wore his
usual cheery face, but Satō was unable to muster a
smile. . . .[2]
Shortly after the close of the conference, Ikeda
Hayato entered the prime minister's residence and held
a reception for all the participants of the party conference to thank them for their labors.[3]

Presidential elections are not new to the conservatives.
The party laws of the major pre-war parties had provisions
for such elections.[4] But there is a major difference between the
prewar and postwar party elections. Before the war, the
elections were an elaborate ritual to justify a more informal
process of selection. The party president was in fact chosen

[2] *Mainichi Shimbun*, evening edition, July 10, 1964, p. 11.
[3] *Ibid.*, p. 1.
[4] Tōyama Shigeki and Adachi Yoshiko, *Kindai Nihon Seiji-shi Hikkei*
[A Handbook of Modern Japanese Political History] (Tokyo: Iwanami
Shoten, 1961), pp. 134-135.

through consultation of the party elders. They were severely constrained in their range of selection because they knew that the ultimate purpose of the party president was to serve as the prime minister, that the power to extend the mandate to form a cabinet lay with the emperor, and the emperor would act only after hearing his personal advisors. The party leaders, in short, had to choose a party president acceptable to the emperor's advisors. During the various periods of prewar history, this power to advise the emperor lay with different groups. During the period of party government in the twenties and early thirties, the power lay in the hands of the *genrō*.[5] As one old politician describes it, "The basis of selection of the party president was whether he would receive the imperial mandate to form a cabinet. The favor of the *genrō*, who were charged with protecting the national polity and the imperial constitution had to be gained. . . ."[6] Later, in the thirties, the military forces became the dominant element in Japanese politics. Through the judicious use of political funds, they were able to influence the decisions, including the selection of leaders, of the parties. In the forties, the parties merged into a single political entity, the Imperial Rule Assistance Association, which was little more than a rubber stamp, and whose leader, although elected, enjoyed no real political power.

After Japan's defeat in the war, the parties were resuscitated and selection of their leaders reverted to a pattern similar to that established during the days of party govern-

[5] The term *genrō* needs definition and I find myself, like a great many other students, unable to offer a precise one. They were men who in their younger days had played an instrumental role in the development of the modern Japanese state. All had served as prime ministers. With the exception of Saionji, all came from the feudatories of either Satsuma or Chōshū. "They had powers which exceeded the constitution . . . they surrounded the emperor . . . and advised him and the government." *Nihonshi Jiten* [A Dictionary of Japanese History] (Osaka: Sōgen-sha, 1961), pp. 157-158.

[6] Tsugumo Kunitoshi, secretary general of the Friends of Constitutional Government Association, quoted in *Asahi Shimbun*, August 17, 1962, p. 2.

ment in the twenties, although the formal election of the party presidents was temporarily forgotten.[7] Who was to rule the nation was formally decided by a majority vote in the Diet, and the president of the party that controlled the Diet could in theory become prime minister. But all politicians realized that no man could become prime minister who met with the disfavor of the occupation authorities. Party leadership went, as it had in the days before the war, to the politician who was acceptable as prime minister.

The Occupation came to an end. In 1955, the socialist parties merged into a single party and the conservatives, worried about losing control of the government, prepared to follow the same road.

At the time, the conservatives were divided into two parties. One was the Liberal party led by Ogata Taketora. The other was the Democratic party headed by Hatoyama Ichirō. After several months of discussion, the principals found that they were in agreement on all save one point: who was to lead the new party. Finally, Ogata suggested that the impasse be broken by holding an election. Hatoyama agreed. On November 15, 1955, the Liberal Democratic party was born.[8]

In April, 1956, the first presidential elections were held. During the interim Ogata had died and his death gave an open field to Hatoyama. He became the first party president. All told, there have been nine presidential elections. I have tried to place most of the essentials concerning these elections in Table 12.

Some knowledge of the rules will be helpful at this point. There are three documents which govern the party presidential elections. They are the Japanese constitution, the party

[7] One of the conservative parties, the Democratic party, held an election on November 9, 1948, among its members in the Diet to decide the party leader. There was discussion among the other conservative groups about holding a party election to decide party leadership but no elections actually took place. Watanabe Tsuneo, *Tōshu to Seitō* [Party Leaders and Political Parties] (Tokyo: Kōbundō, 1961), p. 93.

[8] Watanabe Tsuneo, *Habatsu* [Factions] (Rev. ed., Tokyo: Kōbundō, 1963), p. 141.

151

law, and "Rules for the Public Election of the Party President," which consists of sixteen articles.

The role of the Japanese constitution is inferential. It does not mention political parties, much less establish provisions for choosing their leaders. But the constitution does give qualifications for the selection of the prime minister. Since the ultimate purpose of the party president is to serve as prime minister, these qualifications are observed in the party presidential elections. First, the constitution provides that the prime minister shall be a civilian,[9] a provision prompted by the events leading up to the last war but essentially meaningless today. The second qualification is that "the prime minister shall be designated from among the members of the Diet by a resolution of the Diet."[10] This provision insures that the party president will be a Dietman as well as providing the basis—so long as he is leader of the majority party—by which he becomes prime minister. Finally, the constitution gives the lower house ultimate authority over the selection of the prime minister,[11] passage of the budget,[12] and the conclusion of treaties,[13] thus making it the highest legislative authority and encouraging the selection of the party president (prime minister) from its ranks.

The party law[14] takes up where the constitution lets off. It has two provisions which concern the selection of the party president. Article 82 establishes the term of office of the president as two years but allows for his re-election. Article 6 states, "The president . . . shall be elected at the party conference."

---

[9] Japan. "Nippon Koku Kempō" [Japanese National Constitution] in *Roppō Zensho* [Compendium of Laws] (Tokyo: Iwanami, 1960), Art. 66, sec. 2.

[10] *Ibid.*, Art. 67, Sec. 1.

[11] *Ibid.*, Art. 67, Sec. 2.

[12] *Ibid.*, Art. 60, Sec. 2.

[13] *Ibid.*, Art. 61.

[14] The party law is not a national law but a private law created by the party itself. There is presently discussion in Japan whether the parties should be recognized and their activities regulated by an act of the Diet, but such a law has yet to be passed.

The Dietmen follow several calendars. First, there is the legislative calendar, with the summoning of the Diet in December, its adjournment to the new year, its close in May, followed by the extraordinary session, usually in the fall. Second is the factional calendar in which the months of July and December dominate, since funds are collected and disbursed at this time. There is the electoral cycle: in practice, a little more than two years for the lower house members; in law, six years for the upper house members. Article 82 creates the presidential or party cycle which is completed every two years.

A look at Table 12 shows that this cycle has often been disrupted. Only four of the first eight terms have been completed. Illness has caused the early resignation of two prime ministers, Ishibashi Tanzan and Ikeda Hayato. Politics has also taken its toll. Hatoyama Ichirō found it advisable to resign after reestablishing diplomatic relations with the Soviet Union. Kishi Nobusuke decided on the same course after renegotiating a treaty of mutual security with the United States. During the nine cycles prime ministers have changed five times. The politicians speak of two terms as "normal," but nothing is ordained.

The party conference, the forum for the election, is the "supreme organ of the party."[15] The party conference meets once a year, usually in January before the Diet settles down to taking care of the legislative business of the year. Extraordinary sessions, however, can be summoned by the president at any time.[16] The conference has the responsibility of making the basic decisions of the party. The most important of these decisions is the election of the party president.

During the years when there is no presidential election, the party conference is a formality. The meeting takes only a few of the morning hours. The secretary general makes a report

[15] Jiyūminshutō, "Tōsoku" [Party Law] in *Wagatō no Kihon Hōshin* [Basic Policies of Our Party] (Tokyo: Jiyūminshutō Kōkoku Iinkai, 1966, Art. 26.

[16] *Ibid.*, Art. 27.

153

TABLE 12. RESULTS OF PRESIDENTIAL ELECTIONS OF THE LIBERAL DEMOCRATIC PARTY 1956-1966

Election	Number of Electors	First ballot Results		Runoff Ballot Results		Winner	Remarks
First–April 5, 1956	489	Hatoyama Ichirō	394	None		Hatoyama	uncontested election 95 protest ballots including 69 blanks. 7 months in office.
		Other	19				
		Invalid	76				
		Majority	207				
Second–December 14, 1956	511	Kishi Nobusuke	223	Ishibashi Tanzan	258	Ishibashi	7 vote victory resulting from Ishibashi-Ishii alliance (2nd and 3rd places in first ballot). 3 months in office.
		Ishibashi Tanzan	151	Kishi Nobusuke	251		
		Ishii Mitsujirō	137	Invalid	1		
		Majority	256				
Third–March 21, 1957	476	Kishi Nobusuke	471	None		Kishi	uncontested election 22 months in office.
		Other	4				
		Invalid	1				
		Majority	238				
Fourth–January 24, 1959	496	Kishi Nobusuke	320	None		Kishi	18 months in office.
		Matsumura Kenzō	166				
		Other	5				
		Invalid	1				
		Majority	248				
Fifth–July 14, 1960	501	Ikeda Hayato	246	Ikeda Hayato	302	Ikeda	Ikeda five votes short of victory on first ballot. Forced into runoff, with Fujiyama's votes going to Ikeda. 24 months in office.
		Ishii Mitsujirō	196	Ishii Mitsujirō	194		
		Fujiyama Aiichirō	49	Invalid	5		
		Other	7				
		Invalid	3				
		Majority	251				

Sixth–July 14, 1962	466	Ikeda Hayato	391	None	Ikeda	uncontested election 75 protest votes including 35 blanks. 24 months in office.
		Other	37			
		Invalid	38			
		Majority	215			
Seventh–July 10, 1964	478	Ikeda Hayato	242	None	Ikeda	Ikeda gained majority of only four votes. 7 months in office.
		Satō Eisaku	160			
		Fujiyama Aiichirō	72			
		Other	1			
		Invalid	3			
		Majority	238			
Eighth–December 1, 1964					Satō	Serious illness struck Ikeda after his third election. He made known his intent to resign on October 25. At the assembly of the members of both houses, it was decided to allow the secretary general and the vice president to decide on his successor through consultations. On November 9, Ikeda issued his resignation and announced Satō Eisaku as the single candidate for the party presidency. The assembly of both houses met the same day and elected him to this post. This election was subsequently endorsed by general acclamation at a party conference on December 1st. 24 months in office.
Ninth–December 1, 1966	459	Satō Eisaku	289	None	Satō	
		Fujiyama Aiichirō	94			
		Maeo Shigesaburō	47			
		Other	25			
		Invalid	9			
		Majority	226			

SOURCE: Derived from accounts published in Tsuji Kiyoaki, ed., *Shiryō—Sengo Nijūnen-shi* [A History of the Twenty Years After the War—Documents], Vol. 1 (Tokyo: Nihon Hyōronsha, 1966), pp. 346-351; *Asahi Shimbun*, evening edition, December 1, 1966, p. 1.

on the state of the party, the party budget is presented, a new party song is perhaps heard, the party platform is read, the men who have made special contributions to the party are given scrolls. The proceedings have been carefully planned and everybody knows his part. There are no floor fights and no debates. Every motion is adopted unanimously. "These conferences are boring," a reporter told me at the 17th party conference (January 1966), "The only reason I show up is because several years ago, Prime Minister Kishi got stabbed in the fanny by a thug. This year, with a little bit of luck . . ."[17]

About noon, the conference draws to a close and the participants head for the prime minister's residence. Rimming its back lawn are small catered-food stalls loaded with everything from pancakes to raw fish. Round tables spot the center of the grounds and they are loaded with beer, sake, Bireley's Orange Drink, and Coca-Cola. On the steps leading up and into the residence, local politicians vie with each other and an accordian player over who shall use the microphone set up there. The Dietmen spend most of their time being photographed with the groups from their constituencies against the imposing background of the mansion. Everyone wears a broad smile. The reception seems more in keeping with the mood of the delegates than the conference. Everyone is gay, relaxed, and talkative. "It is a festival," says a newsman.[18] The party is having a party. "When no election is scheduled for the post of party president, the conference itself is largely ceremonial with scant political significance."[19]

The atmosphere changes drastically when the party conference is called upon to elect the party president. Many times, it is an extraordinary session called specifically for this purpose. No party songs are heard, no florid speeches made, all extraneous party business is compressed or forgotten entirely.[20] Many months of planning and maneuver by many

[17] Watanabe Tsuneo, interview, January 22, 1966.

[18] Ikeda Kanjō, interview, October 15, 1965.

[19] *Asahi Shimbun*, January 22, 1966, p. 2.

[20] For the ninth presidential election, for example, the party resolved formally that it would deal with no business save the election. *Yomiuri Shimbun*, evening edition, November 15, 1966, p. 2.

politicians have gone into preparation for this conference. It is a moment of high political drama. As ten o'clock rolls around, the voting starts.

Procedures for the election of the party president are embodied in special rules. Considerable thought was given to their drafting, but the authors were fallible. There is provision in the rules themselves for amendment by the party conference, but most politicians are reluctant to tamper with them. The plans and hopes of some of the party's most powerful politicians hinge on these rules as they are now written.

One peculiarity of the presidential election rules is that there is no provision for the nomination of the presidential candidates. The rules state only that eligibility shall be confined to the Dietmen.[21] But only the purists and the lawyers carp at this oversight. A newsman explains, "Sometimes the candidates make a formal announcement to us of their candidacy, sometimes not. It makes no difference. We know who the candidates are and so does everybody else in the party. For several weeks prior to the election we have been writing stories on little else."[22]

All is not left up to the newsmen, however. There is a presidential election committee which administers the election.[23] It is composed of eleven men,[24] all Diet members;[25] from this group, one is elected as chairman.[26] Each of the factions has its man on the committee. If any dispute should arise over the election, they investigate and make the final decision.[27] They are also empowered to make other rules on a case by case basis to enforce the provisions of the presidential election rules.[28] "They mainly just stand around," says a reporter. "If anything happens, they make sure their faction's interests are represented. When the votes are counted, they cluster around the ballot box and signal the other members of the faction or

<hr />

21 Jiyūminshutō. "Sōsai Kōsen Kitei" [Rules for the Public Election of the Party President] in *Wagatō nō Kihon Hōshin* [Basic Policies of Our Party] (Tokyo: Jiyūminshutō Kōkoku Iinkai, 1966), Art. 4.

22 Senda Wataru, interview, November 6, 1965.

23 Jiyūminshutō, *Sōsai Kōsen Kitei*, Art. 2, sec. 1.

24 *Ibid.*, sec. 2.   25 *Ibid.*, sec. 3.   26 *Ibid.*, sec. 5.

27 *Ibid.*, Art. 13.   28 *Ibid.*, Art. 15.

the factions they are allied with, who has won. It gets pretty tense for the faction leader if he has to wait for the official announcement."[29]

The electors have to register five days in advance of the elections and their qualifications have to be approved by the headquarters of the party.[30] Each elector has one vote,[31] which he must exercise himself.[32] One interesting provision is that the elector must write the name of his candidate on the ballot.[33] During the third election of Prime Minister Ikeda (the one described at the beginning of this chapter), this provision caused difficulties. Since there is no nominating process and there are several Ikedas among the Diet members of the party, an elector who simply scribbled the family name Ikeda on the ballot had his vote invalidated, though it was patently clear that there was only one Ikeda in the running.[34]

The polling is opened by order of the chairman of the presidential election committee.[35] He also proclaims the end of the voting.[36] He reports the results of the poll to the chairman of the party conference, who in turn announces to the conference at large the total number of votes gained by each candidate and the name of the elected.[37] The chairman of the presidential election committee has on occasion assumed other unofficial duties. He is the man who sits nearest to the ballot box. During the party elections of 1964, the chairman was a member of the Ōno faction and several of the other Ōno faction members flashed their votes to him to insure there was a witness who could guarantee that they voted as they said they would.

It is articles three, five, and eleven that have given the presidential elections their unique flavor. These articles deal with

[29] Ikeda Kanjō, interview, October 5, 1965.
[30] Jiyūminshutō, *Sōsai Kōsen Kitei*, Art. 3, sec. 2.
[31] *Ibid.*, Art. 6.   [32] *Ibid.*, Art. 7.   [33] *Ibid.*, Art. 9.
[34] *Asahi Shimbun*, July 10, 1964, p. 1.
[35] Jiyūminshutō, *Sōsai Kōsen Kitei*, Art. 8.
[36] *Ibid.*, Art. 10, sec. 1.   [37] *Ibid.*, Art. 12.

the voting qualifications, the secret ballot, and majority rule.

Article three grants the franchise. By its provisions, each Diet member of the party and one delegate from each of the prefectural federations shall vote for the president. (Originally, two delegates from each of the prefectural federations had the vote, but in 1962, an amendment was passed reducing these votes to one). In the nine presidential elections that have been held, the number of electors has hovered around five hundred. In the second election, there were 511 electors and in the ninth election, there were 459 (see Table 12). Since the number of electors is limited, the candidates for the party presidency have not relied on eloquence, drama and charisma—the tools of mass persuasion—to gain adherents. Rather they have made individual appeals to each one of the voters to win his support. The pledging of allegiance has taken the form of the voter entering the faction of the presidential candidate. "The party presidential elections resulted in the establishment of the factions. More accurately, presidential elections and factional politics are two wheels on the same cart. One does not move without the other."[38]

These five hundred votes can be broken down into three groups. The largest group is composed of the representatives (lower house, Diet) who usually number about three hundred. These men must be ready to stand for election any time, usually every two or three years. They face formidable opponents from other factions of the same party. All the favored party posts except one chairmanship, and all the cabinet seats except three ministerial posts, go to members of the lower house. Political funds, campaign support, and posts in the party and government are subject to the control of the faction leader. A high degree of fealty to the factions among the lower house members is thus ensured.

The second largest group are the councillors (upper house, Diet). During the last election of Prime Minister Ikeda

[38] Watanabe, *Tōshu*, p. 96.

(1964), they cast 143 of the 478 votes.[39] The desire to maintain a separate identity, less concern with the daily affairs of party and government, an election system that does not encourage allegiance to the factions, and an independent system of appointment to high posts conspire to make the councillor less fervid in his factional loyalty than his lower house counterpart.

The third group of electors is made up of the delegates from the prefectural federations. They number forty-six, one from each prefecture. The method of selecting the federation delegate for the election varies from prefecture to prefecture. A general rule is hard to draw. Rank within the federation is of some concern. At the third election of Ikeda, seven of the prefectural delegates were chiefs of their federations, 27 of the prefectural delegates were secretaries of the federation, and three were vice chiefs of the federation. But these positions do not exhaust all the possibilities. In the same election, three chairmen, one from a policy affairs research council, one from an executive council, and one from a discipline committee; three federation advisors, two of whom were former Dietmen; and three prefectural assemblymen with no formal position in the federation represented their respective prefectures. Rank is important only so far as it offers some clues as to who holds the reins of power in the prefecture.

In some prefectures, power is in the hands of the governor. Governors like to maintain an air of being above party politics though, in truth, most of them are members of the conservative party. They will not attend the party conference but will send a delegate to vote their choice. More often, the power in a prefecture lies with a Diet member. In this instance, he will probably be the chief of the federation and the delegate to the party conference will be one of his men, usually the secretary of the federation. The most common case occurs when power is not clearly held by any one person. Heated battles rage over whom the prefecture will sup-

[39] Watanabe, *Habatsu*, p. 145.

160

port in the presidential election and who will cast the prefecture's vote. Many times these conflicts can not be resolved and a senior member of the federation is sent off to vote according to his own best judgment.

The point to be noted is that the factions do not play a direct role in deciding who the prefectural delegate shall be. This is not to say that regional politicians do not have factional affiliations. Many times they do. For example, gubernatorial elections cost money and often these funds come from a faction, to which the governor is then obligated. Other local politicians usually belong to one of the *kōenkai* of the Dietmen, and they will usually follow his lead in the voting. But the factional ties of the prefectural delegates are weaker than those of the representatives or councillors.

The factions are the basis for the presidential elections. Their decisions determine the way the electors vote. The strength of their influence can be illustrated by events shortly before the ninth presidential election.

During the late summer and early autumn of 1966, a series of minor scandals were uncovered in the Liberal Democratic party. The newspapers set out in full cry after the party and the conservative politicians responded by initiating several movements to clean up the party. The factions got their usual raking over the coals. Since the presidential elections were scheduled to be held in December, it was perhaps inevitable that the Dietmen would demand that the stranglehold which the factions have on the elections be broken and that the electors be given a free vote.

Fujiyama Aiichirō, who was opposing Satō Eisaku for the party presidency, made this demand part of his campaign.[40] Satō, of course, could not oppose this movement and it was not long before the executive council adopted a resolution declaring the free vote to be a matter of party policy, a reform that had been urged by both Miki Takeo and Tanaka Kakuei when they were secretary generals of the party. "I feel the fresh breezes of a new conservative party which has broken

40 *Mainichi Shimbun*, evening edition, November 11, 1966, p. 1.

through the old concepts of faction," crowed Ōishi Buichi, a Dietman.[41]

But few shared Ōishi's great enthusiasm. An editorial in the *Yomiuri Shimbun* explained why:

> Looking at the history of the presidential elections to date, the free vote argument has almost always been preached by the factions opposing the prime minister. The reason is that the prime minister's faction has the power both to rule and to reward. Using it, the prime minister's faction works on the leaders of the other factions, who in turn keep their factions united in support of the prime minister. . . . So long as this factional discipline is maintained, an opposition candidate stands no chance of winning. Opposition factions therefore oppose support of a candidate on a factional basis. They urge a free vote."[42]

One Dietman had the rules of the game pointed out to him personally, if the following item, which appeared in the *Asahi Shimbun*, is correct:

> On the tenth of November, Secretary General Tanaka was visited by Kitsukawa Kyūe who was the spokesman for a group of ten or so Dietmen belonging to a party reform group. Kitsukawa presented a resolution demanding that "presidential elections should be decided by a free vote." Tanaka accepted the resolution and then stood shaking his head bewildered for a few moments. "Kitsukawa, you're clearly a member of the Miki faction," he said. "If my understanding is correct, Miki and the others of the faction have already decided to support Satō. . . ."[43]

Even the free vote movement gets enmeshed in factional machinations. The factions are the final arbiter. Every vote, free or not, has been committed. The elections themselves

41 *Yomiuri Shimbun*, November 13, 1966, p. 2.
42 *Ibid.*
43 *Asahi Shimbun*, November 11, 1966, p. 2.

should be just a ceremony. But such is not the case. Article five turns the election from a formality into a hard-fought contest. This article states, "The election shall be conducted by a secret ballot with a single entry."

The single entry clause has caused no major problems, though there have been several instances where voters cast blank or mutilated ballots. At the time of the first presidential election, it was clear that Hatoyama was going to win. A coterie of 70 Dietmen around Ikeda Hayato were adamantly opposed to Hatoyama, but instead of putting up their own candidate who was bound to lose, they chose instead to cast blank or mutilated ballots.[44] Ikeda got a taste of his own medicine in the sixth election when 35 blank or mutilated ballots were cast against his unopposed candidacy.[45]

It is the secret ballot that adds the element of uncertainty. At every presidential election, several of the factions will attempt to subvert the secret ballot. Any political reporter can regale the listener with tales of one faction or another instructing its followers to fold the corners of a ballot a certain way, or write with a ballpoint or a special colored ink so that a tally of who voted for whom can be made. But vote marking is only one of the minor shenanigans that take place during a presidential election, if the newsmen are to be believed. The secret ballot means that the legislators can disregard factional loyalties and prefectural delegates ignore federation instructions and vote for whomever they choose. The task of each faction, then, is to cut mavericks out of the other factions' herds and pick up the strays.

It is open range war. During the third Ikeda election, politics became so rough that a group of politicians banded together and formed the General Federation for the Renovation of Political Conditions. They declared a pox on unbridled vote-snatching and severed themselves from any connection with these politics. Their lofty purpose was cynically interpreted as a new way of putting the squeeze on the factions.

44 Watanabe, *Habatsu*, p. 141.
45 *Sankei Shimbun*, evening edition, July 14, 1962.

These antics goad the press into paroxysms of outrage. Indeed, a special argot has sprung up to describe the presidential elections. The journalists speak of "real bullets" (money), "fishing with one pole" (attempting to influence an individual delegate), and bottles of "Suntory whisky" (Suntory resembles the word *san-tori*, which means to take from three —the last word, factions, being left unsaid). Within each faction are other factions' *ninja* (historically, warriors who operated separately from the regular body of troops; in modern terms, spies and fifth columnists). The factions and the businessmen are connected by "pipes" (to carry the money).

The tone of the press can best be exemplified by the following quotation taken from the *Mainichi Shimbun* shortly after the third Ikeda election:

> Rumor has it that during this campaign, too, great numbers of real bullets flicked about, skulduggery was hatched under the cover of night, slanderous documents were being cast around with abandon. There was haggling over the party and cabinet posts. Lures and threats were handed to legislators who had businesses even remotely connected with the government....[46]

The *Mainichi Shimbun* is not alone in raising these charges. All the newspapers speak with a single voice at the time of the presidential elections. But slander, skulduggery, haggling, threats, and lures are a matter of interpretation. Money is not. Since the press often suspects a zephyr of being a hurricane, the testimony of the politicians is worthy of consideration.

Ōno Bamboku states flatly in his memoirs, "Money is necessary in the presidential elections."[47] Ishibashi Tanzan says, "This problem came up after the time I was Prime Minister. Judging from my experience I don't think that money is be-

---

[46] *Mainichi Shimbun*, July 12, 1964, p. 1.
[47] Ōno Bamboku, *Ōno Bamboku Kaisōroku* [Ōno Bamboku's Memoirs] (Tokyo: Kōbundō, 1964), p. 106.

ing used altogether recklessly."[48] Kuraishi Tadao, one of the senior politicians of the party, is reported as saying that during the first presidential election one vote was worth from $840 to $1400, with payments to the faction leaders being measured in the several thousands of dollars, while today, each vote is worth a minimum of $2800 and a maximum of $8400. During the 1963 elections, when Ikeda, Satō, and Fujiyama were fighting it out, a total from four to five million dollars was spent.[49] Furui Yoshimi, a Dietman who has participated in all the presidential elections, says, "The three evils of the presidential elections are the spreading around of money, the promises of position, and the manipulations of the factions."[50] It seems fairly evident from the above accounts that money played a role at least until the party presidential elections in November 1966. Prior to this election, the press waged a vigorous campaign to prevent money from becoming an arbiter in the campaign. They apparently were successful. All observers, including the ever-suspicious press, agreed that no significant amount of money changed hands in this election.

Article eleven contains the conditions for winning the presidential election. It has two provisions. The first is that the candidate who "wins a majority of the valid vote shall be the winner." The second provision states, "In the event no one receives a majority of the valid vote, there shall be a run-off election between the two persons who received the greatest number of votes. The person who receives the greatest number of votes resulting from this election shall be the winner."

Let me take up the valid vote clause first. I have mentioned earlier that protest votes were cast in several elections. Sometimes, these votes take the form of a blank ballot, a mutilated ballot, or a vote for a candidate who is not qualified for office (i.e., a dead man or a man who is not a member of the Diet). On other occasions, these ballots are cast for men

48 *Yomiuri Shimbun*, November 5, 1966, p. 1.
49 *Ibid.*, November 7, 1966, p. 3.
50 *Ibid.*, November 6, 1966, p. 1.

who are patently not in the running. There is a difference between these two types of ballots. The first ballots are not valid; therefore, they are excluded in computing the majority. The second type of ballot is valid and therefore is included in the total figure from which the majority is derived. This may appear to be a minor point. But these elections are many times very close and this distinction may someday spell the difference between victory and defeat. In the fifth election, Ikeda was only five votes short of a first ballot victory and in the seventh election, he scraped by with a majority of only four votes.

Next, the question of the majority. Since the electors are limited to Dietmen and the prefectural delegates, the total number of votes, and therefore the upper limit of the majority, is known well in advance of the election. The majority is usually in the neighborhood of 250 votes. As Table 3 on page 32 shows, no faction has this many members. Alliances must be made among the factions. Their maneuvers as they fight to build a majority behind a given candidate constitute the heart of the campaign for the party presidency. Table 13 shows the alliances for selected elections. In some elections, one candidate, usually an incumbent prime minister, proves so powerful that the other factions decline to test his strength. The election is uncontested. The election of Hatoyama in 1956, the second election of Kishi in 1957, and the second election of Ikeda in 1962 are cases in point. A slight variation occurs when one man steps forth to serve as a focal point for gathering opposition votes but does not regard himself as a serious challenger. The fourth election (Kishi in 1959) and the ninth election (Satō in 1966) are examples. After the latter election, the press asked Prime Minister Satō how he interpreted the many opposition votes cast against him. He replied that he regarded them as "whips of love." A third pattern is when there is an honest race between several candidates, but one candidate is able to win a majority on the first ballot. The only example of this type of election to date has been the third Ikeda election in 1964. The fourth

166

TABLE 13. FACTIONAL ALLIANCES IN SELECTED ELECTIONS OF PRESIDENT OF LIBERAL DEMOCRATIC PARTY, 1956-1966

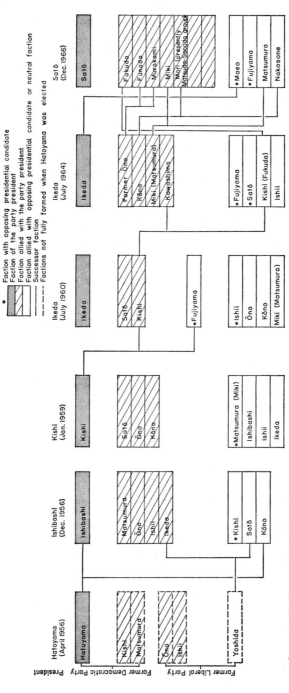

* Faction with opposing presidential candidate
▨ Faction of the party president
▨ Faction allied with the party president
▨ Faction allied with opposing presidential candidate or neutral faction
— Successor faction
--- Factions not fully formed when Hatoyama was elected

President | Former Democratic Party | | | | | Former Liberal Party

Hatoyama (April 1956): Hatoyama — Kishi, Matsumura, Ōno, Ishii, Ikeda — *Kishi, Satō, Kōno — Yoshida

Ishibashi (Dec. 1956): Ishibashi — Matsumura, Ōno, Ishii, Ikeda — *Kishi, Satō, Kōno

Kishi (Jan. 1959): Kishi — Satō, Ōno, Kōno — *Matsumura (Miki), Ishibashi, Ishii, Ikeda

Ikeda (July 1960): Ikeda — Satō, Kishi — *Fujiyama — *Ishii, Ōno, Kōno, Miki (Matsumura)

Ikeda (July 1964): Ikeda — Former Ōno, Kōno, Miki (Matsumura), Kawashima — *Fujiyama, *Satō, Kishi (Fukuda), Ishii

Satō (Dec. 1966): Satō — Fukuda, Funada, Murakami, Miki, Mori (presently Matsuda-Sagoka group) — *Maeo, *Fujiyama, Matsumura, Nakasone

Source: Asahi Shimbun July 19, 1968, p. 28.

pattern is when there are several candidates, none of whom can muster a clear majority. In this case, the two top candidates must submit to a runoff election.

There have been two examples of this type of an election—the second and the fifth. These are the hardest fought elections and the most interesting. In the second election, three candidates appeared: Ishibashi, Kishi, and Ishii. All the observers were freely predicting a victory for Kishi. But Ishibashi, despite numerical weakness, had concocted a clever strategy. First he made a runoff alliance with Ishii. They agreed that if no man received a majority on the first ballot, whichever of them received more votes would get the votes of the other one on the runoff. Ishibashi then went to work on the other electors, particularly the regional delegates, to prevent Kishi from receiving a majority. A senior reporter describes events in his memoirs:

A mood of optimism pervaded the Kishi camp. This won't do, I felt, and warned several of my friends among them. But they wouldn't even hear me out. Huffily, they said, "Just wait and see."

"How's the mood in the regions?" I asked Takechi Yūki, who had just jauntily returned to party headquarters after making a swing around visiting the prefectural delegates.

"There may be two or three exceptions. But of the men I visited, I can guarantee that 90% are OK," he said with absolute confidence.

"I've got my doubts," I said to myself. . . .

Finally election day rolled around. When I arrived at the party conference which was being held in the Sankei Hall, I noted an atmosphere of great tension and caution. I stuck my head in Kishi's headquarters in a room on the second floor. Dietmen whom I knew were showing up one by one, dragging with them the prefectural delegates. But there were a lot fewer people in the line-up than I anticipated. Particularly, hardly any of the prefectural delegates were putting in an appearance. "This is strange," I thought and went over to speak with the reporters covering the Ishibashi camp. "It seems that there are fewer delegates showing up than expected. How is Ishibashi doing with his men?" "They've been sitting it out over there since early morning drinking beer," the reporters answered. . . . After hearing this, I couldn't bear to stay there any longer. I sneaked out of the conference and went home to watch the slaughter on television . . .[51]

Ishibashi's strategy was successful. Kishi was blocked from getting a majority on the first ballot. Ishibashi beat Ishii by 14 votes. The runoff alliance held. Ishibashi slipped into the president's chair by seven votes on the runoff ballot.

The fifth election proved equally dramatic and put a new twist on the runoff alliance. Ōno Bamboku was one of the candidates for this election and he has written a compelling account of his bid for the presidency, making clear the classic strategy of the faction leader. I will allow Ōno to tell his own story, but first let me set the scene.

Prime Minister Kishi's term of office was nearing its end. He had run into strong criticism within the party for his handling of the renegotiation of the security treaty with the United States. In order to secure its passage and ratification, he was obliged on June 23, 1960, to state publicly his intention to resign.

His statement touched off an old fight that had been brewing among the conservatives for many years. Throughout the postwar period, professional bureaucrats had been resigning from office, standing for election, winning, and gradually taking over the party. This trend was strongly opposed by the politicians who had never served in a ministry but had spent most of their lives within the conservative parties. The battle had seesawed. Prime Minister Yoshida had been a bureau-

[51] Kiya Ikusaburō, *Seikai Gojūnen no Butai Ura* [Fifty Years Behind the Political Scenes] (Tokyo: Seikai Ōrai Sha, 1965), pp. 447-449.

crat, indeed, the man who was primarily responsible for starting the movement of the bureaucrats into the party. The next prime minister, Hatoyama, was a party politician, as was his successor, Ishibashi Tanzan. Prime Minister Kishi represented a victory for the bureaucrats. The party politicians were determined to recapture the chair of the prime minister.

The party, however, had experienced four presidential elections and was anxious to avoid a bruising and costly fight if the party president could be selected by consultation. For two weeks, the leading contenders, Ikeda Hayato, Ōno Bamboku, and Ishii Mitsujirō held talks to see if agreement could be reached on a single candidate. Ikeda was a bureaucrat, a product of the Finance Ministry; Ōno and Ishii were both party politicians. A meeting of the minds proved impossible and on July 9, the talks were called off. Two other faction leaders, Matsumura Kenzō and Fujiyama Aiichirō, let it be known that they also were candidates, turning the battle for the presidency into a five-man fight. The Kishi faction, the largest of all the factions, could not agree whether to support Fujiyama, Ikeda or Ōno. Kishi, himself, threw his weight behind Ikeda. One of his lieutenants, Kawashima, an old party politician, chose to support Ōno. The faction loyal to Kōno Ichirō, another party politician, also supported Ōno.[52] With this background, let me turn the narrative over to Ōno.

Tomorrow was July 12, the day of the presidential election. I went to bed late with the clean feeling that comes from finishing a good fight. Many of my friends had expected to fight the night through. But the evening wore on and finally I found myself alone in my bedroom. It was well after two o'clock in the morning. Win or lose —the election was now in the hands of the gods. . . . My eyes had not been closed for long when I was awakened by my friends Murakami Isamu, Mizuta Mikio, and Aoki Masashi.

52 Watanabe, *Habatsu*, p. 143.

The three of them had apparently hesitated before awakening me since they knew I was exhausted. But the problem they brought was a major one.

Aoki reported that he had been called to the Imperial Hotel by Kawashima Shōjirō, the secretary general, around half past two. When he got there, he found Nadao Hirokichi of the Ishii faction waiting to speak to him.

"The Ikeda faction has cut pretty heavily into the councillors in the Ishii faction and they're all scattering. If it comes to a runoff ballot, only twenty or twenty-five votes will swing over to supporting Ōno. We're not going to be able to live up to our promise. It may cause you some trouble!"

I had an agreement with the Ishii faction. Ishii and I had promised each other that the man who got more votes on the first ballot would get all the votes of both factions on the runoff election.

Up until last night I felt certain that I was in first place. I had taken a straw vote and found that I had 170 ballots. Ishii, by another straw vote which was accurate, had been stopped at the seventy vote level. If promises were kept, I had anticipated getting the majority on the second ballot. Even if I had some defections, I had expected to pick up a few of the floating votes in the Fujiyama faction and some of the strays among the neutrals and the Ishibashi faction.

Mizuta reported that the Fujiyama votes were flowing over to Ikeda as a result of some last ditch strategy by Kishi Nobusuke.

It was clear that even if I took first place on the first ballot I had no chance of winning on the runoff.

Shortly after my three men awakened me, Kawashima showed up in my bedroom. The five of us discussed what to do. If the party politicians were to win, there was no other solution but for me to step down and give my votes to Ishii. My votes were solid. Even if I withdrew, I could give these votes in a block to Ishii. On the other hand, if Ishii were not on the runoff ballot, it appeared that most of Ishii's voters would break their agreement with the Ōno faction and give their votes to Ikeda Hayato.

Tearfully, I had to recognize the contradictory logic of having to surrender my candidacy and give my many votes to a lesser candidate because I had twice the number of ballots and they were firm.

I put out a call for Kōno Ichirō and finally he and other members of his faction showed up. When they learned of the new state of affairs, some of them urged, "Triumph or annihilation. Don't give in." But I was determined that I was going to do what was right. . . .

I recalled one by one the faces of how many tens of friends who had worked for me without sleep and without rest for how many tens of days. I thought, how was I ever going to apologize to the many people who had given me their support, both moral and material. I remembered the long bitter struggles I had had in fifty years of political life. But I pushed all these thoughts aside. I had to sacrifice myself for the second best policy—winning the party presidency for Ishii.[53]

Ōno's announcement of withdrawal the following morning threw the plans of all the other factions into confusion. Ōno says: "Because of my withdrawal, the party conference was extended for a day."

Ōno's gesture of self-sacrifice appeared initially to unite the divided forces of the party politicians. The five party politicians, Ōno, Kōno, Ishii, Ishibashi, and Matsumura threw their factions behind the candidacy of Ishii. But the Ikeda forces still had to be reckoned with. They had been given an additional day to continue working on the factions of the party politicians. Ōno says: "The extension was bad. During the space of that day, the allied forces of the party politicians whose ranks had already become ragged, began to crumble away."

53 Ōno, *Kaisōroku*, pp. 107-110.

On the morning of July 13, the party conference opened and the first ballot was held. There were 501 voters. They split their votes as follows:

Ikeda	246
Ishii	196
Fujiyama	49
Other	7
Invalid	3

The Ikeda forces were close to triumph. They were only five votes short of a victory. There should have been more votes for Ishii. What had happened? Ōno's comment is:

"Arrows broken, ammunition spent, the battle ended in a defeat for the party politicians. Simply stated, the reason we lost was that we ran out of money . . ."

The second ballot was a foregone conclusion. Fujiyama had been eliminated from the running and he threw his votes behind Ikeda. The results:

Ikeda	302
Ishii	194
Invalid	5

Ikeda was the next party president and in a few days, after the Diet was called into session, he would be the prime minister. Ōno could be forgiven for harboring resentment against him. Ōno's dream of a lifetime had gone down to defeat. But he says:

"I was cheated by any number of people in the election. But the fight with Ikeda was fair on both sides. Ikeda is basically honest. He is a man after my own heart."[54]

Ikeda was later to nominate Ōno as the vice president of the party.

Since the party elections in effect decide the occupant of the highest office of the land, they have been subjected to close scrutiny. Watanabe Tsuneo offers the following commentary in one of his books on party leadership:

[54] *Ibid.,* p. 110.

When the election of the party president was decided, I thought that the conservative party would in large measure overcome, through this modern and democratic system, its anti-democratic and pre-modern predilections. I welcomed the new system. But as time passed, I realized that I was greatly mistaken in my expectations. As a political reporter covering the conservative party, I have studied minutely from inside the swirl of political controversy, the process of the election of the party president since its inception. In reality, this election corrupts the party, makes money rather than policy or knowledge the important attribute of the party leader, and ultimately poses the danger of enfeebling party authority. The system, as it is, reveals the sickness of the conservative party. If allowed to continue, further complications will develop, not only in the conservative party, but perhaps in Japanese politics as well. There is even the fear of bringing about the death of democracy.[55]

This may appear to be an extreme view, but some of the Dietmen themselves echo Watanabe's sentiments. Utsunomiya Tokuma, a conservative Dietman of fourteen years' standing, says, "All the evils of politics stem from the presidential elections."[56] Maeo Shigesaburō, the present leader of the old Ikeda faction, says, "It's deplorable, but to win, scurrilous measures are indiscriminately taken. We politicians ought to reflect on the fact that by our own hand we are scattering the seeds of suspicion about ourselves."[57] Many responsible citizens have suggested reforms—so many, in fact, that it is most convenient to classify them in groups. There are the legalists, the structuralists, and the moralists.

Tanimura Yuiichirō, a former judge on the Supreme Court, is predictably one of the legalists. He writes, "Since the office of the party president is not a public office, the provisions of the electoral law are not applicable. Bribery is ram-

55 *Tōshu*, p. 1.
56 *Yomiuri Shimbun*, November 5, 1966, p. 1.
57 *Mainichi Shimbun*, July 12, 1964, p. 1.

pant."[58] The *Yomiuri* comments, "It is indeed strange that a person who offers a hundred yen bribe in a village election gets tossed into the pig box [jail] while during the presidential elections in which many millions of yen move about, nobody is even investigated by the legal officers."[59] One solution, then, is to draft a public law regulating the parties. Ōsawa Yūichi, a former governor of Saitama prefecture, pointedly says, "If such a law is drafted, the method of selecting the party leaders should be included in it."[60] Prime Minister Satō Eisaku has charged a group of scholars, bureaucrats, and politicians with investigating the feasibility of this course of action.

More citizens have concerned themselves with structural reform. One group of politicians suggests the establishment of an overseers committee. Kawasaki Hideji, a former welfare minister, says, "A supervisory organ should be created and clean, open elections enforced."[61] Some men would place this organ in the hands of the journalists, others want an ad hoc group of politicians, still others would use existing organs. "It is necessary to revise the party rules so that the discipline committee can deliver warnings," says Setoyama Mitsuo, a Dietman from the lower house.[62]

A second group of politicians wishes to change the electorate. Nakasone Yashuhiro has suggested two reforms. First he has proposed that the party abolish presidential elections. Instead, he urges that the occupant of the highest office be decided by direct popular vote.[63] This plan would require extensive constitutional revision and would mean a fundamental change in the basis of Japanese government.[64] His

[58] *Yomiuri Shimbun*, November 5, 1966, p. 1.
[59] *Ibid.*, November 6, 1966, p. 1.
[60] *Ibid.*   [61] *Ibid.*   [62] *Ibid.*
[63] Yoshimura Tadashi, ed., *Shushō Kōsen-ron* [Discussion of the Public Election of the Prime Minister] (Tokyo: Kōbundō, 1964), pp. 7-68.
[64] Kempō Chōsakai Jimukyoku, *Kempō Kaisei-ron oyobi Kaisei Hantai-ron ni okeru Kihonteki Tairitsuten—Kaisetsu to Shiryō* [Basic Points of Conflict Regarding the Arguments Favoring Constitutional Revision and Arguments Opposing Constitutional Revision—Documents and Analysis] (Tokyo: n.p., 1962), pp. 239-244.

second plan is less visionary. He suggests expanding the electorate from the present five hundred electors to five thousand people, drawing chiefly on the women and the young men who are associated with the party.[65] An alternative would be to give the franchise to all the party members who hold elective office. This would expand the franchise to about 8,000 people. "The results would be closely in accord with popular sentiment and bribes would no longer be effective," he notes.[66]

Uno Sōsuke, another young conservative legislator, has urged reform along similar lines. He would involve all party members in the selection of the party presidency. Through a series of primary elections, first in the villages, then in the towns and cities, the prefecture would decide its candidate and would charge its delegates to the party conference, both the Dietmen and the representative from the prefectural federation, to vote its choice.[67]

Nishimura Eiichi, a conservative who first entered the Diet in 1949, takes just the opposite tack. He would further limit the electorate. He says, "I would like to excuse the regional delegates from the present enfranchised voters. Only the Dietman in the upper and lower house ought to vote. If this is done, money will not be indiscriminately thrown around."[68]

Other men suggest changing the voting procedure. One proposal is to eliminate the secret ballot. Ōno Bamboku, one of the drafters of the present system, urged this change. "In order to make the responsibilities of the voters clear, I have concluded that we ought to have an open vote."[69] Other men affiliated with the party support Ōno's thesis. Kudō Shōshirō, the president of the Tokyo People's Bank and a financial backer, is one of them. He says, "To stop the practice of secretly passing money, there ought to be an open

[65] Nakasone Yasuhiro, "Seiji o Kokumin no Naka e" [Put Politics into the Hearts of the People], *Nihon oyobi Nihonjin*, October, 1963, p. 26.
[66] *Yomiuri Shimbun*, November 5, 1966, p. 1.
[67] *Ibid.*, January 30, 1966, p. 2.
[68] *Yomiuri Shimbun*, November 5, 1966, p. 2.
[69] Ōno, *Kaisōroku*, p. 109.

vote. As matters now stand, the men who supply the political funds are stuck."[70] Most Dietmen oppose Ōno's suggestion. It gives the power to decide the election completely to the faction leader.

Some politicians believe that the elections should be done away with. They advocate a return to consultations among the party leaders. "The English tories seem to have been successful in choosing their leaders. We ought to consider giving their way of doing things a try," says Kurogane Yasumi, one of the senior lieutenants in the Ikeda faction.[71] Hayakawa Takashi, a conservative legislator who has traveled extensively throughout the United States and Europe has concluded, "Party leaders ought not be elected but developed."[72] Kōno Ichirō, whose political power lingers on despite his death, wished to hold on to the system of elections but render them meaningless. "The party president should be recommended. I think it desirable to have careful consultations followed by a ceremonial conference in which the candidate is elected by acclaim."[73] One current scheme is to set up a nominating committee of senior party officials to recommend the party president. "This sounds fine, but you immediately get snagged on the problem of who chooses the nominating committee," notes Fujieda Sensuke, who has served at different times as defense, transportation, and home minister.[74] The present prime minister, Satō Eisaku, is on record as opposing consultations. "Consultations are well and good, but an election is the fair and proper way for a modern political party. The evils of political bosses deciding by consultation outweigh the evils of an election."[75]

Mizuta Mikio, the present finance minister, has suggested separating the party presidency from the premiership. By

---

[70] *Yomiuri Shimbun*, November 6, 1966, p. 1.

[71] Kurogane Yasumi, interview, April 21, 1966.

[72] Hayakawa Takashi, *Shin-Hoshushugi no Seiji Rinen* [Political Ideals of the New Conservatism] (Tokyo: n.p., April 1965), p. 4.

[73] *Mainichi Shimbun*, July 12, 1964, p. 2.

[74] Fujieda Sensuke, interview, April 25, 1966.

[75] *Mainichi Shimbun*, July 12, 1964, p. 1.

his plan, elections for the party presidency would be carried out under the present system. Once elected, the party president would not become the candidate for the prime ministership in the Diet elections.[76] His intent is to remove the august office of the prime minister from the rough and tumble of presidential politics.

Finally, there are the moralists. Rōyama Masamichi, Japan's most eminent political scientist, believes that the difficulties with the presidential elections arise out of the confusion of private and public business. "The great significance of the presidential election has been forgotten. It is being treated as a private matter of concern only within the party." He notes that all the advanced countries as they have gone through their popular revolutions, have had their periods of "loose politics." He looks to the prime minister himself to correct matters. "He must have the faculty to break through the narrow self-interests of the factions, throw aside factional calculations, and think beyond to where the real, long-range interests lie."[77] Former Prime Minister Ishibashi says, "It is necessary to inculcate self-esteem among the Dietmen so that they cannot be bought off.[78] Furui Yoshimi, a former welfare minister, says, "It is not a matter of the system. Matters must be exposed to public criticism. There is no other way of bringing about a thorough reform."[79] Furui aims at shaming the electors into changing their ways.

The great majority of the proposals to clean up the presidential elections put their faith in changing the system. All the propositions assume that reform should be immediate and should come from above. It is more probable that fundamental change will be more gradual, come from below, and will not be the result of tinkering with the presidential election machinery. Japan has a good working parliamentary system and the political consciousness of its citizens, despite the

[76] *Yomiuri Shimbun,* January 30, 1966, p. 2.
[77] *Mainichi Shimbun,* November 10, 1966, p. 2.
[78] *Yomiuri Shimbun,* November 5, 1966, p. 1.
[79] *Ibid.,* November 6, 1966, p. 1.

contentions of some scholars, seems to be roughly equal to the political consciousness of the citizens in any of the western democracies. On the other hand, a sense of party is woefully lacking in Japan. A recent *Asahi Shimbun* survey shows that less than 50% of the population is willing to express a liking for a political party, much less join it and work on its behalf.[80] I have found in my own experience that even many of the secretaries of the Dietmen refuse to identify themselves with a political party. So long as these conditions continue, the parties are going to remain the private preserve of the professional politicians and they will continue to respond to pressures from within the political machinery rather than to demands from outside. Real reform will come only when the average Japanese starts enrolling in the party and insisting on a voice in running its affairs.

[80] *Asahi Shimbun*, April 22, 1966, p. 5.

AUTHOR'S POSTSCRIPT: At the 25th regular party conference on June 21, 1971, representatives adopted new rules for the party's presidential election. By then, Satō Eisaku had been elected party president for four consecutive terms. The other politicians had come to realize that it was nigh impossible to elect a new president under the existing party rules if the incumbent was determined to remain in office. (See Nathaniel B. Thayer, "The Election of a Japanese Prime Minister," *Asian Survey*, Volume IX, Number 7, July 1969, pp. 477-497.) The new rules (1) extended the term of office for the party president from two to three years, (2) effectively limited the number of times a party president could serve by specifying that an incumbent party president must secure the endorsement of at least two-thirds of the LDP Dietmen if he wished to run for a third term, and (3) established a nominating procedure: Candidates for the party presidency had to register willingness to be nominated and to secure the endorsement of ten Dietmen. These revisions have not solved the problem of removing an incumbent from office. They only limit his stay to six years. The nominating procedure fulfills two purposes—it closes a loophole since the earlier law had no provision for nomination, and it discourages the use of frivolous nominations.

On July 5, 1972, Tanaka Kakuei was elected party president under these provisions.

CHAPTER VII

Making a Cabinet

"IT IS not an exaggeration to say that the greatest political power that the prime minister possesses is to appoint and remove ministers," a *Yomiuri Shimbun* reporter writes. "Even an unpopular prime minister can last a long time if he distributes the ministerial chairs adroitly."[1]

The power to select the cabinet is given to the prime minister by the constitution.[2] It places only two restrictions upon him. No military officers may be appointed[3] and a majority of the cabinet must be drawn from among the members of the Diet.[4] The first provision is designed to prevent the military from dominating the government as it did in the decade before the war. The second provision is designed to insure a government accountable to the electorate. Although the cabinet is responsible collectively to the Diet, the prime minister has the power to remove ministers as he chooses. The only function of the emperor in this matter is to attest to the selections of the prime minister.[5] More specifically, he attests to their appointments as ministers of state. The actual division of labor, that is, the appointment of a minister of state to a particular ministry is again made by the prime minister. "When it comes to the cabinet, the prime minister is almighty," says Hori Shigeru, a politician who has served in the Diet throughout most of the postwar period.[6]

Prime ministers have made increasing use of these powers.

[1] *Yomiuri Shimbun*, January 9, 1966, p. 2.
[2] Japan. "Nippon Koku Kempō" [Japanese National Constitution] in *Roppō Zensho* [Compendium of Laws] (Tokyo: Iwanami, 1960), Art. 68, sec. 2. Hereafter cited as Japan, *Constitution*.
[3] *Ibid.*, Art. 66, sec. 2.
[4] Article 66, section 3 of the constitution states, "The cabinet, in the exercise of the executive power, shall be collectively responsible to the Diet." Article 68 gives the prime minister the right to "remove ministers of state as he chooses."
[5] Japan, *Constitution*, Art. 7, sec. 5.
[6] Hori Shigeru, interview, January 12, 1966.

MAKING A CABINET

It is possible to work out a historical production schedule for the making of ministers. Since the inception of the cabinet system, Japan has had a grand total of 1,101 ministers (leaving aside holdovers and acting or temporary ministers). From the Meiji era until the end of the World War II, there were 629 ministers. From the end of the war to August 1966, there were 472 ministers. Breaking these figures down still further, from the first cabinet of Itō Hirobumi (1885) until the second Saionji cabinet (1911), that is, during the Meiji era, a period of 26 years, there were 79 ministers appointed. From the third cabinet of Count Katsura (1912) until the Wakatsuki cabinet (1926), that is, during the Taishō era, a period of 15 years, there were 61 new ministers appointed. From the Tanaka Giichi cabinet (1927) until the Suzuki cabinet (1945), that is, during the Shōwa era before the end of the war, a period of 18 years, there were 137 new ministers appointed. From the Higashikuni cabinet (1945) until the first cabinet of Satō Eisaku, that is, during the Shōwa era after the war, a period of twenty years, there have been 232 new ministers appointed.

Working out the production rate, we find that an average of three ministers a year were produced during the Meiji era, four new ministers a year during the Taishō era, and a little better than seven ministers a year during the Shōwa era before the war. In the twenty years after the war, an average of just under 12 ministers have been produced a year. More specifically, 11.4 ministers a year were produced prior to 1955 and 11.7 new ministers a year were produced in the ten years after 1955, the period in which we are most interested. This figure is four times greater than that of the Meiji era. Table 14 gives the number of ministers which each postwar prime minister appointed. Because of the mass production of ministers, more than one-fourth of the conservative members of the Diet in 1966 had had ministerial experience.[7]

The great increase in the number of ministers indicates

[7] Yomiuri Shimbun Seiji-bu, *Seitō* [Political Parties] (Tokyo: Yomiuri Shimbun-sha, 1966), pp. 29-30.

181

TABLE 14. NUMBER OF MINISTERIAL APPOINTMENTS OF THE POSTWAR PRIME MINISTERS, AUGUST 1945 TO DECEMBER 1966

Prime Minister	Total Appointments	New Appointments
Higashikuni	16	9
Shidehara	21	11
Katayama	23	16
Ashida	17	6
Yoshida	80	73
Hatoyama	33	25
Ishibashi	17	12
Kishi	61	28
Ikeda	69	45
Satō	55	33

SOURCE: Yomiuri Shimbun Seiji-bu, *Seitō* [Political Parties] (Tokyo: Yomiuri Shimbun-sha, 1966), p. 30; *Yomiuri Shimbun*, August 2, 1966, p. 1; *ibid.*, December 4, 1966, p. 1.

that cabinets have turned over at an increasing rate. In the Meiji era, cabinets changed once every 1.9 years. In the Taishō era, cabinets changed once every 1.4 years. In the Shōwa era before the war, there were seventeen cabinets in eighteen years. In the twenty-one years after the war, there have been twenty-two cabinets.

Some of the reasons for changes in the postwar cabinets are specified in the constitution. Whenever the House of Representatives passes a resolution of no confidence or rejects a resolution of confidence, the cabinet must resign.[8] When a new prime minister is selected, the cabinet must resign. After a general election of the lower house, the cabinet must resign.[9]

Other reasons for a change in the cabinet are based on politics. The prime minister may decide that the present cabinet is not working well, that the present government policies are not going smoothly, or that the public is tired of the same old faces and the same old voices. A threatened revolt by the factions may be quelled by the appointment of a new cabi-

[8] Japan, *Constitution*, Art. 69.
[9] *Ibid.*, Art. 70.

net. In the postwar era, the political instances have by far exceeded the constitutional instances in the making of a new cabinet. Since the term for all party posts, with the exception of the party president, is one year, the prime minister will, if possible, use the occasion when new appointments must be made in the party to form a new cabinet.

The frequency of cabinet changes has given rise to a solid body of tradition and an almost unchanging procedure. The prime minister, acting as party president, first selects the men to serve in the four highest party posts. These are the vice president (if there is to be one), the secretary general, the chairman of the executive council, and the chairman of the policy affairs research council. Acting as head of government, he will also choose a chief cabinet secretary. These men will usually serve as an advisory board for the prime minister's further nominations. After the prime minister has decided what sort of a cabinet he intends to choose, he will call for recommendations of lower house members from the faction leaders and of upper house members from party leaders in the House of Councillors. Factional balance and the selection of able men will be the two principles which guide the prime minister in the selection of his new cabinet. Particular attention will be paid to the economic posts. After the prime minister has selected his new officers, they will be attested to by the emperor, a proclamation of the new cabinet will be issued, and the cabinet will formally be set in motion. The rest of this chapter will be devoted to explaining these steps in greater detail.

We will inquire later into the precise considerations that the prime minister makes in the selection of the top four officers of the party. We need only note here that these men are drawn from his own faction or from factions closely aligned with him. Since the merger of the conservative parties in 1955, all these men have been experienced politicians and their advice is invaluable. Nevertheless, the use of the four top men in the party as an advisory body is a relatively new practice. Indeed, the name of this advisory body, the *sokaku sambō*, which translates awkwardly into English as the cabinet formation staff, was invented by the newspapers. Although the *sokaku sambō* is not mentioned in any party document, it plays an integral part in the process of making a cabinet.

The cabinet formation staff owes its birth to the development of factionalism within the conservative party. Prior to the merger of the conservative parties in 1955, it did not exist. Prime ministers, of course, held consultations before selecting a new cabinet. Every prime minister had his advisors. But these advisors were not always even politicians. Many of them were simply personal friends of the prime minister or, in the case of Yoshida Shigeru, members of his family. They rarely met as a group.

With the formation of a single conservative party, factionalism became a major issue, and the prime minister found it expedient to discuss the candidacy of the cabinet members with the various strong men of the party. Thus a new qualification was added to these previously amorphous consultations. Position in the party, even though it was informal position, became important.

It was Prime Minister Kishi who gave final impetus to the formal creation of the cabinet formation staff. Wishing to emphasize the role of the party rather than the factions, he stated that he would meet with the four highest party officials and hold consultations on the selection of the cabinet. Each succeeding prime minister has followed this practice. Thus a new organ was created and formal position in the party determined its composition.

The cabinet formation staff has no established procedure, no vote, no power save that of being able to discuss. And even this power of discussion is circumscribed. The prime minister does not limit his consultations solely to this group, and "usually the prime minister has a clear idea who he wants in his cabinet by the time he summons the cabinet formation staff."[10] Once met, the staff rarely proposes candidates on its own initiative, but restricts itself to commenting on the proposed cabinet lineup given it by the prime minister. Once the cabinet is decided, the cabinet formation staff often has the task of justifying the selections to the disgruntled elements in the party.

The importance of this group is a matter of some dispute. One politician maintains that this body had its real meaning during the heyday of factionalism. With the gradual withering away of the factions, a process he maintains is well under way, this organ will fall into disuse.[11] Others, unwilling to predict the future, try to describe the cabinet formation staff's importance in terms of its past performance. One group notes that Prime Minister Ikeda Hayato was willing to leave the selection of one of his cabinets almost entirely in the hands of the cabinet formation staff and from this draw the conclusion that it is powerful or is potentially powerful. Others point to the Satō cabinets of 1965 and 1966 (December) and note that the prime minister formed these cabinets almost singlehandedly. They draw the opposite conclusion. Miura Kineji, a former assistant political editor on the *Asahi Shimbun*, says, "The only objective statement that can be made about the cabinet formation staff is that after their discussions, there have always been at a minimum two changes in the prime minister's suggested lineup."[12]

The cabinet in Japan is limited by law to the prime minister and eighteen ministers of state. However, the posts they fill number twenty. There are one "office on the ministerial level," twelve ministries, and seven commissions or agencies of which the head is a minister of state.[13] Since the number

10 Sutō Hideo, interview, January 18, 1966. Sutō served on the cabinet formation staff under Ikeda Hayato.

11 Hori Shigeru, interview, January 12, 1966.

12 Miura Kineji, interview, October 15, 1965.

13 The office on the ministerial level is the *sōrifu* or office of the prime minister. Formerly a ragtag collection of offices which did not fit comfortably into any ministry, it was given its present status in 1965. The twelve ministries are Justice, Foreign Affairs, Finance, Education, Health

of ministers and the number of posts do not jibe, it is necessary for the ministers to receive concurrent assignments. It is not unusual for the construction minister also to be head of the National Capital Region Development Commission. The home minister is usually placed in charge of the National Public Safety Commission. One of the other ministers may be assigned responsibility for two of the agencies or commissions.

Custom has it that the chief cabinet secretary is the first selected in the making of a cabinet. Some politicians describe him as the "political wife" of the prime minister. Others call him the "chief clerk in the store." Both metaphors are apt. The chief cabinet secretary is the politician who will work most closely with the prime minister during the life of his cabinet. Broadly speaking, he has three major tasks, although Hayashi Shin'ichi, a counselor of cabinet, says, "There is considerable dispute about what the chief cabinet secretary's duties are or should be."[14] First, he runs the secretariat attached to the cabinet. He has two deputies, liaison officers from each of the ministries, and a group of about eighty people to do the staff work. In this capacity, the chief cabinet secretary arranges the agenda for the cabinet meetings, coordinates important matters for cabinet decision, and is in charge of research and the collection of information.[15] The second major function of the chief cabinet secretary is to serve as the window between the party and the cabinet. His

---

and Welfare, Agriculture and Forestry, International Trade and Industry, Transportation, Posts and Telecommunications, Labor, Construction, and Home Affairs.

The seven commissions and agencies are the National Public Safety Commission, the National Capital Region Development Commission, the Administrative Management Agency, the Defence Agency, the Hokkaidō Development Agency, the Economic Planning Agency, and the Science and Technology Agency. The most important of these organs are the Defence Agency and the Economic Planning Agency. *National Government Organization Law* (Law No. 120, 1948 as amended), Art. 3, sec. 2.

[14] Hayashi Shin'ichi, interview, January 5, 1966.

[15] Japan. "Naikaku Hō" [Cabinet Law] in *Roppō Zensho* [Compendium of Laws] (Tokyo: Iwanami, 1960). Arts. 13, 14, 15, 16.

role is to ensure that the voice of the party is heard in the cabinet and that the various elements within the party receive satisfaction. The third major duty of the chief cabinet secretary is to meet with the press. Since no record or transcript is kept of the cabinet deliberations, theoretically the only public report of what transpired is what the cabinet secretary chooses to announce, although many of the ministers hold press conferences for the reporters assigned to their ministry shortly after the cabinet meeting is concluded. He also serves as spokesman for the prime minister.

Because of his close relationship with the prime minister, few in the party question the prime minister's selection for chief cabinet secretary. He is invariably a long-time friend and trusted confidant of the prime minister. He usually comes from the prime minister's own faction, although there have been exceptions. His selection is not subject to the usual rules of factional balance, which are a major consideration in the appointment of other members to the cabinet. That the cabinet secretary is considered apart was clearly illustrated when Ikeda Hayato resigned and Satō Eisaku became prime minister in his stead. Because of the extraordinary circumstances surrounding Satō's appointment—he was selected through consultation rather than election in November 1964—the new prime minister agreed to maintain the Ikeda cabinet, with the exception of the chief cabinet secretary. Ikeda's cabinet secretary resigned and was replaced by a man more congenial to the new prime minister.

Although the chief cabinet secretary is usually chosen first, his name is not announced formally until all the other members of the cabinet have been selected and have informed the prime minister that they will accept the appointment. At this time, the old chief cabinet secretary calls a press conference. The new chief cabinet secretary's first task is to announce the names of the new cabinet officers.

It is with the selection of these other seventeen ministers that all the difficulty lies. Before the prime minister begins consultations on these posts, he must decide what kind of

187

cabinet he wishes to make. Basically, there are two types. One is a "cabinet of strong men," alternatively known as a "cabinet with factional balance." Ideally, in such a cabinet, all the faction leaders are included and other seats are given to their followers, the number of which is decided in accord with the faction's size. The second type is called the "one-lunged cabinet."[16] In this cabinet the prime minister gives seats only to the factions—leaders and followers—who support him or are allied with him.

A good example of the one-lunged cabinet can be found in the cabinet formed by Satō Eisaku in December 1966. During the previous summer, a series of minor scandals had been exposed in the Liberal Democratic party. Several of the factions which had become disenchanted with Satō's leadership seized upon these scandals as an issue and demanded that Satō take responsibility and resign. A party presidential election was in the offing and these forces organized around Fujiyama Aiichirō to push his candidacy. The factions in the forefront of the insurgency were the Fujiyama faction, the Matsumura faction, and the Nakasone faction. Satō won the presidential election handily and immediately formed a new cabinet. None of the members of the dissident factions became ministers. Other examples of the one-lunged cabinet can be found, but they are not numerous.

The principle that a prime minister more generally follows is to create a cabinet of strong men in which all the faction leaders—whether they are enemies or allies—have seats. A typical example is the third cabinet of Kishi Nobusuke:

It was midnight of June 12, 1958—no, it was the early morning of the 13th. In the lobby of the main entrance

16 The terms, "cabinet of strong men" and "cabinet with factional balance," have been used in the Japanese political world for some time and are widely accepted. There is no commonly accepted term for the alternate form of cabinet. I have used the term, "one-lunged cabinet," which, as far as I know, first appeared in the *Yomiuri Shimbun* to describe the third cabinet of Satō Eisaku. See *Yomiuri Shimbun*, December 4, 1966, p. 5.

to the prime minister's residence, seventeen ministers, bathed in the brilliance of floodlights and dappled with flashbulbs, stood arrayed. They all wore different expressions. Among the flushed faces, the brothers Kishi Nobusuke, the prime minister, and Satō Eisaku, the finance minister, showed white teeth in irrepressible grins. But Ikeda Hayato, a minister without portfolio, Miki Takeo, the head of the Economic Planning Agency, and Nadao Hirokichi, the education minister, looked as if they had bitten into a worm and stood impatiently waiting for the ranks of photographers to break. It was a study in contrasts.

That night, the brothers Kishi and Satō could not hide the smiling faces of victors. Ikeda, Miki, and Nadao were in the position of defeated generals suing for peace.

But barely six months were to pass when on another night, December 27th, the position of the victors and the vanquished was about to be reversed. Prime Minister Kishi had been hard pressed . . . and now these three cabinet officers had appeared at the prime minister's residence to thrust their resignations upon him. Like the spurned ugly suitor importuning the beautiful woman, Prime Minister Kishi pleaded insistently for better than an hour trying to get them to withdraw their resignations. But the three men ·adamantly refused. With glowing countenances, exactly the opposite of their faces six months earlier, they departed the prime minister's residence.[17]

The reason that the prime minister likes to include all the faction leaders in his cabinet is implicit in the above excerpt. So long as the faction leaders are safely encompassed in the cabinet, there will be no overt attempt to force the prime minister out of office. Faction leaders may play rough, but as cabinet officers they are responsible for the formulation of

[17] Watanabe Tsuneo, *Daijin* [Minister] (Tokyo: Kōbundō, 1959), pp. 1-2.

189

national policy and are answerable for it. If one or more of the faction leaders intends to oppose the prime minister—Ikeda, Miki, and Nadao are a case in point—they will resign their cabinet posts.

Sometimes the circumstances are such that the faction leaders do not become cabinet officers. Generally faction leaders who have vigorously opposed the prime minister at the party elections do not enter into his new cabinet even though the prime minister is willing to give them a seat. Satō Eisaku, for example, stayed out of the last Ikeda cabinet since he had fought Ikeda for the prime minister's chair at the party conference. Policy differences may preclude a faction leader from joining a cabinet. Kōno Ichirō, for example, was regarded as "soft on communism" for his role in entering into closer relations with the Soviet Union under the Hatoyama regime. Aside from the question of whether the accusation was justified or not, it was sufficient to keep him out of the first Kishi cabinet. Differences of opinion between a faction leader and the prime minister over appointments are also frequent. If a faction does not receive the number of cabinet seats it feels rightfully entitled to, its faction leader finds it difficult to assume a cabinet post. The likes and dislikes of the prime minister must also be taken into consideration. The political joustings between faction leaders sometimes harden into personal animosities. When Kōno Ichirō and Yoshida Shigeru met and chatted civilly together at a hotel reception for a few minutes, it became of great interest to the newspaper pundits. Kōno Ichirō, despite his great political power, was never invited to sit in one of Yoshida Shigeru's cabinets. Finally, a prime minister in the declining days of his stewardship has difficulties drawing the faction leaders into his cabinet. None of them wants to be hampered by a cabinet post in the race for succession. In reality, then, there are few cabinets which actually achieve perfect factional balance. But a prime minister strives towards this goal. And it is a test of his ability as a politician to see how close he can come to this target.

One of the first steps that the prime minister will take is to ask each of the faction leaders to submit a list of names of the men whom he would like to have appointed to the cabinet. These faction lists are of great concern to every party member. In some of the factions, there are meetings among the members to decide who shall be nominated as a cabinet officer. In other factions, the leader may consult with only a few trusted lieutenants within the faction. Occasionally, the faction leader will make his list without consultation. Generally, the stronger the faction leader and the greater the discipline within the faction, the less the discussion.

The faction leader does not have complete liberty in making his recommendations. He faces several restrictions. Nowadays, the candidate must be a member of the Diet. Although the constitution makes provision for the appointment of men to the cabinet from outside the Diet, actually, with one exception, all ministers have been Diet members since the Ishibashi cabinet of 1956. The second customary restriction is that the faction leader will select only men from the lower house. There is another process to choose candidates from the House of Councillors which will be described shortly. Finally, the faction leader will recommend only members of his own faction. The competition is too keen to allow a faction leader the luxury of considering other party members.

In choosing among the faction members, there are further customary qualifications. A prospective minister will have been elected to the Diet on the average of five times. Priority is given to those who have not yet served in a cabinet. The length of time a man has been in the faction carries great weight. A new faction member, no matter how long he has been in the Diet, will have to wait until the other faction members with seniority have been recommended for ministerial posts before he will be considered.

The intangible considerations of whether a man has the ability, experience, and stature to serve as a cabinet officer are also evaluated. The contribution a man has made to the party is considered. Finally, the likes and dislikes of both

191

the faction leader and the prime minister will receive due measure. Since cabinets change every year, this process of selection has been repeated many times in each faction. There is a generally accepted order of succession of faction members awaiting their turn to become ministers.

When the faction list is finally prepared, there are more names than there are posts which the faction leader can reasonably expect to receive. This practice satisfies some of the desire for a cabinet seat built up within the faction and also gives the prime minister some latitude in making his selection. On the other hand, there is no wholesale listing of all the qualified candidates within the faction. One faction leader, Ōno Bamboku, unwilling to turn down any of his faction members, once presented a list with nine names when it was apparent that his faction would receive at the most two posts. This, in effect, was no recommendation at all, and when this ploy became known, the faction leader was criticized by his followers for failing to weed out some names, present an appropriate number, and urge their appointment. The ministries desired are not generally listed, but the order in which the candidates should be chosen is indicated. With a properly selective list, the first man believes that he has a good chance of becoming a minister.

Since the composition of the faction lists is known within the faction, the names of the candidates soon spread throughout the party and gradually make their way into the outside world. Indeed, sometimes the faction lists are distributed to the newsmen because it helps a good deal in elections for a certain candidate to be known as a prospective minister. It must be added that sometimes the real list and the published list are different. Shaky election districts force this stratagem on a faction leader. Finally, there are occasions when attempts are made to keep the faction lists confidential. There is no rule; the exigencies of the moment dictate.

When the faction leader has finally made up his mind whom he wishes to recommend, he meets with the prime minister and hands over his list. A brief discussion between

192

the two men ensues, during which the faction leader explains his choice of candidates and perhaps verbally crosses off one or two candidates whose names were written down on the list to satisfy intra-factional requirements. The conversation is invariably terminated with the prime minister formally asking the faction leader to leave the decisions to him. While the faction leader is meeting the prime minister, other lieutenants of the faction are making sure that the cabinet formation staff is fully informed of the faction's wishes.

Since the Ishibashi cabinet in 1956, it has been customary for three members of the House of Councillors to serve in the cabinet. Before 1956, the practice was to select two members. At the present time, there is a conflict of opinion within the upper house over how many seats the councillors should occupy. Kōno Kenzō, a former vice speaker, maintains that no councillors should become ministers.[18] A seat in the cabinet compromises the ability of the upper house to fulfill what most councillors regard as their fundamental duty—criticizing the government and correcting its errors and excesses. Other councillors reject Kōno Kenzō's views as too idealistic and urge that four men of the upper house should serve in the cabinet, a position which does not meet with great favor among the conservative members of the lower house. For the time being at least, it appears that three councillors will continue to be the quota.

The candidates for the posts in the cabinet are selected by the three conservative factions in the upper house: the Konwakai, Mizuho Club and the Seishin Club. Since each upper house faction is composed of three lower house factions, each upper house faction selects three candidates. Their names are given to the chairman of the assembly for the House of Councillors, the highest party post in the upper house. He consolidates the names into one list, and gives them to the prime minister together with his recommendations. During the Kishi, Ikeda, and Satō cabinets, the prime minister further discussed the faction selections with the speaker

18 Kōno Kenzō, interview, January 25, 1966.

193

(Gichō) of the upper house. From this group of nine men, the prime minister selects the three councillors to serve in the cabinet.

There are several criteria which customarily guide the factions in the selection of candidates. A councillor must have been elected to the upper house twice before he is considered eligible. He will have had to demonstrate his ability in the Diet. A candidate will have had experience either as a parliamentary vice minister or as a chairman of standing or special committees. He will also have had to serve the party. The chairman of the Diet policy committee and the secretary general of the party in the upper house are usually regarded as running on an inside track for the cabinet. Finally, it is a general rule that a councillor can occupy a cabinet seat only once.

Because of this last condition, and because there are generally only 140 or so conservatives in the upper house, a councillor usually becomes a minister long before his counterpart in the House of Representatives. This pleasant state of affairs for the upper house member is somewhat dampened since in all likelihood he will not serve in any of the major cabinet posts. These go to lower house members because the major legislative battles will take place in the House of Representatives and it is felt that a lower house member will fare better than a councillor.

Some Dietmen have managed to get around this rigid system. There are three examples of members of the Diet who were first elected as members of the upper house, served as ministers, and then campaigned and won elections to the House of Representatives. Two of these men have again become ministers. The third is waiting his turn.

With all the recommendations heard, with the cabinet formation staff waiting quietly in the wings, the prime minister turns to the delicate task of choosing his new ministers. Since he is human, his own likes and dislikes will influence him. Since he is also the supreme political leader, the needs of the nation at this particular juncture of history will be thoughtfully considered. These are the variables in the decision. The two constant principles that guide all prime ministers in their deliberations are the maintenance of factional balance and the selection of men of ability.

The first step in the selection process is to decide how many men are to come from each faction. The general rule in correctly balancing the factions is that two or three men are selected from the large factions, one or none from the small factions, and as we have mentioned earlier, three from among the factions of the upper house. If the prime minister has promised seats in the cabinet to secure votes in the presidential elections, he may choose to honor them. Conversely, factions which opposed the prime minister may find one or two seats whittled away from what they regard as their due allotment. The prime minister will not unduly favor his own faction. Usually, the faction leaders are more concerned with the number of seats they receive rather than with the ministries that they will control. Ōno Bamboku crows in his memoirs about receiving four seats in the Ishibashi cabinet because of his support during the presidential elections. He was willing to allow the Finance Ministry to go to Ikeda Hayato, although that post, too, had been promised him.[19] It is the giving of one post to this faction leader rather than that faction leader which calls upon the full political powers of the prime minister and will determine whether he will be able to maintain harmony within the party.

The second step is to decide which men to select from each of the factions. The faction leaders have made known their desires regarding both the men and the priority in which they should be appointed. The prime minister has his own ideas about the acumen, talent, and predilections of the men in the party. Rigid adherence to the faction lists may produce a mediocre cabinet. Disregard of them may disrupt party harmony. A prime minister's skill can be measured by the success of the compromise he reaches.

19 Ōno Bamboku, *Ōno Bamboku Kaisōroku* [The Memoirs of Ōno Bamboku] (Tokyo: Kōbundō, 1964), pp. 94-95.

If the prime minister flouts a faction's list, he arouses the faction leader's deepest suspicions, since "the most effective way for a prime minister to strengthen his leadership within the party and to weaken the other factions is to disrupt the order of men within a faction awaiting appointment."[20] The prime minister, by selecting a man not on a faction list, by appointing a faction member who has recently been a minister, or by holding a man in office for another cabinet, causes factional strife, and "the legislators have doubts about the favor of their faction leaders or are disillusioned with his political strength."[21]

On the other hand, the factional leaders are senior politicians who have a stake in the success of a conservative government and recognize that the making of a cabinet is not a game of musical chairs. If the prime minister can justify his choice in terms of ability or special talent, the faction leader will acquiesce in his disregard of the faction list. Every prime minister has faced this challenge.

For example, Prime Minister Satō, in the cabinet shuffle of August 1965, clashed with the Kōno faction. Kōno had suggested that Mori Kiyoshi be appointed to the cabinet, but the prime minister demurred. When Kōno came to complain, the prime minister stated his intention of appointing Nakamura Umekichi—another Kōno faction member, to be sure, but one who was not included on the Kōno list—to the post of education minister, and requested Kōno to join his cabinet as the minister of health and welfare. Kōno rejected the offer and made clear his intention of not cooperating with the Satō administration.

The third step is to decide which post is appropriate for the men selected to serve in the cabinet. In theory, all the ministries are equal. "There is no difference in the cabinet posts," says Sutō Hideo, who has served in several cabinets. "The ministers all have the same power in a cabinet meeting."[22]

---

[20] Watanabe Tsuneo, *Habatsu* [Factions] (2nd rev. ed., Tokyo: Kōbundō, 1963), p. 4.

[21] *Ibid.*   [22] Sutō Hideo, interview, January 18, 1966.

His views are seconded by others in the party. Certainly the law recognizes no distinction. Japanese protocol officers, who have to grapple with this problem daily, usually choose the easy way out by ranking the ministries according to their age with the oldest ministry, Justice, heading the list.

In talking with the press and politicians, however, it soon becomes clear that each ministry has its own flavor and that an unofficial hierarchy exists. Watanabe Tsuneo, a reporter on the *Yomiuri Shimbun*, recounts the following story:

> When Ishibashi formed his cabinet, he offered the Finance Ministry to Ikeda but was unwilling to give his faction any other ministerial post. Ikeda made clear his dissatisfaction to the cabinet formation staff. Ōno Bamboku, who was leading this staff, closed off Ikeda's complaints by remarking, "The Finance Ministry is worth four of the other unimportant ministries." Later, when Ikeda was forming his second cabinet, he limited the Ōno faction to one post—Mizuta Mikio was appointed finance minister. When Ōno went to complain, Ikeda, without looking up, said, "As I remember it, the Finance Ministry is worth four other ministries." For once in his life, Ōno was without words. Ōno told me this tale himself before he died.[23]

The ranking appears to be based on four factors. The first consideration is how much power a ministry exercises in deciding the basic policies of the nation. The second consideration is how much prestige it enjoys in the public eye. The third is the nature and quality of the work connected with a particular ministry. The press alleges that the fourth consideration is the degree of opportunity a ministry offers for the collection of political funds.

The minister of state who heads one of the agencies or commissions will not find his work too arduous. Postwar decentralization of education is said to have reduced the Educa-

---

[23] Watanabe Tsuneo, *Seiji no Misshitsu* [The Backroom of Politics] (Tokyo: Sekka-sha, 1966), p. 128.

tion Ministry to the point where the ministerial responsibilities can be fulfilled in half a day. The Justice Ministry is unpopular since its principal task is enforcing the law. One writer has suggested facetiously that the reason the post is not highly regarded among the politicians is because it has precluded them from violating the election law.[24] On the other hand, the Foreign Ministry and the Finance Ministry are popular. Their ministers are noted for the long hours they keep and for the heavy responsibilities they carry. The press watches the Finance and other economic posts in particular. "Connected with the economic ministries are powers of license and regulation which amount to tremendous concessions. A few simple and easy-to-understand examples will make the point. The Finance Ministry pegs the price of state-owned land. The Agriculture Ministry sells farmland and gives permission to convert farmland into residential sites. The Defense Agency lets contracts worth millions of dollars for military weapons. . . . The Transportation Ministry has concessions that are of great value to the land and sea transport industries . . . [such as] shipbuilding subsidies and [everything] from bus routes to rights of way for railroads."[25]

Ask ten politicians to rank the ministries and you will have ten different lists in hand. Each man sees the cabinet from a different perspective. But all the lists will have two things in common. At the bottom of the pecking order will be the agencies and the commissions. At the top of the list will be the Ministries of Foreign Affairs, Finance, Agriculture, and International Trade and Industry (MITI), although their order will vary. Perhaps the top two posts are the Finance Ministry and the Ministry of International Trade and Industry. Every prime minister since the Ishibashi Cabinet has served in one of these two posts. Kishi Nobusuke rose from the bureaucracy of the prewar equivalent of MITI, serving first as the administrative vice minister and finally as the minister. Ikeda Hayato was a bureaucrat in the Finance Ministry

24 Watanabe, *Habatsu*, p. 5.
25 *Yomiuri Shimbun*, October 19, 1966, p. 3.

and later its minister. Satō Eisaku was initially a bureaucrat in the Transportation Ministry, but later served at different times as minister to both MITI and the Finance Ministry. The press and the politicians debate whether it is essential to serve in these two posts before having a shot at the post of the prime minister, but in any case, "the guts of the cabinet are the foreign and economic posts."[26]

The importance of appointments to the agencies and the commissions should not be slighted. Many times, the faction leaders can be found sitting in these chairs since it gives them a voice in the cabinet without too many administrative duties. But the prime minister will pay the greatest attention to the economic and foreign ministries. It is almost a general rule that these posts will go to men in factions aligned with the prime minister, but this is not the only consideration. The prime minister will try to insure that men of talent and ability occupy these positions. Since these posts require technical knowledge and experience, it is not unusual for the prime minister to appoint former bureaucrats to these posts, although administrative experience is not the only criterion. "If a man has bureaucratic experience it is taken into consideration, but bureaucrats are not accepted at their face value. They must prove their competence in the party," says Sutō Hideo.[27] The Finance Ministry is particularly noted for having ministers who have served as bureaucrats within the ministry. Both the Finance and the Foreign Ministries have highly skilled and competent bureaucrats who are inclined to take matters into their own hands if not held under tight rein by an equally skilled minister.

That factional balance is not the sole consideration in selecting ministers can clearly be illustrated in the case of the Labor Ministry. Two men within the party have served a number of times as head of this ministry. One of them, Kuraishi Tadao, has changed his factional affiliation several

26 Mizuta Mikio, interview, January 10, 1966. Mizuta has served on two occasions as finance minister.
27 Sutō Hideo, interview, January 18, 1966.

times, and by the rules of the game, he should be at the bottom of the waiting list for a ministerial appointment. The other, Ishida Hirohide, is one of the few men in the party who belongs to no faction, which should also place him out of the running. However, both these men are recognized as genuine labor authorities, smart, and having the trust of labor circles. Their appointment to successive ministries has not been questioned within the party.

Miyazawa Kiichi, a former member of the upper house, was appointed to two successive Ikeda cabinets as the head of the Economic Planning Agency. Despite complaints by other councillors, the prime minister prevailed in his choice and succeeded in keeping this immensely talented and brilliant politician by his side. There have been other appointments to the cabinet which did not reflect factional considerations and can only be explained in terms of ability.

The opinion of the economic community is given consideration in the case of the economic and foreign posts. No prime minister accords to business the right to suggest candidates for the cabinet posts, although a prime minister may value the suggestions of an individual businessman with whom he has had long acquaintance. It is generally recognized that business has a particular interest in the selection of the finance minister and the minister of international trade and industry. Most prime ministers will solicit the opinion of the economic community regarding the candidates he contemplates appointing to these posts. Business is also recognized as having an interest in the appointment of the foreign minister, the economic planning minister, and the agriculture minister, and business views regarding these appointments are given adequate consideration. Labor has chosen to ally itself with the opposition parties and therefore its views are not solicited. No other pressure groups are consulted during the making of a cabinet.

After the prime minister has decided whom he wishes to appoint, he calls the prospective ministers one by one to his official residence and informs them of his intention. Although the press soon learns who the new ministers will be by the parade going in and out of the residence, no formal announcement is made until all of the new ministers have given their acceptance. These confrontations are surrounded by their own body of legend. There is a case on record of one lady Diet member who was called on the phone by a prankster to come to the residence. She showed up dressed to the teeth and embarrassed all concerned. Another story relates to Fukuda Tokuyasu. Since his name was on no faction list and he did not expect to be appointed, he had departed for his constituency and could not immediately be found.

After the ministers have met with the prime minister, they change into cutaways and striped pants, and, at the convenience of the emperor, are summoned to the palace. A simple ceremony takes place. Each minister receives a small piece of paper signed by the emperor and stamped with his vermilion seal attesting to his appointment as minister of state.

The new cabinet then returns to the prime minister's residence where the first cabinet meeting is held. The prime minister gives them documents assigning them to their respective ministries. The chief cabinet secretary has been busy drafting a document characterizing the new cabinet. If age predominates, he may characterize the new cabinet by emphasizing its "lofty serenity." If young men are in the majority, the chief cabinet secretary may call attention to its "energy and new spirit." With perfect factional balance, the cabinet is one which "strengthens cooperation." If the factional balance is slightly askew, then "selecting the right man for the right slot" may be the theme. The new ministers discuss this document, and authorize its release to the press. A *banzai* is given and the ministers troop out to the front of the residence to have their pictures taken for posterity and the evening papers.

Many conservatives are critical of one or more aspects of the present cabinet system. Most of them agree that there has been a decline in the authority of the ministers. Aoki Kazuo

201

says bluntly, "I have no desire to be appointed to a cabinet today."[28] Aoki was finance minister in 1939. Although he leads the conservatives in the upper house today, he wishes to have his service in an antebellum cabinet remembered as the high point of his illustrious career. The conservatives attribute this decline to the postwar constitution, the mass production of ministers, and the factions.

Under the prewar constitution, the ministers were appointed and dismissed by the emperor, who was "sacred and inviolable."[29] Since they acted in his name, "they were nearly as far above reproach as their sovereign."[30] Compared to the present system by which the ministers are appointed and removed by the prime minister, a mortal subject to daily political pressures, the contrast is great. "The difference between a prewar minister and a postwar minister is the difference between the moon and a turtle," says Masutani Shūji, a legislator who has served in the lower house since 1920.[31]

The party elders particularly regret this attrition of power. Occasionally, they speak vaguely of restoring the glory a Japanese minister once had through constitutional revision. The younger politicians may share this concern with ministerial prestige, but reject constitutional reform as politically impossible, if not undesirable. For the near future at least, the constitution will not be the vehicle for bolstering the authority of the ministers.

Most conservatives regard the mass production of ministers as detrimental. While trying to satisfy the demand of all the politicians for a seat in the cabinet has resulted in some inferior appointments, the real damage has been done in not having the capable ministers serve long enough. One political commentator notes, "Cabinet officers don't have any time to make policy. They are new to their jobs and have to

28 Aoki Kazuo, interview, January 19, 1966.
29 Japan. "Teikoku Kempō" [Imperial Constitution] in *Roppō Zensho* [Compendium of Laws] (5th rev. ed., Tokyo: Iwanami, 1934), Art. 3.
30 Hugh Borton, *Japan's Modern Century* (New York: The Ronald Press, 1955), p. 155.
31 Masutani Shūji, interview, January 6, 1966.

spend all their time boning up on answers to questions in the Diet. By the time they are experienced, they are out of office. The result is that policy is made by the bureaucrats."[32] The *Yomiuri Shimbun* shares these views and has written a tart indictment of the present system. I quote it at length:

> From the point of view of the bureaucrats, there are two types of ministers. One is the "chapeau minister" and the other is the "muscle man minister." The "chapeau minister," during his term of office, simply wears the hat of the ministry. He does not interfere with the formation of policy or with administration. His only task is to grunt affirmatively to explanations and reports of the bureaucrats and try not to advance any ideas or thoughts of his own. . . .
>
> The "muscle man minister" is just the opposite. He has complete and direct control over the high officials. He uses two methods. First, he uses the power to appoint, transfer, and promote personnel. . . . Second, he has a close understanding of policy and administration, and through this ability, he controls the bureaucrats. Most of these ministers are Dietmen who are former bureaucrats. . . .
>
> But usually, the life of a minister is about one year. The bureaucrats make great efforts not to tell these ministers about the implementation of important policies or administrative secrets. . . . A clumsy explanation and the minister may change things to suit his own wishes. The administrative vice minister secretly instructs other bureaucrats at the working level how to implement policies. And then, after a while, the ministers change.[33]

The conservative politicians also point out that the rapid turnover of ministers does not benefit Japan in her foreign relations. The pace of international negotiation is never swift and by the time a problem is resolved there may have been

[32] Miura Kineji, interview, January 18, 1966.
[33] *Yomiuri Shimbun*, May 15, 1966, p. 1.

several cabinet reshuffles. New ministers, not only to the Ministry of Foreign Affairs but also to the Ministries of Labor, International Trade and Industry, and the Defence Agency, have no first hand knowledge of the history of a problem, little time to study it, and less time to establish an intimate working relationship with the other nation's representatives. The result is that negotiations are more protracted than necessary and the Japanese minister is at a decided disadvantage vis-à-vis his foreign counterpart to the detriment of Japan's interests and prestige.

Many conservatives are content with exhorting the prime minister to lengthen the life of a cabinet to change this state of affairs. "The prime minister must take a sterner position and resist changing the cabinet every year."[34] Mizuta Mikio, who has been active in formulating plans for party reform, suggests the way to lengthen the life of a cabinet is to extend the term of the party president.[35] Instead of the present two-year term of office, Mizuta would have the party president stay in office for a three-year term. Since two terms for a party president are regarded as "normal," this would mean that each party president would serve for a period of six years. Politics would proceed at a much slower pace than at present and the prime minister would not have to be constantly bolstering his support within the party, which is the most common cause of a cabinet change.

The conservatives recognize that the factional bickering over cabinet seats has contributed to the decline of ministerial prestige. Men within the party advocate the dissolution of the factions and look to the prime minister to take the initiative. "If the Liberal Democratic party is to become a modern party, the prime minister must discard the factions. No doubt this will cause confusion and disorder within the party, but it must be done."[36]

None of the prime ministers has failed to respond to this

34 Sutō Hideo, interview, January 18, 1966.
35 Mizuta Mikio, interview, January 10, 1966.
36 Hori Shigeru, interview, January 12, 1966.

challenge. Recognizing that the method of selecting ministers constitutes one of the fundamental reasons for the existence of the factions, every prime minister proclaims shortly after assuming office that the first step in dissolving the factions is to abolish the orders of succession within the factions and to select ministers on the basis of merit. "This pronouncement is absolutely without effect," notes one newspaper. "Even if the order of succession in the other factions is abolished, the prime minister appoints members of his own faction to the cabinet in proper sequence."[37]

The blame for the continued existence of the factions should not be laid solely at the prime minister's door. It can be argued cogently that he will benefit most if the factions are abolished. Institutions with such deep economic and political roots cannot be ripped up and discarded overnight. If the factions are eventually abolished then another system will have to be created to take their place. Few politicians have given this any thought. Appointment by merit is a splendid political principle, but few nations have been able to transmit this principle into an effective political system.

The Japanese political critics dream of a system in which the prime minister sits down and with broad strokes of his pen draws up a cabinet in which all talent in the party is recognized and placed in office. Aside from whether the prime minister's and the critics' ideas regarding the most talented men would coincide—it's a safe bet they wouldn't —the real question is: would the Japanese nation be served better with a prime minister who was able to wield so much power—particularly under present conditions, when there is no acceptable opposition party to take power and when the prime minister is not directly elected by all the people?

There is no denying that the factional system places restraints on the prime minister in the selection of his cabinet. But it can be argued that the factional system works to give the talented politician the opportunity to serve within the cabinet. The factional system is, in effect, a dual sifting

[37] *Yomiuri Shimbun*, January 9, 1966, p. 2.

operation. The faction leader shakes the first sieve in making his recommendations. Perhaps conditions within his faction will cause him to try to push some inferior candidate off on the prime minister. But usually the faction leader will resist these pressures. He wishes to have his recommendations accepted. It makes him look good. He will try then to come up with names of candidates attractive to the prime minister.

After the faction leaders have made their recommendations, the prime minister himself is given the opportunity to winnow the chaff out further. The prime minister cannot appoint all the men who have been recommended to the cabinet. He will have to pick and choose. This picking and choosing gives him the opportunity to come up with the talented politicians. Nor does the prime minister have to restrict himself to the recommendations of the factions. All the prime ministers have at one time or another chosen men who were on nobody's list. So long as he can justify these selections in terms of ability there will be no major revolt. In sum, by adjudicating the conflicting claims of the factions and at times causing the factions to give way to the claims of ability, the prime minister gives himself the freedom to select the right man for the right spot.

If everything worked out the way the preceding two paragraphs have outlined it, all Japanese cabinets would be composed of men of genius. But such is not the case. Minor men get appointed to minor posts. But the observer would be hard put to find a "chapeau minister" among the foreign and top economic posts, and they are at the heart of the government. Despite the complaints, the Japanese people get as good a crop of ministers as they can expect.

206

CHAPTER VIII

Formulating Policy

THE explanation of a politician's real motives is best left to the historian, the psychologist, and the politician's wife. We take refuge in the classic view that the purpose of being a politician is to run the country. Running the country means making policy, and in this and the next chapter we turn to an examination of the making of Japanese policy.

Japanese think small. While the western democracies regard the formulation and decision of policy as a single function, the Japanese regard it as two. Formulating policy is one act and in the conservative party, its forum is the policy affairs research council, the subject of this chapter. Deciding policy is another act and its forum in the conservative party is usually the executive council, the subject of the next chapter.

I asked several men if they could clarify this division of function. Iwano Miyoji, one of Miki Takeo's secretaries said, "If you want to put it in American legislative terms, the policy affairs research council is the same as the committees in the Senate. The executive council is the Senate in plenary session."[1] Yamamoto Katsuichi, an economics professor who has served in the lower house, said, "The policy affairs research council is where the specialists' decisions are made. The executive council is where the political decisions are made."[2] Both definitions need refinement, but they make the difference clear enough to start an investigation into the policy affairs research council.

The policy affairs research council is not a new institution. Before the war, both the major conservative parties had policy organs almost identical in structure, though not as

[1] Iwano Miyoji, interview, May 13, 1966.
[2] Yamamoto Katsuichi, interview, June 6, 1966.

207

highly developed as the present council. The major difference between the prewar and the postwar policy councils lies in the stature of the chairman. In the present conservative party the chairman of the policy affairs research council is regarded as one of the four senior party officials, along with the vice president, the secretary general, and the chairman of the executive council. In the prewar political parties, the chairman of the policy affairs research council was clearly one rank below the secretary general and the chairman of the executive council; there was usually no vice president. For example, the party law of the Constitutional Democratic party stated: "The Chairman of the Policy Affairs Research Council shall be permitted to sit with the Executive Council and humbly to present his views."[3] In the Friends of Constitutional Government Association, the president customarily selected a policy chairman each year shortly before the opening of the Diet, but the party did not believe the post important enough to mention in its party law even as late as 1927.

As time passed, however, the stature of the policy chairman began to grow, and one discovers some of the major politicians of the day sitting in this chair. An old politician who belonged to the Friends of Constitutional Government Association tells an anecdote about Yamamoto Jōtarō, a powerful politician who served as policy chairman in 1932.[4] One day Yamamoto, sitting in his office on the first floor of the party headquarters, imperiously commanded his staff, "Go fetch Mori Kaku." Mori was the secretary general of the party, a post in which Yamamoto had previously served. An underling went to Mori's office on the second floor and relayed the command. Mori's reply was brusque. "What's this business of summoning the secretary general. If Yamamoto has something to say, tell him to come up here and see me

3 Rikken Minseitō, "Tōsoku [Party Law] in *Gendai Seijigaku Zenshū* [Collection of Studies on Modern Politics] by Takahashi Seigo. (Tokyo: Nihon Hyōronsha, 1930), Vol. 10. Art. 6.
4 Ōta Masataka, quoted in *Asahi Shimbun*, August 28, 1962, p. 2.

in person." The chairman of the policy affairs research council was never to become powerful enough to approach the secretary general as an equal in the days before the war.

The reason the chairman of the policy affairs research council was held in such light regard was that he did not really have very much to do. Drafting statutes was more a prerogative of the government than of the parties. "In the making of law, the government was overwhelmingly more powerful than the parties," recalls one of the legislators of the day.[5]

Since the parties only marginally shared in the power to create law, their policy deliberations were aimed at another purpose. "There were not a few cases where policy was used as a tool to overthrow cabinets."[6] Slogans and speeches rather than statutes and research were the substance of that day's policy. "To debate the state of the nation, to denounce the government, to set forth their own political opinions on the main floor of the Diet—this was both the purpose and pride of yesterday's party politicians."[7]

Nemoto Ryūtarō, a conservative politician who has served several times on the policy affairs research council, summed up the approach of the prewar politicians toward policy as follows: "In the days before the war, policy was writ large. The old politicians were not interested in the daily considerations of policy or the drafting of laws. They left this up to the government. Policy was used as a way of protesting. The old politicians didn't have the same passion towards policy that the present politicians have."[8] Given this attitude, it is small wonder that the chairman of the policy affairs research council was not held in high repute and elaborate policy machinery was regarded as superfluous.

Today, the name of the policy affairs research council remains the same but a much more formidable structure has

[5] Uchida Nobuya, quoted in *Asahi Shimbun*, August 28, 1962, p. 2.
[6] *Asahi Shimbun*, August 28, 1962, p. 2.
[7] *Ibid.*, September 1, 1962, p. 2.
[8] Nemoto Ryūtarō, interview, February 5, 1966.

grown up for the study, research, and planning of policy. This structure is organized like a pyramid, with a welter of divisions, special committees, and investigative commissions at the lowest level, a deliberation commission at the next level, and a group of five vice-chairmen at the third level. At the top sits a chairman.

The basic unit of the policy affairs research council is the division. There are fifteen of them and they effectively span the range of government activity. There is a division for each of the ministries.[9] These divisions also have their counterparts in the standing committees of the upper and lower houses of the Diet. The conservative members of the standing committees in the two houses are members of the divisions. In short, what the party members decide in the divisions they will have to defend in the Diet. These divisions have existed from the days before the war.

Many of the divisions have subcommittees. In December 1965, the forestry and agriculture division had six subcommittees, the social welfare division had seven subcommittees, and the communications division had five subcommittees. In total, there were 31 of these subcommittees.[10] These subcommittees are formed on an ad hoc basis; their number varies from time to time. They will be formed to study anything from a new intern program for Japanese hospitals to stimulation of the Japanese poultry industry.

According to the party law, every conservative member of the Diet must belong to one of the divisions.[11] Since the personal interests of the Dietmen and the political needs of their constituencies vary, the choice of which division to join is

[9] The divisions of the policy affairs research council are: cabinet, regional administration, defense, justice, foreign affairs, finance, education, social welfare, labor, forestry and agriculture, marine products, commerce and industry, transportation, communications, and construction.

[10] Jiyūminshutō *Seimu Chosakai Meibo* [Membership List of the Policy Affairs Research Council], December 1, 1965.

[11] Jiyūminshutō, "Tōsoku" [Party Law] in *Wagato no Kihon Hōshin* [Basic Policies of Our Party] (Tokyo: Jiyūminshutō Kōkoku Iinkai, 1966), Art. 45, par. 3.

210

left up to each legislator. To be sure, this results in some unbalance in membership among the divisions. As one might expect, the agricultural and forestry division has a surplus of members. In October 1967, there were 124 members in this division.[12] But even the Justice Division, which has little popular or political appeal, managed to pick up thirty-nine members.[13] No division is under-represented. As the reader may surmise from these figures, most of the Dietmen belong to several of the divisions. Each of the divisions has a chairman and two or three vice chairmen who are selected by the chairman of the policy affairs research council in consultation with the secretary general of the party.[14]

Besides the divisions, there are special committees and investigative commissions. It is hard to distinguish the difference between them. The scope of a commission seems to be larger. For example, there is a labor investigative commission, an economic investigative commission, and a foreign affairs investigative commission. The special committees seem to be more concerned with a particular problem. For example, there are special committees for public safety, natural disasters, and tourism. But many times the difference is solely in the name. For example, there are special committees for science and technology and for youth and women's affairs. Either of these two special committees could just as easily be an investigative commission. To confuse matters further, the party has from time to time created conferences, but so far they seem to be little different from special committees.

With one exception, all the special committees and investigative commissions are functional. The exception is the national land development commission, which has ten subcommittees, each representing a geographical section of the country. This is the only instance in which geography has been given consideration in the policy affairs research council. In the next chapter we shall discuss regionalism in the exec-

12 Jiyūminshutō, *Seimu Chosakai Meibo*, pp. 18-20.
13 *Ibid.*, pp. 12-13.
14 Jiyūminshutō, *Tōsoku*, Art. 45, par. 2.

211

utive council, one of the decision-making organs. It should be noted here that the regional divisions in the policy affairs research council and in the executive council are not identical.

Unlike the divisions, the members of these special committees and investigative commissions are selected by the chairman of the council, often in consultation with the secretary general. The chairman of the council will try to select Dietmen who have experience or special knowledge in the area of the organ's jurisdiction. Former ambassadors are chosen to serve on the foreign affairs investigative commission. Five former labor ministers presently serve on the labor investigative commission. A former governor of the Bank of Japan now heads the special committee for overseas economic cooperation. Sometimes membership is limited to these men. But more often, Dietmen who express an interest can find seats.

There are many special committees and investigative commissions. In December 1967, 19 investigative commissions and 25 special committees were on the books.[15] Some of the committees and commissions have responsibilities outside the competence of the divisions. Neither the constitution investigative commission nor the election system investigative commission would fit comfortably into any of the divisions. The special committee for science and technology and the special committee for public safety, which were created to cover the activities of the Science and Technology Agency and the National Public Safety Commission are also cases in point. But many of the commissions and committees duplicate the efforts of the divisions. For example, there is a labor investigative commission and a labor division. There is a foreign affairs investigative commission and a foreign affairs division. I asked what the necessity was for this overlapping of functions. I received four answers.

Ikeda Kanjō, a reporter for the *Asahi Shimbun*, put forward one explanation. The divisions, he argued, are study groups. A Dietman who is interested in a subject but knows

[15] Jiyūminshutō, *Seimu Chosakai Meibo*.

212

little about it, will join one of the divisions to inform himself. Here he can review the studies of the bureaucrats, listen to testimony, and question witnesses. The commissions, on the other hand, are the gathering points of the experts and specialists. By Ikeda's account, the commissions are the place where policy is hammered out.[16] I took this argument to the legislators for confirmation. Some of the Dietmen agreed with Ikeda, particularly noting the foreign affairs investigative commission as a case in point. Other Dietman disagreed and pointed out many exceptions, where the actual drafting of policy had taken place in the divisions. Ikeda's thesis, then, will not fit all cases.

A second reason given for the large number of commissions and committees was that there have been many matters which overlap the jurisdictional boundaries of several of the divisions. To avoid squabbles over which division should have primary responsibility, the politicians have found it expedient to set up special committees. The most recent example is the creation of a special committee to oversee the plans and development of a world's fair to be held in Ōsaka in 1970. This project could have been given to one of the divisions. But since all the divisions would ultimately be concerned, it was decided to establish a special committee.

The actions of the pressure groups constitute a third reason for the creation of overlapping commissions and committees. "No politician likes to turn down a bundle of votes," says Yoshimura Katsumi, the political editor of the *Sankei Shimbun.* "When the pressure groups put the heat on, the politicians temporize by setting up a committee to study the matter."[17] This political tropism is not unique to Japan.

A fourth reason is that none of the chairmen of the policy affairs research council has seen any great virtue in trying to keep the number of committees and commissions down. Clean flow lines, orderly procedures, clearly defined responsibilities are the concern of hidebound bureaucrats and fusty

16 Ikeda Kanjō, interview, February 14, 1966.
17 Yoshimura Katsumi, interview, June 24, 1966.

political scientists. Another high-sounding title added to a politician's biography might do some good at the polls. Until recently, whenever a group of politicians wished to form a new committee, permission was always granted.

This attitude has now changed. It is increasingly recognized that the crazy quilt of committees and commissions has created confusion about who is running the show. In the spring of 1966, an effort was made to renew the declining prestige of the division chiefs by rationalizing the party structure and altering Diet procedure.

There are two ways of introducing a bill into the Diet. One way is to introduce it as a cabinet bill. The other way is to introduce it as a bill sponsored by an individual Dietman. In the lower house, private bills need the endorsement of at least twenty other representatives, and if the bill will require funds, the endorsement of at least fifty representatives. In the upper house, regular private bills require the endorsement of at least ten councillors and money bills the endorsement of at least twenty councillors.[18] Because of this cumbersome procedure, most bills are introduced by the government.

Government bills are defended by the government. When a measure is introduced into the Diet committees, the opposition parties will immediately demand that the prime minister answer their questions. If he puts in an appearance, they are assured of a good story in the newspapers. Failing to get him, the opposition parties will level their attack against one of the ministers. Press coverage is not assured, but if the attack is well aimed and forcefully delivered, the newspapers will make space for it. The role of the members of the ruling party is to sit dumbly on the sidelines and when the debate is over, to vote the measure into law. The publicity and the glory go to the opposition and the government.

The conservatives decided in May 1966, that they had given the opposition parties enough of a field day in generat-

[18] Japan. Kokkai Hō [National Diet Law], in *Roppō Zensho* [Compendium of Laws] (Tokyo: Yuhikaku, 1967), Art. 56, par. 1.

ing publicity for themselves. In the future, they decreed, legislation would be sponsored by individual legislators and the defence of these bills would be in the hands of the division chiefs. Credit, if there was any, would redound to the party. To increase the prestige of the divisions chiefs, the party ruthlessly eliminated the special committee and commissions whose functions overlapped with the divisions.[19]

The reform was short-lived. Bills never did get introduced by the division chiefs. The elimination of the special committees and commissions lasted only until August, when the prime minister reshuffled the cabinet and new men were appointed to all the party posts. A general election was widely being predicted for the fall, and each of the legislators wanted to become chairman of something to help him at the polls. "There have never been so many requests for posts as now," reported Tanaka Kakuei, then secretary general.[20] Special committees and commissions, supposedly abolished, were quietly rejuvenated.[21] When Mizuta Mikio, then chairman

[19] *Asahi Shimbun*, May 28, 1966, p. 2.
[20] *Asahi Shimbun*, August 11, 1966, p. 2.
[21] As of August 1966, the commissions are *constitution, foreign affairs,* administration, *economic, price problems,* educational system, *election, tax system,* new agricultural basic problems, small and medium industry, basic policy, *labor problems,* social welfare, roads, *national development, mutual security,* national railroads basic problems, telegraph and telephone basic problems, *medical care basic problems.*

The special committees are *science and technology, public safety policy, tourist industry, overseas economic cooperation,* Okinawa problems, *conciliation, women and youth policy,* snow bound and cold regions policy, people's nutrition policy, public monopoly, military base policy, housing and land, coal policy, off shore islands development, *natural disasters, public nuisances, world's fair.* The names of these committees adequately describe their function, with the exception of the conciliation special committee. This organ deals with the problems of the Eta, a minority group in Japan.

There is only one conference, the overseas capital and industrial production problems conference. This organ deals with the problems Japan will face when it liberalizes the importation of capital.

The commissions and special committees in italics are the organs kept in existence after the May reform. The other organs were restored in August 1966. *Asahi Shimbun*, August 11, 1966, p. 2.

215

of the policy affairs research council, proposed abolishing the vice chairmanships of the divisions he met with adamant refusal.[22]

Pressure groups and elections encourage the Dietmen to increase the number of special committees and the commissions. Party spirit and the desire for order and rationality urge cutting them back. Each of these conflicting moods has its moments of ascendancy. The number of the special committees and commissions rises and falls. There seems to be nothing that can break these rhythms of the party.

None of these organs—subcommittee, division, special committee, or commission—has regularly scheduled meetings. They come together when the occasion demands. During the fall, when the budget is being put together, they may meet twice a week. In the early winter, when budget deliberations are reaching a climax, they may find themselves in almost constant session. During other times of the year, their conferences are less frequent. There is rarely a day, though, that several of these policy groups do not meet. "The conservatives are more concerned with policy than most people give them credit for," says Ikeda Kanjō.[23]

The party law also provides for the appointment of a research staff.[24] The men on this staff are divided into three groups. First are the senior researchers, of which there are six at present. They are assigned directly to the chairman of the council and receive their instructions from him. The second group includes the specialists. They are assigned to the various divisions; sometimes they serve in more than one division. At present, they number ten men. The third group comprise the clerks who take care of the housekeeping duties. At present, there are twenty of them. All the members of the research staff are salaried employees of the party.

On the second level of the pyramid sits the deliberation

[22] *Ibid.*
[23] Ikeda Kanjō, interview, February 14, 1966.
[24] Jiyūminshutō, *Tōsoku*, Art. 48.

commission.[25] Its task is to examine the policies that have originated with the committees, commissions, and the divisions. In some instances, it changes the recommendations that come from below. The conclusions of the deliberation commission must, in turn, be submitted to the executive council, an organ we shall discuss in the next chapter. From there the policy goes to the cabinet for the final stamp of approval. Any of these superior organs may reject or modify the recommendations of the deliberation commission, but as a general rule the recommendations of the deliberation commission carry the day.

Although the party law permits twenty men to be appointed to the deliberation commission,[26] the actual membership is usually less than that; there are presently sixteen members. Some of these men come from the upper house, but most come from the lower house. Each member is selected, with due regard to faction, by the chairman of the policy affairs research council in consultation with the secretary general. Actually, "the factions do not have much significance in either the deliberation commission or the council as a whole," said Fujieda Sensuke, then one of the vice chairmen on the council.[27] All the factions are represented to insure balance and harmony within the party, but rarely is the deliberation commission involved in factional squabbles.

The credentials of the members of the deliberation commission are impressive. These men have all demonstrated their ability to work with and create policy. They have an intimate knowledge of the ministries and their inner workings. Previously former ministers monopolized this commission, but nowadays younger men who are regarded as having ministerial talent are given the opportunity to serve. The members from the lower house have usually won at least five elections and those from the upper house two elections, and thus they have a good understanding of what is politically sound or feasible.

[25] *Ibid.*, Art. 43, par. 1.   [26] *Ibid.*, Art. 43, par. 2.
[27] Fujieda Sensuke, interview, February 23, 1966.

217

Above the deliberation commission sit five vice chairmen.[28] When the deliberation commission convenes, they sit with it. On other occasions, they meet as a group with the chairman of the council. Their formal duties are described in the party law as "assisting the chairman."[29] They also have the power to speak and negotiate on behalf of the council. One of the vice chairmen comes from the upper house, no faction gets more than one vice chairmanship, and the senior vice chairman comes from the prime minister's faction if the chairman of the council is not a member of his faction. Aside from these qualifications, the vice chairmen share the same credentials held by the members of the deliberation commission. The power to appoint these vice chairmen rests with the chairman of the council who will consult with the secretary general.

On top of the pyramid sits the chairman of the policy affairs research council. Together with the vice president, the secretary general, and the chairman of the executive council, he is considered one of the four top officials of the party. We have already discussed in some measure the appointment of these officials. The vice president is a faction leader in his own right and is closely allied with the president. The secretary general, as a general rule, comes from the prime minister's faction. The chairman of the executive council comes from one of the factions allied with the president at the time of the party elections, and it is suggested by close observers of the party that the chairman of the policy affairs research council is similarly chosen.

The chairman sits in on all the top conferences of the party. As a senior member of the party, his views carry great weight. When it comes to policy, however, it would be more correct to regard him as the speaker for the five vice chairmen and deliberation commission who sit under him. While there are no rules, and a great deal will depend upon the chairman's personality, he will rarely suggest an action

[28] Jiyūminshutō, *Tōsoku*, Art. 42, par. 1.
[29] *Ibid.*, Art. 42, par. 3.

unless he has these men's assent. In policy matters, no single man, short of the president, is accorded the right to make decisions for the party.

Policy is suggested by four sources in Japan: the Dietmen themselves, the pressure groups, the opposition parties, and the bureaucracy. Hayakawa Takashi, a politician who has served as a vice chairman on the policy affairs research council, estimates that 60% of the policy suggestions come from the bureaucracy, 20% from the Dietmen themselves and 20% from interest groups. He did not speak of the role of opposition.[30]

I have tried to pin these estimates down. To see how many innovations came from the Dietmen themselves, I have collected the figures for government and private bills for selected years since the merger of the conservative parties in 1955. These figures should by no means be regarded as definitive. Policy originating with the pressure groups and the opposition is also hidden within these figures. There is no easy or certain way to separate it out. While a pressure group may get a ministry to sponsor its ideas, it is more likely that they will get a Dietman to do so. Dietmen may also convince a ministry to introduce their bill, since a cabinet-sponsored bill has a greater likelihood of becoming law. This rarely happens, however. The figures in Table 15 can be regarded as a rough estimate on which to base a comparison between the number of policies originating with the ministries and the number introduced by the politicians. They put a general outside limit on the number of policies conceived by the politicians.

Despite the imprecision of this table, the percentage of proposed legislation sponsored by the Dietmen proves to be remarkably stable. In the 24th regular session, 33% of the proposed legislation came from the Dietmen; in the 38th regular session, 30% of the legislation came from the Dietmen; in the 48th regular session, 33% of the legislation came from the Dietmen; in the 51st regular session, 35% of the

TABLE 15. SPONSORSHIP OF LEGISLATION INTRODUCED INTO THE DIET

	Bills sponsored by Cabinet	Bills sponsored by Dietmen	
		Upper House	Lower House
24th Regular Session 1955-1956			
Bills introduced	173(1)	26(13)	77(6)
Bills passed	141	4	16
38th Regular Session 1960-1961			
Bills introduced	211	35(1)	60(2)
Bills passed	150	2	8
48th Regular Session 1964-1965			
Bills introduced	139(6)	24(5)	64(19)
Bills passed	125(1)	4	10
51st Regular Session 1965-1966			
Bills introduced	156	18	60
Bills passed	136	0	11
55th Special Session 1967			
Bills introduced	152	13	43
Bills passed	131	0	6

NOTE: Figures in parentheses show number of bills brought forward from previous session.

SOURCE: Table compiled from statistics of Shugiin Hoseikyoku [House of Representatives, Legislative Bureau].

proposed legislation came from the Dietmen; and in the 55th special session, 27% came from the Dietmen. These figures are higher than the estimate made by Hayakawa. When I mentioned these percentages to other Dietmen, they, too, were surprised. The Dietmen do not disclaim their role as the originators of policy, but they are more inclined to regard themselves as the judges of other people's ideas.

The opposition also plays a role in the formation of policy. Each opposition party has a policy organ which produces policy recommendations. "For example, the minimum wage law, the yearly income law, and the agricultural industries basic law were first drawn up by the Socialist party and the law relating to small and medium industries was conceived by the Social Democrats. These bills never became law, but later legislation based on these bills and introduced by the conservatives has become the law of the land."[31] Since the renovationist parties are closely connected to labor, they respond to labor's demands and make many policy suggestions beneficial to labor's interests. "Particularly there are many instances in the field of education, labor, and social welfare where the conservatives have made the policy of the opposition parties their own."[32]

Pressure groups are also a source of policy. These groups are largely a postwar phenomenon. "In the old days," says Kōno Ichirō, "Diet members were men of great standing and power. They would not permit the existence of pressure groups."[33] Despite the Japanese penchant for new things, these pressure groups have been subjected to heavy public criticism. The popular attitude is best expressed by Nagai Yōnosuke, who wrote while he was a professor at Hokkaidō University: "The ordinary people of Japan feel that it is ethically wrong for various organized, extra-parliamentary forces to bring pressure to bear on the government."[34] Their attitude is understandable. Given the primitive stage that Japanese pressure groups are now in, the Japanese people have not yet had the opportunity of seeing the real benefits that the pressure groups can bring to government.

Dislike of pressure politics does not, of course, prevent participation. The Japanese, with their genius for organiza-

[31] *Yomiuri Shimbun*, February 21, 1966, p. 3.
[32] *Ibid.*
[33] *Nihon Keizai Shimbun*, Oct. 31, 1963, p. 5.
[34] Nagai Yōnosuke, "Structural Characteristics of Pressure Politics in Japan," *Journal of Social and Political Ideas in Japan*, December 1964, p. 101.

221

tion, have belatedly but whole-heartedly, adopted the forms of extra-parliamentary persuasion. To watch a group of small land-owners or middle-aged housewives, the most orderly and conservative of citizens, trotting docilely at the heels of their leaders through the crowded streets of Tokyo on their way to the Diet hill to stage a "mass demonstration" complete with red flags, slogan-inscribed banners and chanted protests is unnerving. The Japanese politicians, however, view these proceedings with equanimity. A high party official, perhaps the chairman of the policy affairs research council, will meet with the group's leaders and may say a few words to the group at large. He would do the same at any village festival.

Some of these mass demonstrations are taken more seriously. The Agricultural Cooperatives Association came up with a new way to persuade the Dietmen to raise the producer's price of rice. On June 28, 1966, one day before the rice deliberation council started its final consultations in establishing the amount of government support, the association called a Tokyo convention of the 16,000 local cooperative officials. These tactics proved too blatant for Tanaka Kakuei, then the secretary general of the party, and he issued a notice to all the legislators to stay away. Nevertheless, "better than two hundred Dietmen showed up in the guest seats on the main speaker's platform, waved to the cooperative officials from their election districts and were all smiles for everyone."[35]

The farmers continued their pressure on other fronts. On July 2, the agricultural cooperative from Akita prefecture gathered in the street outside the chambers of the rice deliberation council. Armed with an accordion and drum, they danced to the refrain of "One bag, ten thousand yen."[36] Meanwhile busloads of farmers were being disgorged outside of the party headquarters to lay siege to it.[37]

35 *Asahi Shimbun*, evening edition, June 28, 1966, p. 10.
36 *Ibid.*, evening edition, July 2, 1966, p. 3.
37 *Ibid.*, July 3, 1966, p. 2.

222

FORMULATING POLICY

If protest is one approach, humility is another. A second form of pressure politics is the petition group or *chinjōdan*, usually country folk with the village mayor, sometimes local officials alone, or, on major occasions, the prefectural officials and the governor. They come to Tokyo to plead their case in the offices of the bureaucrats and the politicians, the officials usually coming at the taxpayers' expense. The *chinjōdan* are particularly active during the months of December, January, and February when the national budget is being welded together and farm activity is slack.

The press never fails to note their arrival, usually on the city pages rather than in the political columns. One reporter writes of the 1965-66 season: "Boxes of Fukushima pears and Aichi tangerines are piled up in the corridors of the Construction Ministry. These gifts of the regions are the thing this year. The Home Ministry is said to have sent notices to each of the prefectures requesting that gifts not be brought. . . . One of the busiest men in the Construction Ministry, the section chief of the road bureau says, 'During the height of the season I haven't got time to sit down. If I let the *chinjōdan* in to speak with my men, all work would stop. I regard myself as a dike. . . .' The Public Welfare Ministry is reported to have had 1,500 people, some mothers with babies strapped on their backs, on November 25 asking for a doubling of the livelihood protection payments."[38] Matsuda Takechiyo, sitting in his suite in one of the two office buildings for lower house members, gestured with exasperation toward the door leading to the corridor and told me, "Last January, there was a day when 10,000 petitioners crowded into this building."[39]

The *chinjōdan* are certainly much in evidence. But how seriously they should be taken is another matter. The lady critic Inukai Michiko, daughter of a minister and granddaughter of a prime minister, tartly says, "I learned one thing from my father. The petitioners come in great crowds but

38 *Ibid.*, December 1, 1965, p. 15.
39 Matsuda Takechiyo, interview, May 23, 1966.

223

better than half of them are using the *chinjōdan* as a cover. They just tag along with the others and don't say anything. Afterwards, they go shopping in the department stores or go watch a strip show."[40] The *chinjōdan* are also a waste of money. The *Asahi Shimbun* cites a case of a *chinjōdan* which came to Tokyo from Kyūshū. After repeated visits, they finally got their money. But when they sat down and figured it out, they discovered their expenses were more than the funds obtained.[41] The politicians like the *chinjōdan*, however. A Dietman says, "Elections are coming up. I should be the one going through the countryside bowing and scraping. Instead they come to see me. Petition groups are welcome guests."[42]

The *chinjōdan* get more than their fair share of criticism from the press, but they are important as a means of giving the people a closer identification with their government and politicians. Their major failing is that they and the mass demonstrators do not seem to realize that their rough political tools cannot always be honed fine enough to carve out effective legislation.

There are other pressure groups that are in another league entirely. The National Federation of Housewives Associations, the National Veterans Association, the Japanese Medical Association, the Agricultural Cooperatives Association, the League for Government Compensation of Expropriated Agricultural Land are a few examples of a score or so pressure groups that are nationally organized, control a hefty number of votes, have large secretariats with competent research staffs. Their leaders are in constant touch with the politicians, and they can present a rational and effective brief. Their efforts have been remarkably successful.

The League for Government Compensation of Expropriated Agricultural Lands has received a handsome settle-

40 *Asahi Shimbun*, September 6, 1964, p. 19.
41 *Ibid.*
42 Yomiuri Shimbun Seiji-bu, *Seitō* [Political Parties] (Tokyo: Yomiuri Shimbunsha, 1966), p. 149.

ment. The Agricultural Cooperatives Association may hold conventions at opportune times but it supplements this activity with detailed and extensive agricultural studies that will hold up before any group of experts. The National Federation of Housewives Associations nags the cabinet so diligently that they won't let the public bath operators jack up their price even a few pennies. One triumph in 1966 was blocking a phony sanitation measure—proposed, incidentally, by another pressure group, the Dry Cleaners Association—which would have almost doubled the price of the dry cleaners' mortal enemies, the do-it-yourself establishments. The Japan Medical Association has been powerful enough to elect its own representatives to both houses of the Diet.

Japanese politicians are particularly susceptible to organized pressure groups. We have seen in earlier chapters, the weakness of the party organization in the countryside. A conservative politician must put together his own organization if he is to win in the elections. He relies in some measure on the existing organzations of the pressure groups. The pressure groups, in return, use him to represent their interests and introduce their bills in both the party and the Diet.

The fourth source of policy is the bureaucracy. They play a most important role. The *Yomiuri Shimbun* says, "The services of the government offices are exhaustive. The truth of the matter is that practically all the divisions of the policy affairs research council are carried piggyback by the bureaucracy through all the phases of policy making, from the supplying of basic research documents to the drafting of bills."[43] The conservative Dietmen do not deny that they are heavily dependent on the ministries, but they maintain that they are running the show. Fujieda Sensuke says, "There is a strong determination on the part of the legislators not to let the bureaucrats lead them around by the nose."[44]

Fujieda may have spoken too sharply. He makes it sound as if there were a confrontation between the bureaucrats and

43 *Yomiuri Shimbun*, February 21, 1966, p. 3.
44 Fujieda Sensuke, interview, February 23, 1966.

the politicians. There is not. Relations between the conservative politicians and the bureaucrats are both close and cordial. They are two peas in the conservative pod. The bureaucrats realize the great power of the politicians. The politicians recognize the usefulness of the bureaucracy. In no other place are the close ties between the bureaucrats and the politicians so readily apparent as in the policy affairs research council.

Theoretically, the bureaucrats could stand aloof from the political parties. They could request their ministers to bring their policy recommendations to the attention of the cabinet. They could rely on committee hearings in the Diet to present their views. But the Japanese cabinet is composed of conservative ministers and the Diet committees are led and dominated by conservative politicians. No minister would introduce, no cabinet would pass on, and no committee would hold hearings concerning a policy that did not have the full approval of the appropriate party organs. The road to party approval starts in the divisions of the policy affairs research council.

Most of the bureau directors of the various ministries are on intimate terms with their respective committees, divisions, and commissions in the policy affairs research council. They spend a great deal of time testifying, and their staffs spend a great deal of time preparing research for them. No bureaucrat who hopes to have ministry ideas translated into law will fail to touch base early and often with the party organs. And aside from legislation, the party organs hold the ministries responsible for keeping them informed of recent developments in their respective areas of interest.

Professional pride of the bureaucrats, then, demands that they be in close contact with the party. Personal ambition also encourages them to work with the conservatives. To make room for the younger bureaucrats to climb the steps of the bureaucratic staircase, senior officers in the bureaucracy are required to retire when they reach fifty or so years of age. Retirement is perhaps not the correct word. These men are at the height of their energies and abilities and few desire, look forward to, or can afford, a life of leisure. Upon leaving their ministry, most of them will take up employment elsewhere. They usually head in one of three directions. They may become senior officers in one of the major business firms, they may take up posts in one of the public corporations, such as the Japan Monopoly Corporation, or they may—this choice is reserved for a limited few—choose to stand for public office, for a seat in the Diet.

The first two courses for the senior bureaucrats are relatively easy to pursue. Long experience in the ministries has brought them in contact with a great many business firms and these firms highly value the bureaucrats' abilities and contacts. A number of posts in the public corporations are reserved for the bureaucrats. The head of the Japan Telegraph and Telephone Corporation, for example, will always come from the senior ranks of the Finance Ministry. The third choice—becoming a politician—is extraordinarily difficult. The bureaucrat to whom this course is open will be no lower in grade than bureau chief, and may well be administrative vice minister, the highest bureaucratic rank in the ministry. Since the party is weak organizationally, the bureaucrat will have had to develop by himself an election district, and usually during the last few years before his retirement he will have been using the advantages of his position to assist him. The Agricultural and Forestry Ministry, the Construction Ministry, and the Home Ministry officials are particularly fortunate in this respect since they have a strong "clientele" in the regions. The Foreign Office officials, on the other hand, have no strength in the regions, and thus few of them become politicians.

But developing an election district is not enough to win an election. The bureaucrat must also have the backing of the party, and to get the backing of the party, he must have the backing of a faction. Imai Kazuo, a political critic and a former bureaucrat from the Finance Ministry, says, "Many of the top bureaucrats become politicians. They are good at running the country but terrible at winning elections. They need the help of professional politicians, campaign funds, and the party endorsement. If a bureaucrat is considering going into politics he must have close connections with the party from the time he is promoted to be a section chief [*kachō*]. He will usually be about forty years of age at that time. Although there are exceptions, most bureaucrats won't be in a position to run for office until they have become division chiefs [*kyokuchō*]. They usually make this post at about fifty years of age. This gives the bureaucrat ten years to establish himself with the politicians."[45] The *Asahi Shimbun* in 1968 made a study of the backgrounds of the politicians and found that of the 273 conservative Dietmen in the lower house 78, or a little less than 30%, had risen from the bureaucratic ranks.[46]

This description would make it appear that the bureaucrats are completely under the thumb of the politicians. But such is not the case. The bureaucrats have their own strength which permits them to stand as at least equals in the process of making policy. This strength comes from organization.

The great power of the bureaucrats is their control of information. The ministries have the responsibility of systematically collecting data for the formulation of policy and there is no agency within the party or society as a whole that can effectively challenge them in this function. No one in the party openly accuses the bureaucracy of consciously doctoring information—at least, I have not heard the charge. But bureaucrats, despite the popular image of hard faces and cold hearts, are human and information which buttresses a ministry position will certainly get more prominent attention than those niggling facts which weaken its argument. The politicians, particularly those who have risen from the bureaucratic ranks, are aware of this predilection. Kurogane Yasumi, once a Finance Ministry official and now a member

[45] Imai Kazuo, interview, November 11, 1966.
[46] *Asahi Shimbun*, July 19, 1968, p. 19.

of the lower house, has put the case simply. "Ask the bureaucrats for research and what you get is an opinion."[47]

In common with bureaucracies the world over, Japanese public officials do not air their internal differences. The relation between the conservative politicians and the ministry officials may be close but it does not extend to the point where the ministry washes its linen in front of the party. No policy is presented to the party until the ministry's ducks are all in a row. When the ministry chooses to speak, it will be with a single voice.

"To be sure," says Kurogane Yasumi, "The bureaucrats are always careful to give a series of options. They list them across the page. One, two, three, four, five. But the reasoning leads to only one acceptable conclusion."[48]

The only time this system breaks down is when two or more ministries are involved. The ties of bureaucracy are strong but they do not extend between the ministries. The Ministry of International Trade and Industry is often at loggerheads with the Foreign Ministry over foreign economic policy, particularly trade with Communist China. The Education Ministry squabbles with the Science and Technology agency over who controls Japan's space program. All of the ministries have unkind words to say about the Finance Ministry and its niggardly control of funds. When the ministries begin speaking with different voices, it is not unusual for the divisions within the council to begin squabbling, each representing its ministry's position.

The members of the party have been dissatisfied with the present policy affairs research council and have from time to time suggested reforms to improve and strengthen it. One of the major criticisms has centered on its membership. The council is composed of Dietmen, and many apparently believe that membership should be broadened to include other elements of the party. True, the party law specifies

47 Kurogane Yasumi, interview, February 22, 1966.
48 *Ibid.*

229

that "the policy affairs research council shall be constituted of members of the Diet and other men of knowledge and experience especially entrusted by the president."[49] The latter clause was designed to enmesh heavy financial backers further into the workings of the party by giving them a forum to express their views. The financial backers, however, have been content to remain a little bit away from the party and have not risen to the bait. The provision has not otherwise been exploited. In 1964, Miki Takeo, then secretary general, chaired a committee looking into the structure of the party and one of his recommendations was to make use of scholars outside the party.[50] The recommendation was accepted, but little has been done to put it into effect. A former secretary general, Tanaka Kakuei, speaks of creating a "supporting party member system," by which scholars, economists, financiers, and former bureaucrats will be brought into the colloquies of the party. "These influential party members will deliberate on an equal basis with the Dietmen, the ministers, and the prime minister when important policies are being drawn up."[51] Tanaka's plan also has not passed the talking stage.

Given this control by the bureaucrats and the legislators, it is not surprising to discover that the major concern of the council is the fashioning of law and policy to meet the needs of government. In this respect, the council does its job extremely well. No matter is too small for it to investigate. The construction of a rural airport on an offshore island, the exploitation of the resources of a small river in Kyūshū, the awarding of disaster funds to fishermen shipwrecked in the Marianas—all these matters receive the careful consideration of the council. The party millstones of policy grind a fine

[49] Jiyūminshutō, *Tōsoku*, Art. 41.

[50] Jiyūminshutō, *Soshiki Chōsakai Tōshin* [Report of the Organization Investigation Commission] (Tokyo: Jiyūminshutō, 1964), p. 60.

[51] Kokumin Seiji Kenkyūkai, "Kanjichō Shian to Tōkindaika" [The Secretary General's Proposal and the Modernization of the Party], *Getsuyōkai* [Monday Club Report], October 11, 1965, p. 10.

political grist which, with the yeast of Diet debate, makes excellent government bread.

Modern political parties, however, must be concerned not only with bread but with dreams. They must fashion a complete and credible image of where the nation stands and where it should be going. None of the committees, divisions, or commissions gropes seriously with this problem. To change our previous metaphor just slightly, the party is greatly concerned with the quality, taste, and cost—particularly the cost—of the doughnut; nobody is investigating the hole. But the hole gives the doughnut its unique shape.

To be sure, the conservative politicians are concerned with tomorrow. They talk about it constantly among themselves. But the talks are at night on the tatami mats of the restaurants in Akasaka with a cup of sake in the hand and a slightly aging geisha at the elbow. Nobody has thought about shifting the venue to the policy affairs research council and the time to the cold, hard morning. The prime minister occasionally delivers a speech which permits a foggy glimpse of his vision of the future. An energetic party member may publish an occasional article delineating his views in a magazine with low circulation or a book which gets distributed only in his election district. A new party slogan is released which may or may not catch the fancy of the public. But slogans, and speeches, and occasional articles do not shape a destiny. As yet, sustained and systematic investigation of where Japan is going or ought to go remains outside the party's ken.

Politics abhors a vacuum, and the opposition parties have enunciated their view of Japan's future; but none of them has, as yet, captured the Japanese imagination. The newspapers are the only group which has even partially filled the void. They regularly give the vision of a noted intellectual on page five of their evening editions, report party news on page two of their morning editions, and hold space open on page one of both editions for a political scandal. Since the conservatives have the congenital weakness, common to all long-entrenched ruling parties, of being susceptible to corruption,

231

they are the ones usually caught. This willingness to be bludgeoned by the press rather than capture the imagination of the press is one of the major causes for the particularly unfavorable image of the conservative party in Japan.

Domination of the policy affairs research council by the Dietmen also vitiates the party in another respect. We have seen earlier that the great flaw in the party is the lack of a strong organization. One reason is the isolation of the regional branches from the policy-making apparatus. Since they do not have a direct voice in the formulation of policy, they tend to work through individual Dietmen to get their interests recognized, thus further encouraging division within the party. What is true of the local politicians is also true of the Japanese voters at large. They, too, are excluded from the policy organs and must work through individual Dietmen. One of the major reasons for joining and working for a political party is denied both to the regional politicians and the general public. As long as these conditions continue, the party cannot hope to build a strong, popular base.

The second major criticism of the policy affairs research council is that it is too dependent on the bureaucracy. There have been various recommendations over the years to give the politicians a greater degree of freedom. Most of them have centered around the establishment of a secretariat within the party to do research. This idea first surfaced when the party was formed in 1955. Provision was made for employing a modest number of researchers, but little else came of the suggestion. In 1964, Miki Takeo, then the secretary general, managed to have the party laws revised to permit the establishment of a "general institute of policy studies for the purpose of studying fundamental problems of democratic government and basic policies of the party, as well as collating basic research materials."[52] But nothing has been done to put teeth into this provision. None of the politicians I talked to objected to the formation of an institute for policy studies. All believed it to be a good idea in princi-

[52] Jiyūminshutō, *Tōsoku*, Art. 49.

232

ple. But the politicians cited great difficulties in creating such an organ. Some wondered about who would run it, others questioned whether the party could gather men of high enough caliber to staff it. Few failed to mention the staggering costs such an institute would entail. In short, what the proposal means is setting up another bureaucracy parallel to the government, and none in the party is willing to undertake this huge task.

A research institute within the party does not seem to be the answer. Nor can the politicians turn to the academic world to recruit talent and ideas. The scholars and other intellectuals are engaged in a noisy debate over their role in Japanese society, but the great majority are agreed that cooperation with the politicians, particularly the conservative politicians, is out. Kobayashi Katsumi, a secretary to Nakasone Yasuhiro, who is actively interested in fostering a better relationship with the scholars, says, "Some of the young scholars have ideas that they would like to see put into action. They are willing to work with the politicians but they are afraid of being ridiculed by their colleagues and cut down by their seniors. It gets pretty ridiculous sometimes. They write letters which they instruct us to burn after reading. They sneak into the office and make us promise to tell no one that they have been there."[53] The Japanese academicians will not soon leave their closed world. It will be many years before the conservative politicians can tap this group of brilliant and capable men.

The economic community undertakes research and makes policy recommendations to both the ministries and to the conservative party. Their research is generally held to be good, and while they stress economic problems, they also investigate other fields. The party accords their views great weight. But they are only one group and thus have limitations.

The consolidation of local governments into larger units may give them the size and strength to undertake independent policy studies, an area that they have been willing to leave

[53] Kobayashi Katsumi, interview, April 13, 1966.

in the hands of the bureaucrats of the central government so far. But this hope is dim, since money is scarce in the regions, raising taxes is politically impossible, and research funds would have to be obtained from the central government. It would appear that the party will have to depend on the pressure groups.

This is not as bad as it sounds. True, the present pressure groups are intent on raiding the national treasury. Most of them rely more on sound and fury than they do on fact and reason. Few have developed the facilities for research. They can play rough, as the example of the agricultural cooperatives convention cited earlier in the chapter attests. But their structure, style, and tactics are changing rapidly.

Such groups are no longer limited to those concerned with getting a bit of the budget. Most Japanese have become aware of the benefits that special interest groups can obtain, and all segments of the society—conservation groups, education groups, youth groups are organizing for political action; rumor has it that a national flower arranging association is considering trying to put one of its officers into the Diet. The lobbying of these groups will soon cover the complete range of government activity.

Inevitably many of these groups will become competitive and their conflicting goals will give the politicians space to maneuver. Furthermore, the realization is growing that diligent research on behalf of the politicians rather than mass lobbying against the politicians will pay more dividends in the long run. Finally, the gradual growth of the party's regional organization will eventually make the politicians less beholden to the pressure groups for votes. The pressure groups may well end up playing a positive role in Japanese politics by giving the politicians healthy alternatives to the policies suggested by the bureaucracy.

A third criticism can be made concerning the policy affairs research council. But this criticism is directed not so much at the politicians as at the press. They pay entirely too little attention to the council's deliberations.

234

The fault is partially the politicians. The council makes little effort to draw attention to its efforts, primarily, one suspects, because the council members find it easier to work outside the glare of publicity. "After a Dietman has gotten into the inner circles of the council, he becomes closemouthed. The freewheeling opinions that he spouted before are forgotten,"[54] says Yamamuro Hideo, an assistant editor on the political desk of the Japan Broadcasting Corporation. The politicians' behavior is understandable. Nobody can expect them to strike the match to the hay in their own barn.

Politics, to the political reporters, means first of all covering the factions. There is not a reporter worth his salt who cannot explain in detail the shifting front of the factional wars, the plottings of the generals, the flurries of guerilla action, the defections, and the casualties. Their second interest centers on the Diet and they joyously pummel the politicians for the occasional rhubarbs that disrupt its proceedings and worry publicly about the parlous state of Japanese democracy. They have a third passion, which usually goes unsatisfied. It is trying to figure out where the political funds come from and where they go. Few pay much attention to the sober deliberations of the policy affairs research council and little appears about them in the newspapers.

I took this criticism to Yoshimura Katsumi, the political editor of the *Sankei Shimbun*, and asked his views. He said, "I have one reporter covering the council at all times. He picks up a lot but he can't get to everybody. Usually, the papers will cover the major matters that come before the council. Space prevents us from printing everything. But still, we ought to be doing more."[55]

It can be argued that the council is more important than the Diet because it is in the council where the real deliberations on policy take place. Quiet wars in its chambers are a daily occurrence, as all the elements of the party fight to have their interests recognized. But once the council has reached a

54 Yamamuro Hideo, interview, April 6, 1966.
55 Yoshimura Katsumi, interview, June 24, 1966.

decision and obtained the formal approval of the executive council, the party members dutifully close ranks and support it.

If no legislation is necessary, the cabinet announces the decision as national policy. The opposition parties issue critical statements and may try to drag the matter into the proceedings of the Diet committees, but the cabinet rarely reconsiders. If legislation is necessary, a bill is presented to the Diet. The opposition may force minor concessions or cause the bill to be held over by threatening to impede the passage of other necessary legislation. But the cut and thrust of debate rarely changes the essence of the bill. Hayakawa Takashi says, "There is very little revision of a bill after it has been introduced into the Diet. The Japanese are more like the English than the Germans in this respect."[56] A ballot is taken. Voting discipline among the conservatives is rigid. Crossing the aisle is unheard of. Their overwhelming strength carries the day. The measure becomes the law of the land.

The role of the Diet as a forum for the making of policy is limited. The council is the seat of the action. The Japanese people should be more informed about its deliberations. They should be cut in on the take-offs as well as the landings. And this responsibility lies with the newspapers.

[56] Hayakawa Takashi, interview, February 24, 1966.

CHAPTER IX

Reaching a Decision

"How does the party reach a decision? That's a good question." Sakata Michita, a conservative politician from Kumamoto prefecture, thought for a moment, then hunched over in his chair and said, "I won my first election in 1946, which means I have been active in the party for twenty years. During this time I have been a minister and I guess I have served on every committee in the party." He paused again. "I don't have the slightest idea how the party makes up its mind." He looked up through his thick-lensed glasses and smiled beatifically.[1]

Decision-making among the conservatives is like a floating crap game. The players remain pretty much the same but the action keeps changing scene. "It's hard to tell who is really making the decisions," says Koyanagi Makie, a conservative now in the upper house who served many years in the lower house and as governor of several prefectures. "Sometimes the factions are important and sometimes the party organs. Sometimes everything may hinge on the party leaders and sometimes on a group of legislators who have gotten together to push a cause."[2] Decision-making among the conservatives is complicated, but like the crap game, tightly organized and played with an involved set of rules.

In this chapter, we shall concentrate on the official decision-making organs of the party. "No matter where the deliberations are started or where they are decided, they will always pass through one of the decision-making organs of the party before they become party policy," says Sakata Michita.[3] I shall hang my discussion on the framework of the

[1] Sakata Michita, interview, May 18, 1966.
[2] Koyanagi Makie, interview, May 30, 1966.
[3] Sakata Michita, interview, May 18, 1966.

party law. No matter how much the politicians twist, fracture, and ignore this law, they all return to it in the end. It is a fair guide to the decision-making process.

In the present conservative party there are three "decision-making organs." They are the party conference, the assembly of the members of both houses of the Diet, and the executive council. All three of these organs have their antecedents in the conservative parties of the days before the war, although their names and functions were slightly different.

Both the Constitutional Democratic party and the Friends of Constitutional Government Association had a party conference. Their meetings, however, were few and far between, and when they were convened, their functions were chiefly ceremonial. "From talking with the old politicians and from studying the documents of the day, it is fair to conclude that there were only rare instances of dispute in the party conference."[4] Each of the two prewar parties had an assembly of the members of both houses. Since many of the members of the upper house (the House of Peers in the days before the war) were appointed directly by the emperor, held their seat by virtue of the taxes they paid, or were members of the nobility, the number of party members was small. An assembly of the members of both houses of the Diet differed little from a meeting of the members of the lower house.

Both the prewar parties had executive councils. In fact, the executive council can be dated back at least to the founding of the Friends of Constitutional Government Association in 1900.[5] The executive councils of those days were composed of five men—at the most, ten men—and once admitted to the executive council, the men rarely left. They were the leaders of the party. Two Dietmen with memories of these prewar parties, Fukunaga Kenji and Nemoto

[4] *Asahi Shimbun*, August 24, 1962, p. 2.
[5] Rikken Seiyūkai, "Kaisoku" [Association Rules] in *Rikken Seiyūkai Shi* [History of the Friends of Constitutional Government Association] by Kobayashi Yūgo, Vol. 1 (Tokyo: Rikken Seiyūkai Shi Shuppan Kyoku, 1923), Art. 2.

Ryūtarō, both stated that the executive council was regarded as more important than the cabinet.[6] One reporter compares the prewar executors to the faction leaders of today.[7] Particularly in the Friends of Constitutional Government Association, the executive council was the most important of party organs.[8]

Some of the old politicians describe how decisions were made in the prewar parties. The late Matsuno Tsuruhei, a speaker of the House of Councillors, served two terms as the secretary general of the Friends of Constitutional Government Association. He describes decisions of that party as follows: "Important matters were first decided by the executive council. These men would then meet informally with other members of the party and, when the groundwork was fully prepared, a meeting of the assembly would be called and the matter would be passed by acclamation."[9]

The decisions in the Constitutional Democratic party were made in much the same manner. Noda Takeo, now a member of the Diet but at the time a young political reporter, describes the process: "The secretary general would first decide how he felt about the matter. He would then talk to the important members on the executive council. While the members of the executive council were deliberating, the secretary general would approach the party elders individually and obtain their approval. Then a meeting of the assembly of the members of both houses of the Diet would be called."[10] Since the secretary general had done his spadework most carefully, "there was little that the assembly could do even if they opposed the measure."[11] All these maneuvers will strike the observer of the current conservative party as very familiar.

There were instances when agreement within the party was not so easily reached. Both Noda and Matsuno agree that the

---

[6] Fukunaga Kenji, interview, June 3, 1966; Nemoto Ryūtarō, interview, May 18, 1966.

[7] *Asahi Shimbun,* August 19, 1962, p. 2.

[8] *Ibid.,* August 21, 1962, p. 2.   [9] *Ibid.,* August 24, 1962, p. 2.

[10] *Ibid.*   [11] *Ibid.*

most common solution to a deadlock was to refer the matter to the president of the party for a decision.[12] Rather than risk a vote, another tactic was to call upon the members who supported the resolution to applaud. "It didn't matter whether there was a great deal of applause or not," recalls Tsugumo Kunitoshi, "it would be announced that the measure had been passed by general acclaim and the meeting would be immediately closed."[13]

Matsuno recalls adopting pressure tactics himself when he was secretary general. "The assembly had been in turmoil for two days and there was not a decision in sight. I whispered to the chairman of the assembly to declare it to be the sense of the meeting that there was unanimous support for the measure and to close the meeting. He followed my instructions. Afterwards, I remember my actions being roundly denounced as the tyranny of the secretary general."[14]

A third tactic was to call a recess in the proceedings of the assembly, break the members up into small regional groups, and have the party leaders circulate among these groups to gain approval for the measure. In 1927, there was a general agreement reached among the party leaders to call a truce in political warfare. This agreement was immediately challenged at a meeting of the Assembly. Whereupon "the meeting was closed to the public and temporarily recessed. During the recess, the various regional bodies met, discussed the matter, and collected their views. At two o'clock that afternoon, the Assembly was reconvened and support for the matter was unanimous."[15] Although regionalism has ceased to be a major consideration in postwar politics, these regional blocs can still be found in the executive council of the present conservative party.

No matter how the parties reached their decision, the party members were obliged to support it. Discipline in the prewar parties was rigid. Failure to comply with the party dictates meant either expulsion or forced resignation. For example, the cabinet of Count Ōkuma decided to increase the

12 *Ibid.*   13 *Ibid.*   14 *Ibid.*   15 *Ibid.*

Japanese army by two divisions. The Friends of Constitutional Government Association opposed this decision. Within the party there was, however, a group of eighteen legislators who were willing to go along with the cabinet. They were summarily thrown out of the party. This instance was to be repeated many times in the years before the war.

The party conference of the Liberal Democratic party differs little in spirit from the party conferences of the pre-war parties in the years when there is no presidential election. We have already described the new role of the party conference, in the chapter dealing with the election of the party president. Our task here will be to describe its other functions.

The party conference is designated "the supreme organ of the party" in the party law.[16] Its membership is made up of all the Diet members of the party and four delegates from each of the prefectural federations. Of these four delegates, two must come from the youth bureau and the women's bureau.[17] The origin of the other two delegates is not specified. Judging from the list of delegates to the 17th party conference, the other two men are usually the secretary general, the vice chief of federation, or the executive council chairman of the federation. But there are enough exceptions to make drawing a rule hazardous. While the delegates' formal positions in the federation may vary, they can all be regarded as the leading local political leaders.

The party conference is regularly convened once each year by the president of the party.[18] Customarily the conference is called in January. Provision is also made for special sessions to be called at the request of the assembly of the members of both houses of the Diet or by one-third of the prefectural federations.[19] In practice, special sessions of the conference are called only to elect a new president.

16 Jiyūminshutō, "Tōsoku" [Party Law] in *Wagatō no Kihon Hōshin* [Basic Policies of Our Party] (Tokyo: Jiyūminshutō Kōkoku Iinkai, 1966), Art. 26.
17 *Ibid.*   18 *Ibid.*, Art. 27.   19 *Ibid.*

The format of the party conference changes very little from year to year. I have chosen to describe the 17th party conference, held in January 1966, though the description would be applicable to any of the party conferences held in previous years. The party conference opens with the party dignitaries arrayed across the stage of one of the large Tokyo auditoriums. The national anthem is played over the loudspeaker system. A temporary chairman is appointed and he, in turn, supervises the elections for the permanent chairman and vice chairman.

The secretary general of the party then delivers a lengthy report on the state of the party. The report rarely covers new ground. But it is not an encomium; mistakes and failures are frankly admitted. Tanaka Kakuei, the secretary general in 1966, castigated the infighting within the party in Miyagi and Gifu prefectures, admitted the loss of popular confidence in the party in Tokyo, and blamed weak organizational strength for the poor showing in the upper house elections.

The report of the secretary general is followed by greetings from the party president, who is usually brief, and from a whole series of guests, who are not. The distinguished guests start with the head of the People's Association, the principal fund raising organization associated with the party, and with the president of the Liberal Democratic party of Okinawa, over which Japan has sovereignty but which is presently under United States administration. They are followed by representatives from the agricultural cooperatives, the Small and Medium Sized Business Federation, youth and women's organizations. Since votes, money, and national prestige are involved, nobody gets left out or cut short.

With the fulsome words of greeting out of the way, the party conference settles down to business. First comes the election of party officials. The party law stipulates that the party discipline committee shall be composed of eight members of the House of Representatives, four members of the House of Councillors, and not more than four men drawn from outside the Diet and recommended by the president.

These members shall be elected at the party conference. The party law also makes provision for the members of the committee to choose from among themselves a chairman and vice chairman.[20] The system of selection envisaged in the party law has been modified with the passage of time. Custom decrees that the chairman of the committee shall be drawn from the conservative members of the upper house, and his selection as well as that of the other two upper house members will depend upon the recommendations of the conservative leadership in the upper house. Lower house members will be selected by the secretary general. "Factional balance is, of course, considered, since it would not do to have the committee overbalanced in favor of any faction or alliance of factions," says Nemoto Ryūtarō, who has served on the discipline committee, "but the important criterion is to select men who have had long party experience and can be relied upon to give an unbiased, level-headed judgment."[21] Until the 1967 party conference, the president ignored the provision permitting him to recommend men from outside the Diet. Throughout the previous autumn and into the winter, the party had been bombarded by charges and scandals, and Prime Minister Satō apparently felt that he had to make some gesture. Acting on the assumption that senility meant rectitude, he recommended that two ancient and retired Dietmen, Kimura Tokutarō of the upper house and Hoshijima Nirō of the lower house be added to the committee. The slate of members to compose the discipline committee is offered to the party conference and they approve it by acclaim.

Party law states that there "may be a vice president of the party"[22] and that he "shall be elected by ballot at the party conference."[23] In actuality, the party is content to leave the judgment of whether there is to be a vice president and who

20 *Ibid.*, Art. 62.
21 Nemoto Ryūtarō, interview, May 18, 1966.
22 Jiyūminshutō, *Tōsoku*, Art. 5.
23 *Ibid.*, Art. 6.

he should be to the president of the party. On the occasions when the president chooses to have a vice president, he will rise at the party conference and in a brief, graceful speech, make his nomination for the post. The delegates will elect the candidate by acclaim, the new vice president will stand, murmur a few words pledging his fullest efforts to the tasks at hand, and sit down. Personnel problems have been taken care of.

The party conference next addresses itself to policy. There will be an explanation of legislation that is pending in the Diet. During the 17th conference, the discussion revolved around the new national budget. The conference returns to party affairs with the adoption of some policy positions. During the last conference the party adopted a women's charter and a youth charter. In the women's charter, the party pretty much limited itself to saying what splendid creatures women are. In the youth charter they went a bit further and pledged themselves to helping youth create a better Japan and a more peaceful world. Both documents will receive considerable exposure in future elections. A lengthy statement of party plans for the coming year is next presented to the conference. In 1966, this statement outlined the party position on various foreign policy questions, on strengthening parliamentarianism, on advancements in social development, and on measures to recover from an economic recession. A large part of the plan suggested ways for modernizing the party and for strengthening its organization.

The party leaders then ask for approval of the party's budget. Finally, a proclamation and a resolution are read out. The January 1966 resolution pledges the party's efforts in responding to the hopes and trust of the Japanese people in the trying days that are facing Japan. The proclamation covers pretty much the same ground, but stresses the need for Japan to contribute to the peaceful solution of the Vietnam question and the creation of a peaceful Asia. All measures put before the delegates—the plan outlining the basic directions of the party, the charters, the approval of the budget, the resolution, and the proclamation—are adopted unanimously by voice vote without debate.

Next, the party conference spends a good half hour reading out the names of various individuals who have made a significant contribution to the party. Some of the most outstanding of the group are called to the stage and given scrolls of appreciation by the president. Others must be content with having their names published in a pamphlet distributed to all the delegates. Finally, the conference is called to a close. The delegates rise and give three banzais—one for the country, one for the party, and one for the party president. There is a scramble to get out of the building and over to the prime minister's official residence, where a reception awaits them.

The Japanese press is critical of the party conference. After the 1966 party conference, for example, the *Asahi Shimbun* wrote in an analytical column: ". . . As usual, the party conference completed its business in a scant three hours. The party conference is the supreme decision-making organ of the party and its convocation offers the most important occasion for deciding the basic policies of the party. Therefore . . . it is natural for there to be extensive debate. But in actuality, in a series of rapid-fire moves, without pause for debate and without an objection voiced, everything was tidied up. The ruling party, which has responsibilities toward the people, needs to reconsider the role of the party conference."[24]

There is no denying the charge that the party rarely uses the party conference to come to grips with the real problems it faces. There is hardly ever any real debate. During the first meeting of the party conference in 1956, there was significant discussion of the position the party should take on restoring relations with the Soviet Union and on revising the constitution. Several years ago, Ishida Hirohide, a former labor minister who is known as a lone wolf within the party, decided to kick up a fuss by introducing a labor charter for approval in the party conference. His efforts got him no-

[24] *Asahi Shimbun*, January 23, 1966, p. 2.

245

where. The labor charter was thrust back into his hands for further consideration at a lower level of the policy making apparatus in the party. Other than these occasions, debate has been virtually nonexistent in the nineteen sessions of the party conference that have been held to date.

The lack of debate indicates clearly how completely the party is controlled by the members of the Diet. The party conference is the only meeting in which both the regional members of the party and the Dietmen meet to adjudicate party policy. In theory, all it would take to spark debate would be for one of the regional delegates to ask for the floor and present his views. But to date, not one of them has had the temerity or desire to raise his voice. They have been content to leave the direction of the party in the hands of the legislators of the central government.

The Dietmen, on the other hand, have ample occasion for hammering out differences in policy at a lower level. They will place nothing on the agenda unless it has been discussed adequately and substantial agreement has been reached within other policy organs. For them, the party conference is the forum where the highest stamp of approval can be placed on the most important policy decisions.

The *Asahi Shimbun* claims, in the analysis I have just quoted, that the party members are taking a second look at the role of the present party conference. "Criticism is starting to grow within the party over the role of the party conference. To measure views in circulation both in the capital and the countryside and to firmly establish a system incorporating all elements of the party, the regional legislators who are delegates to the conference ought to be accorded the . . . opportunity of voicing their opinions. The party conference ought to be extended for two or three days, subcommittees ought to be formed, and the basic courses of action of the party ought to be dug into and debated."[25]

During my discussions, I found conservative politicians to be fully aware that the relations between the party and the

[25] *Ibid.*

prefectural federations were not as deep or as intimate as they should be. There was frank recognition that local politicians were not consulted on any matters except elections. Some Dietmen believe that there are already too many hands stirring the pot of policy. Some deride the local politicians, saying that their idea of decision-making is to concoct a new scheme for squeezing money out of the central government to build a new road in their district. Others feel that they adequately represent the people of their district and that the local politicians are superfluous. Tanaka Kakuei, a former secretary general of the party, notes that decision-making is an intimate process that takes place between the central government, meaning the bureaucrats, and the Dietmen, and that cutting the prefectural federations in on the process would be difficult.[26] For one reason or another, the Dietmen are unwilling to allow the local politicians to participate in the decision-making process.

Reform of the party conference—changing it from a ceremony into a vital part of the decision-making process—will have to come from below, from the regional politicians themselves. I return to a theme that I have struck time and again in this study. The sense of party is weak in Japan. If this is true of the populace at large, it is also true of the regional politicians. While they pay lip service to the party, their real allegiance is to individual Dietmen. So long as this state of affairs continues, the Dietmen will reign supreme. The day that a regional politician stands up in the party conference, demands the floor, and introduces a resolution, another mile-post will have been passed in changing the conservative body from a parliamentary club into a popularly based party.

The second formal decision-making organ of the party is the assembly of the members of both houses of the Diet.[27] It has a chairman, who is customarily chosen from the upper house and two vice chairmen, one from the upper house and from the lower house. Provision is made for the election

<hr>

26 *Ibid.*   27 Jiyūminshutō, *Tōsoku*, Art. 31.

of these men by the assembly itself,[28] but in reality, the upper house chairman and vice chairman are decided by the upper house leadership and the lower house vice chairman is selected by the secretary general.

The party law assigns two responsibilities to the assembly. One is "to examine and decide especially important questions concerning party management and activities in the Diet." The second responsibility is "to substitute for the party conference in matters requiring an urgent decision."[29] A third function has been added over the years. The assembly now has a liaison or reporting responsibility.

Let me take up the informal function first, since it is only of marginal interest to us in examining the role of the assembly in decision-making. Although the party law created an assembly of the members of the House of Representatives and an assembly of the members of the House of Councillors to consider matters relating to the Diet, it never established a joint body of all the Dietmen. The need for such a body became apparent and the assembly of the members of both houses of the Diet, although originally conceived as a decision-making organ, was bent to this purpose.

Since the upper house holds itself aloof from many of the daily political struggles and usually considers legislation after it has passed the lower house, the assembly is convened less often than one would anticipate. It is usually called together when the party leaders wish to whip up enthusiasm or in order to report actions that have been or are about to be taken. In December 1966, for example, Prime Minister Satō summoned an assembly to drop the broad hint that a general election was in the offing. "Since forming my first cabinet, I have not received the judgment of the people. The time has come for me to give serious thought to dissolution."[30] Although the seats of the councillors were not at stake, the prime minister felt the occasion important enough to have them informed. Sakata Michita comments, "One function of the as-

28 *Ibid.*, Art. 33.   29 *Ibid.*, Art. 32.
30 *Mainichi Shimbun*, December 22, 1966, p. 15.

sembly is to keep everyone informed and in line on the important actions of the party."[31]

Regarding the formal responsibilities of the assembly, all the politicians to whom I talked believed that the party law, as far as it goes, is a fair statement of the actual functions. But they all added qualifications.

The politicians emphasized that the assembly was little more than a ceremony. "The assembly is used for formal decisions," said Koyanagi Makie, a former chairman of the assembly.[32] "The approval of the assembly is the final step in making party policy," said Yamamoto Katsuichi, a former economics professor who has served in the lower house. "The real decision has been made long before."[33] "The assembly is convened not to make decisions but to ratify decisions," said Sakata Michita.[34]

I asked why they did not refer such matters to the party conference. The politicians' answer was that the matter usually had to be resolved quickly. "Many of the questions concern policy in the Diet and the party can't wait a year for a decision," said Hara Kenzaburō.[35] All the politicians waved aside the idea of calling a special party conference, pleading trouble, time, and expense. "I grant you that formal assent by the party should be obtained at the party conference," said Koyanagi Makie, "but the conference can't be called on short notice. So for ease the assembly is used instead."[36]

Why not use the executive council, if it was too much trouble to convene a party conference, I asked. The politicians replied that the executive council was good enough for most decisions but not for all. Hara Kenzaburō said, "Most of the important party decisions are subject to a great deal of controversy and you have to add a little more weight to make

31 Sakata Michita, interview, May 18, 1966.
32 Koynagi Makie, interview, May 30, 1966.
33 Yamamoto Katsuichi, interview, June 6, 1966.
34 Sakata Michita, interview, May 18, 1966.
35 Hara Kenzaburō, interview, May 25, 1966.
36 Koyanagi Makie, interview, May 30, 1966.

the decision stick."[37] Sakurauchi Yoshio, a veteran legislator who has served in both the upper and the lower houses since the late forties, said, "Something a little extra special is needed to nail these decisions down."[38]

I asked if there was debate at the assembly meetings. The politicians could remember one or two times when there had been meaningful exchanges. But they noted that this was the exception, not the rule. "If there are any real problems, the matter is usually not put before the assembly," said Sakurauchi Yoshio.[39] "There is always debate but it is not significant. Don't go to the assembly expecting to change anybody's mind. There is little doubt to the outcome of the proceedings," says Hara Kenzaburō.[40]

I asked if the assembly met regularly. The answer was negative. The general consensus of the politicians seemed to be that a meeting was called once or twice a year. Koyanagi Makie explained it this way: "Usually there is a meeting just before the opening of the regular Diet session, when the prime minister presents his views on what the party hopes to accomplish during the session. Other than this occasion, meetings are called when something comes up."[41]

If the assembly does not meet regularly, I asked, who determines when the assembly should be convened and what constitutes an especially important matter? Sakurauchi Yoshio answered the latter part of my question first by ticking off some of the questions that had been brought before the assembly: the visit of Prime Minister Hatoyama to Russia, the renegotiation of the security treaty with the United States, and the reopening of diplomatic relations with South Korea were some of the foreign policy questions; the passage of a police reform bill and the role of the government in managing the nation's coal mines were two domestic matters; the suspen-

37 Hara Kenzaburō, interview, May 25, 1966.
38 Sakurauchi Yoshio, interview, May 24, 1966.
39 *Ibid.*
40 Hara Kenzaburō, interview, May 25, 1966.
41 Koyanagi Makie, interview, May 30, 1966.

sion of the rules for the election of the party president to allow the successor to the prime minister to be chosen by consultation was an example of a party issue.[42] Koyanagi Makie answered the first part of my question. He noted that the party law gives the chairman responsibility for convoking the assembly.[43] "But he doesn't exercise this power on his own. Usually, he is called by the president or the secretary general and they discuss whether there ought to be a meeting of the assembly."[44] In short, what constitutes a matter important enough to be brought before the assembly is decided by the party leadership.

Finally, since the party law stipulates that "decisions of the assembly shall be made by a simple majority of those present, and in case of a tie, the chairman shall decide the issue,"[45] I asked whether the assembly actually voted on questions. The politicians said no.[46] Japanese decisions are reached by *hanashiai*, which literally means talking together. The ideal solution is to reach a unanimous decision, and the Japanese politician will spend many hours trying to reach a compromise that will satisfy all the interests concerned. In a large group such as the assembly, it is never an easy matter to reach a unanimous verdict. A great deal depends on the skill of the chairman in guiding the discussions. Koyanagi Makie gave me a full explanation of how he resolved questions in the assembly. I quote it at length since it has application to all Japanese discussions.

Any matter which is presented to the assembly is supposed to be passed by the assembly. The task of the chairman, then, is to secure the approval of the other Dietmen. Although the decision of the assembly is

42 Sakurauchi Yoshio, interview, May 24, 1966.
43 Jiyūminshutō *Tōsoku*, Art. 33, par. 2.
44 Koyanagi Makie, interview, May 30, 1966.
45 Jiyūminshutō, *Tōsoku*, Art. 34.
46 This has not been the case in all the conservative parties. Nakasone Yasuhiro notes, for example, that the Progressive party, a conservative party which disappeared in the merger of 1955, used to reach party decisions by voting. Nakasone Yasuhiro, interview, June 3, 1966.

supposed to be a formality, there is often debate. There are three ways to guide this debate to a successful conclusion.

In some cases when a Dietman stands up and gives his opinion, it is clear that he is against the proposal, but his opposition is general and not always to the point. I hear the man out and then announce that his opinion has been "registered." Actually, no record is made of the discussion and there is no way to register his opinion. But the Dietman is usually satisfied that his voice has been heard.

In other cases the Dietman may be directly to the point in his opposition. If the point he raises is a simple one, a question that can be answered yes or no, I usually ask for a show of hands. I don't bother to take a count. The Dietman has had his say and the assembly has responded.

After the meeting has gone on for a while, everyone who wants to has had a chance to speak his piece. If the opposition are in a small minority, you can rule it to be the sense of the meeting that the measure has passed and adjourn.

If there are too many voices in opposition, however, the task of the chairman will be to put off making a decision. When several of the Dietmen raise the same criticism, I promise the point will be restudied. This move accomplishes two ends. First, it limits the subject under debate. To restudy does not mean to reopen the entire question but simply to reach agreement on the point being disputed. Secondly, it moves the power to make the decision outside the assembly. After an appropriate period of time has passed, someone can talk to the Dietmen who raised the objection, compromise if necessary, secure their assent, and make a decision that will be to the benefit of the party.[47]

47 Koyanagi Makie, interview, May 30, 1966.

This method of reaching a decision is not always as easy or smooth as Koyanagi makes it appear. In June 1966, Nakayama Fukuzō, the vice chairman from the upper house, had his problems, as the following excerpt from the "Reporter's Chair," a light political column published daily in the *Asahi Shimbun*, attests. I have translated the item in full because it shows another facet of the *hanashiai* and tells what happened to the labor charter, a question left unresolved in our discussion of the party conference:

> Yesterday when the assembly of both houses convened at the party headquarters in Nagata-chō, the labor charter was adopted, but the method of adoption was peculiar. After Sakata Michita, the chairman of the organization research committee, delivered his report, Yamamoto Katsuichi started to argue against it. But Nakayama Fukuzō, the chairman, followed the prepared script exactly. With a look of innocence, he declared, "It's decided according to the report. It's adopted unanimously." Because of his steamroller tactics, the meeting broke out in an uproar. However, Nakayama, by interpreting the objections as "considerations" and by repeating three times, "It's unanimous," brought the issue to a close. This left a bad taste in the mouth of Sakata Michita, but he couldn't do anything about it. With a forced laugh, he said, "They were kind enough to adopt the charter three times. . . ."[48]

None of the politicians to whom I talked offered any suggestions for reforming the assembly. Since the politicians are usually bubbling over with ideas to modernize the party, this lack of comment is, in itself, significant comment. When I asked them if the assembly should be abolished as superfluous, they demurred. When I asked them if it should be strengthened, they shrugged their shoulders. In short, the politicians were not interested in changing the assembly.

48 "Kishaseki" [Reporter's Chair], *Asahi Shimbun*, June 29, 1966, p. 2.

253

Since there are no complaints, we may cautiously assume that the assembly is fulfilling its functions. But its role as a decision-making organ is decidedly limited. It is one of the methods available to the party leaders to add further gravity to an important decision.

The third decision-making organ of the party is the executive council. The party law stipulates that it shall be composed of thirty executors.[49] Fifteen of these executors shall be selected by ballot by all the members of the House of Representatives. Seven of these executors shall be selected by ballot by all the members of the House of Councillors. The remaining eight executors shall be selected by the president of the party.[50] The party law further decrees that the executive council shall have a chairman and four vice chairmen and that these members shall be elected by the members of the executive council itself.[51]

The party law does not tell the whole story. In fact, that part of the story it does tell, it tells backward. The selection process starts with the chairman of the executive council.

We have briefly touched on the selection of the chairman of the executive council in the chapter dealing with the making of the cabinet. This chairman is regarded as one of the four top officials in the party and his selection is made by the party president himself. The occupant of the chair will be one of the most powerful politicians in the party, and will invariably come from one of the factions allied with the prime minister. Of the twelve executive council chairmen who have served since the formation of the Liberal Democratic party in 1955, five have been faction leaders in their own right. Shortly after his nomination, the executive council chairman will huddle with the secretary general of the party and together they will select the other members of the executive council.

Their first concern will be with the eight presidential appointments to the executive council. In making these

49 Jiyūminshutō, *Tōsoku*, Art. 35.
50 *Ibid.*, Art. 37.   51 *Ibid.*, Art. 38.

appointments, balance between the factions will be a major consideration. Each of the factions will recommend the men it wishes to have occupy a seat. However, a presidential appointment to the council may prove a mixed blessing. On the one hand, the council carries great prestige and can play a decisive role in determining what position the party will take on a given issue. This prestige and power rubs off on the politicians occupying its chairs. On the other hand, several politicians told me that presidential appointments to the council are usually consolation prizes for politicians who, for one reason or another, will not be offered the opportunity of serving in the cabinet.

It is virtually impossible to demonstrate the validity of this statement. I have gone over the membership lists of the councils since 1955 and in each council I have found politicians who not only served on cabinets but who constitute the backbone of the party. I reversed the process and selected men whom I considered to be leaders in the party and checked their political history. Many of them, I found, had served at one time or other on the council. In short, there are enough exceptions to the rule to make it doubtful whether there is a rule.

While an invitation to join the council is subject to various interpretations, one fact is clear. The council is not for young politicians. Politicians who have not served as parliamentary vice ministers and as committee chairmen in the Diet will rarely be considered for the executive council. In terms of political age, this means surviving at least four general elections.

In an earlier section of the chapter, we noted that the executive council was one of the few party organs that attempted to maintain geographical balance. The fifteen members of the lower house are selected according to geography. In Japan there are nine major regions, each region comprising several prefectures. Every region will have its representatives on the executive council. At present, the Kantō region has three representatives; the Tōhoku, Tōkaidō,

Hokuriku-Shin'etsu, and Kyūshū regions have two representatives; and the Chūgoku, Shikoku, Kinki, and Hokkaidō regions have one representative. I asked why the imbalance and Yamamoto Katsuichi answered, "Preference is given to regions which have a greater number of conservative legislators."[52] Within each region, an informal order of rotation has been established among the prefectures. Finally, the selection of which legislator should represent the prefecture is decided by consultation. Complying with the provision of the party law that calls for selection by ballot of all the representatives in the party is simply a formality.[53]

I asked why geographical balance is maintained, and the politicians gave the answer I anticipated. "If all regions are represented," explained Fukunaga Kenji, a former chairman of the executive council, "then no regions are overlooked."[54] Perhaps this explanation is correct. But in my personal experience, I have found that the politicians are concerned with the fate of the nation and of their own election district but do not waste too much time on the regions. Yoshimura Katsumi, the political editor of the *Sankei Shimbun*, says bluntly that geographical balance no longer has any meaning. Any policy which ignored a region would be blocked long before it reached the executive council.[55] Geographical balance, I suggest, is the continuation of an old custom which had meaning in the prewar conservative parties.

The secretary general and the executive council chairman have little to do with the selection of the seven members of the council who come from the House of Councillors. The selection of these men rests clearly with the leaders of the Liberal Democratic party in the upper house, and the criteria they use in selecting the men to serve in the executive council are not clear. "The basis for selection varies according to the political conditions existing at the time in the upper

52 Yamamoto Katsuichi, interview, June 6, 1966.
53 Jiyūminshutō, *Tōsoku*, Art. 37.
54 Fukunaga Kenji, interview, June 3, 1966.
55 Yoshimura Katsumi, interview, June 3, 1966.

house," says one reporter who has followed the councillors' activities for many years.[56] Certainly the upper house leaders consider the number of times the councillor has been elected. Factional balance is also brought into consideration. Whether a man has been a minister or not does not seem to matter. One politician suggests that appointment to the executive council can, indeed, sometimes be regarded as a step to a ministerial post.[57] If a personal observation may be allowed, the appointment to the executive council does not seem to be regarded by the councillors as an important assignment. The only clear fact in the selection process is that the election by all party members of the House of Councillors, called for in the party law, is a formality usually honored in abeyance.[58]

Finally, the secretary general and the executive council chairman will select four men to serve as vice chairmen. Three of these vice chairmen will be from the lower house and one from the upper house. They will be the most senior politicians in the executive council. Of the four politicians serving in this post in early 1966, three won their first election to the Diet in 1947 and one won his first election to the Diet in 1949. Their duties are formally described as assisting the chairman and acting in his stead when necessary. In actuality, the position of vice chairman carries more prestige than additional responsibility.

Article 36 of the party law assigns to the executive council the responsibility to "examine and decide important matters concerning party management and activities in the Diet." With regard to party management, the specified duties can be roughly divided into three categories: personnel, discipline, and ceremonial. The executive council also has undefined responsibilities in the area of organization and propaganda. The executive council must give its consent to the recommendations of the policy affairs research council before

[56] Okino Mitsu, interview, May 18, 1966.
[57] Nabeshima Naotsugu, interview, February 3, 1966.
[58] Jiyūminshutō, Tōsoku, Art. 37, par. 2.

they become official party policy. Diet strategy is generally left by the executive council to other hands. Finally, there are several matters—elections, party finance, cabinet appointments, dissolution of the Diet—that the executive council does not touch at all.

More than ten provisions of the party law deal with the role of the executive council in appointing personnel to the various party posts.[59] Although there are exceptions, it is fair to state that virtually all appointments to party posts in the central headquarters must have the consent of the executive council.

The president himself will make the nominations to the top positions in the party. The executive council rarely raises any questions about these posts. However, the president will usually give the task of making the other appointments to the secretary general. In the case of party posts, the secretary general will consult with the appropriate chairman (who has been appointed by the president) and they will draw up a list of the men they wish to see appointed to each of the party committees. The secretary general, however, is obliged to meet with the executive council and submit these appointments for its approval. This approval is not always given automatically.

Custom does not permit the executive council to comment on the individual recommendations on the secretary general's list or make its own recommendations for the various party posts. But they do give their opinion in general, and on occasion refuse to give their consent, leaving the secretary general no recourse but to reconsider the appointments. When this custom was first explained to me, I could readily understand the reluctance of the secretary general and the executive council to discuss individual appointments. Thirty politicians arguing over better than two hundred party posts could turn into a fruitless and ugly spectacle. But, I wondered, how does the secretary general know how to revise the list if the executive council members only give abstract argu-

[59] *Ibid.*, Arts. 10, 11, 14, 16, 44, 45, 47, 53, 71, 73, 75, 77.

ments of disapproval? I put the question to Sakata Michita. His answer was: "Any secretary general who needs to be told why a particular politician is objecting to the list should not be secretary general."[60] Discipline is another of the responsibilities of the executive council. The lack of party spirit, the infighting among the factions, the peculiarities of the election law, the disparate ideologies, the weak organizational strength—all the factors that make the conservative polity more an alliance than a party—and make discipline a major headache. In the steady flow of plans for party reform that the secretary general, the organizational research committee, the individual politicians, and the press issue from time to time, few fail to make recommendations to strengthen discipline within the party.

The party law has elaborate provisions "to maintain discipline and to raise the morale of the party."[61] The enforcement of these provisions is entrusted to a discipline committee whose members are chosen at the party conference. The crimes are: violation of a party law, disregard of a party decision, or action demeaning to the dignity of a party member. The punishments are two: suspension from official duties or expulsion from the party.[62] For the discipline committee to function, two-thirds of its members must be present. For the committee to reach a decision, at least two-thirds of the members present must be in accord. Rights of appeal are guaranteed, and the appeal is made to the president, who, acting through the executive council, can cause the discipline committee to reconsider its judgment.[63]

If these procedures sound elaborate and the punishment harsh, it should be noted that no one has ever been tossed out of the party. The discipline committee is amazingly tolerant. For example, Kōno Ichirō, one of the major faction leaders before his recent death, was suspected of running six candidates of his own choosing against the party-endorsed

60 Sakata Michita, interview, May 18, 1966.
61 Jiyūminshutō, *Tōsoku*, Art. 61.
62 *Ibid.*, Art. 94.   63 *Ibid.*, Art. 63.

candidates in the general elections in 1963. The matter was brought up before the discipline committee. "I investigated the case for the committee," says Nemoto Ryūtarō. "There was nothing that could be proved. Besides, even if Kōno did everything that he was accused of, he went no further than the other faction leaders."[64] Kōno was exonerated.

Utsunomiya Tokuma, one of the lone wolves in the party, has teetered on the edge of disciplinary action many times. He has publicly urged the recognition of Communist China; he took the occasion while in Indonesia to proclaim that 90% of the Japanese people opposed the American bombing of North Vietnam; and announced himself opposed to the reopening of relations with South Korea, positions which delighted the socialists and were all against established party policy. There is constant mumbling in the party, particularly among the right wing, that some one ought to clip Utsunomiya's wings, if not pitch him out of the conservative rookery. Perhaps it is respect for the principle that every Dietman has the right to speak his mind, that has restrained the discipline committee from acting so far.

In 1966, the discipline committee girded itself to advise two politicians who had been exposed in election irregularities in Niigata Prefecture to resign from party membership. The two politicians spiritedly retorted that they had no intention of resigning from the party. The discipline committee did not feel obliged to follow up this rebuke with a harsher sentence.

"The bulk of the cases that come before the discipline committee are concerned with election offenses," says Aoki Kazuo, who has served as chairman of this committee.[65] Election offenses stem as much from flaws in the election laws as they do from excesses of the candidates. "The discipline committee is willing to and does hand out sentences short of expulsion. But they are extremely reluctant to toss a man out

---

[64] Nemoto Ryūtarō, interview, May 18, 1966.
[65] Aoki Kazuo, interview, January 19, 1966.

of the party," says Nemoto Ryūtarō.[66] Given the state of internal tension within the party, they are perhaps wise in their present course of action.

A third specified responsibility of the executive council is policy. In the previous chapter, we reviewed the activities of the policy affairs research council. For their deliberations to become party policy, the consent of the executive council is needed. This consent is not always readily given.

Hasegawa Shirō, formerly one of the vice chairmen of the policy affairs research council, says, "Getting the approval of the executive council is not simply a formality. Many times they refuse to accept our recommendations."[67] I asked Ōkuma Ryōichi, one of the senior researchers for the policy affairs research council, what policies the executive council was willing to approve and what policies it would object to. He was at first reluctant to offer any guidelines. "It's hard to anticipate the actions of the executive council." After further questioning and further reflection, he offered the following general rule: "In domestic affairs, policies that cost money—particularly, social welfare measures, construction projects, and agricultural bills—have rough going in the executive council. Foreign affairs are always delicate. While there are many opinions, nobody wants to take the responsibility of overruling the Foreign Ministry. Its opinion will usually carry the day."[68] Yamamoto Katsuichi said, "There is little chance of the executive council completely changing a plan. They may refuse to approve it. But if the plan has enough pressure behind it, it will get through."[69]

After a measure has received the approval of the executive council, it is passed on to the cabinet and then introduced into the Diet. Because of the heavy legislative load, political decisions have to be made about what legislation to push

66 Nemoto Ryūtarō, interview, May 18, 1966.
67 Hasegawa Shirō, interview, February 28, 1966.
68 Ōkuma Ryōichi, interview, June 4, 1966.
69 Yamamoto Katsuichi, interview, June 6, 1966.

and what legislation to let slide. Usually, the executive council is willing to let other committees make these judgments. Diet strategy usually is the responsibility of the steering committee, a Diet organ; the Diet policy committee, a party organ; the Dietmen's conference, another party organ; and the secretary general.[70] On occasion, if the matter is of importance and interest to both houses, an assembly of the members of both houses will be called, but this meeting will usually be used to obtain ex post facto approval for actions already taken. Fukunaga Kenji, former member of the steering committee and chairman of the executive council, describes the role of the executive council in Diet strategy this way: "The executive council does not get involved in the day-to-day affairs of the Diet. If something becomes a major issue, it will get into the act. Even then, the council will not try to make decisions but will limit itself to encouraging others to get on with the tasks at hand."[71]

The executive council has some other scattered responsibilities, which I lump under the category of ceremonial. The party law specifies that the party president, with the consent of the executive council, may award commendations to persons who have "performed meritorious deeds for the party,"[72] grant a variety of honorary ranks and titles,[73] and establish special organs within the party if the need arises.[74] The party has established a central academy of politics where party workers, chiefly regional organizers, are trained.[75] The party law specifies that the chairman of the executive council shall be one of the academy's advisors.[76] The role of the executive council in all these tasks is simply to provide the party presence.

[70] The Dietmen's conference (Daigishikai) is formally called the assembly of the members of the House of Representatives (Shūgiin giin sōkai), LDP, *Party Law*, Art. 54. Few politicians use this formal title. The party organs concerned with the Diet will be discussed in the next chapter.

[71] Fukunaga Kenji, interview, June 3, 1966.

[72] Jiyūminshutō, *Tōsoku*, Art. 93.

[73] *Ibid.*, Arts. 73, 75, 77.

[74] *Ibid.*, Art. 81.   [75] *Ibid.*, Arts. 15, 20.   [76] *Ibid.*, Art. 84.

Surprisingly, the party law does not assign any responsibilities to the executive council in the areas of propaganda and organization, the two major concerns of a modern political party. The party law does establish two committees to handle these matters: the public relations committee[77] and the national organization committee.[78] These committees are large and active. Decisions are usually made by their respective chairman or by the chairman in consultation with the secretary general.

I asked why the executive council does not play a large role in these two areas. Hara Kenzaburō pointed out that the party law specifies that the executive council shall examine and decide important matters for the party. While the organization and the public relations committees make many day-to-day decisions, few of these decisions rise to the level at which the executive council should contribute its counsel. Hara noted that when something major does come along, the executive council is usually called upon to give its judgment.[79]

There are several matters on which the executive council is not consulted. The first of these is party finances. How the party shall disburse its money is left almost entirely to the secretary general, the finance committee, and the director of the financial accounts bureau. The reason is that the party does not wish to have its finances publicized. As Hara Kenzaburō put it, "The party takes a low posture on finances. We've got enough to talk about with the opposition without debating the finances of the party. There are thirty men in the executive council and if finances were discussed there, in no time flat every newsman in town would know about it and feel obliged to write a story. There are some party matters that are best left unsaid."[80]

Although elections profoundly affect the fortunes of the party, the executive council has relatively little to do with

[77] *Ibid.*, Art. 20.   [78] *Ibid.*, Art. 15.
[79] Hara Kenzaburō, interview, May 25, 1966.
[80] *Ibid.*

them. The dissolution of the Diet is a prerogative of the cabinet, shared with no one. Party endorsements are decided by the election policy committee. We shall see in the next chapter that the overall campaign is conducted by the secretary general. In preparing for the general elections of January 1967, the only thing that the executive council did was to pass formally on the party slogans for the campaign.

Finally, the executive council is not consulted on appointments for the cabinet. This power, we have seen, lies in the hands of the prime minister.

The executive council meets frequently. Fukunaga Kenji says "While the Diet is in session, the executive council meets twice a week, on Tuesdays and Fridays at eleven o'clock in the morning. When the Diet is not in session, it usually meets once a week. There are sometimes special sessions. When the budget is reaching the last stages of being put together, the council may meet every day. Members of the executive council are like firemen. When they are busy, they are very busy. But in between fires they can take it easy."[81]

The sessions of the executive council are semi-restricted. "Any Dietman can attend and, if he wishes to, can stand up and give his opinion," says Yamamoto Katsuichi.[82] Bureaucrats from the interested ministries and officials from the party secretariat are also present. Newsmen and spectators are kept out. "If there are no newsmen present," says Fukunaga Kenji, "none of the Dietmen feels obliged to make speeches for the record. If the newsmen want to find out what went on, they can poke around and find out later. Many times there is a press conference to announce the results of the deliberations."[83]

I asked if there was a formal agenda or whether any studies were distributed in advance. Hara Kenzaburō said, "On some of the larger issues, materials are distributed in advance. But usually not. The agenda is in the hands of the chairman. It

[81] Fukunaga Kenji, interview, June 3, 1966.
[82] Yamamoto Katsuichi, interview, June 6, 1966.
[83] Fukunaga Kenji, interview, June 3, 1966.

isn't usually announced ahead of time. But everyone generally knows what is coming up for decision."[84]

The party law stipulates that decisions of the executive council shall be decided by majority vote of those present and that in the case of a tie, the chairman shall decide the issue.[85] As in the case of the assembly of the members of both houses of the Diet, this is one of the provisions of the party law that has not been exercised. The executive council does not vote on issues but resolves the question by *hanashiai*, that is, talking it over in search of consensus. The chairman will either allow discussions to continue until a small minority has been isolated and then rule in favor of the measure, or put off decision until a compromise can be reached outside the council among the interested parties, or secure agreement from the council to leave the decision up to the senior members of the party.

This difficult process of deliberation is sometimes further compounded by the factions. Although the factions were quiescent during 1965 and 1966, they have in the past, and they may in the future, use the executive council to contest party leadership.

Fukunaga Kenji notes that when factional wars start, deliberations in the executive council become much more vigorous.[86] Sakata Michita recalls that the executive council has been one of the major battle fields for the factions in the past. "Some of the factional fights got pretty hot. But of course, nobody admitted to factional interests being at stake. I don't remember the word 'faction' ever passing anyone's lips at these meetings of the executive council."[87] Hara Kenzaburō, recalls, "I served on the executive council during the latter days of the Ikeda regime. We had a chairman who was not particularly friendly to the prime minister. I don't know if it was conscious policy on his part or not, but anybody who

84 Hara Kenzaburō, interview, May 25, 1966.
85 Jiyūminshutō, *Tōsoku*, Art. 39.
86 Fukunaga Kenji, interview, June 3, 1966.
87 Sakata Michita, interview, May 18, 1966.

opposed a measure got ample opportunity to stand up and make his opposition known."[88]

That the factions are able to manipulate a decision-making organ of the party has brought forth criticism from many of the conservative Dietmen. Many of them would like to see the executive council restored to its prewar stature as an organ to which even the cabinet listened. One recommendation has been to limit the number of executors and to raise their caliber.

In 1964, a committee of almost a hundred conservative Dietmen studied the internal workings of the party. One of the organs which received their critical attention was the executive council, and they recommended, "In order to create a decision-making organ that would accord with the important matters that the party must decide, greater care should be given to the selection of its members. The number of members should be limited to twenty, five of whom would be selected by the president, five of whom would come from the upper house, and ten of whom would be selected regionally."[89] Watanabe Tsuneo, one of the party's critics, has recommended that the executive council be limited to ten men and that these men include the faction leaders. "It is not sensible not to have these men participate in deliberations over the highest decisions of the party."[90]

These proposals have not been acted on, chiefly because of the elections. The executive council—more importantly, the title of executor—carries great prestige among the voters, and the politicians who have not served as ministers or as Diet or party committee chairmen wish to serve as something that sounds important. It is most likely that their wishes will effectively halt any attempt to reduce the membership in the council. Including the faction leaders in the executive council

[88] Hara Kenzaburō, interview, May 25, 1966.

[89] Jiyūminshutō, *Soshiki Chōsakai Tōshin* [Report of the Organization Investigation Commission] (Tokyo: Jiyūminshutō, 1964), p. 60.

[90] Watanabe Tsuneo, *Habatsu* [Factions] (2nd ed., Tokyo: Kōbundō, 1964), p. 172.

may appear to be a good suggestion. But as we have noted in the case of the cabinet, many times the faction leaders find it to their benefit not to join. There is nothing to suggest that the executive council would be any different from the cabinet in this respect.

In a sense, both these proposals are an attempt to turn back the clock. The prewar executive council was authoritative, not because of any strength inherent in the organ itself, but because the members were powerful politicians. Once a politician joined the prewar executive council he rarely left. The executive council of the present Liberal Democratic party changes its members every year. Whatever strength it has is derived from the organ itself. To say that it is weak is to say that the party is weak. Any attempt to bolster the authority of the council by enlisting the party strong men in its ranks would render the making of decisions easier but would not strengthen the structure of the party.

It can be argued that the council should stay as it is. As the party itself grows strong, so will the council. In the meantime, there are other informal organs where party decisions can be made. We will turn to an examination of these institutions in the next chapter.

CHAPTER X

Running the Party

TANAKA KAKUEI jotted down the following thoughts for a small column of recollections that appears regularly on the front page of the *Sankei Shimbun*:

> On the third of this month [December 1966], I resigned from the post of secretary general. I was appointed to this post on July 2, 1965. It has been exactly a year and a half that I have occupied the position.
>
> Looking back, I can best describe the post of the secretary general as a traffic cop standing at a crossroad with no signal light trying to direct a flood of trucks and pedestrians. If the people and problems steadily pushing in on you are not taken care of with dispatch, everything soon comes to a standstill.
>
> I had a set schedule. But politicians, scholars, labor leaders, company officials—every sort of person from every occupation and station—would appear without warning and lecture, argue, cajole, and demand. To all of them, a responsible answer and a correct decision had to be given. I was scolded and I was scorned. I was rarely praised. At night, when I finally got home and began to relax, the newsmen would descend on me in a horde. They had their responsibilities and I couldn't brush them off lightly.
>
> That's the way it was. Over the past year and a half, I was really busy.[1]

Although there were no traffic cops in Japan at the turn of the century, there were secretary generals. It is one of the oldest positions in the conservative parties. The post first made its formal appearance on September 15, 1900, when the Friends

[1] *Sankei Shimbun*, evening edition, December 9, 1966, p. 1.

of Constitutional Government Association was formed.[2] Article four of this party's constitution decrees, "There shall be a secretary general and several secretaries in the party. They shall be selected by the president of the party. . . ." "Prior to this time, there had been men in the earlier political parties who held the title of secretary. Among them had been men of ability and learning who performed the duties of the secretary general. But the existence of a secretary general was not recognized by party law."[3] The Constitutional Association also made provision for a secretary general when it was launched in October 1916, and the post continued when this party became the Constitutional Democratic party in 1927.[4]

The authority of the secretary general was different in the two parties. In the Friends of Constitutional Democratic Government Association, the secretary general was clearly the most powerful leader, with the exception of the party president. In the Constitutional Democratic party, the chain of command was party president, first executor [hittō sōmu], executors, and the secretary general. Uchida Nobuya, a prewar politician, says, "Compared to the Friends of Constitutional Government Association, which made the secretary general the central figure, the Constitutional Democratic party gave greater status to the executors."[5]

The difference between the two secretary generals can best be illustrated by listening to the descriptions of some of the prewar secretary generals. One of the secretary generals of the Constitutional Democratic party was Ōasa Tadao, who occupied the chair in 1934. Noda Takeo, at that time a newspaper reporter and now a member of the lower house, describes Ōasa as follows, "He wasn't one of the so-called

[2] Tōyama Shigeki and Adachi Yoshiko, *Kindai Nihon Seiji-shi Hikkei* [A Handbook of Modern Japanese Political History] (Tokyo: Iwanami Shoten, 1961), p. 134.
[3] Togawa Isamu, *Seiji Shikin* [Political Funds] (Tokyo: Uchida Rōkakuho, 1961), p. 92.
[4] Tōyama, *Hikkei*, p. 135.
[5] *Asahi Shimbun*, August 21, 1962, p. 2.

brains of the party, but he really worked hard. Rain or shine, no matter whether he had anything special on his mind or not, he showed up at the private residence of Machida Chūji, the president, at nine o'clock every morning. He would sound out the president's views on each party matter and then, with this as a base, visit each of the party leaders. Because he listened to all their opinions, there was never a soul in the party who complained. He was careful in personnel matters and was most considerate even when the back benchers came to him with their tales of woe."[6] Another secretary general was Nagai Ryūtarō. "When Nagai toured the countryside, shouts of 'Nagai is coming' would go up and a crowd of one or two thousand people would gather in an instant. But Nagai hated to collect political funds or look after party responsibilities other than making speeches in the Diet or the countryside. He was frosting on the party."[7]

Secretary generals of the Friends of Constitutional Government Association were men of a different stamp. The names heard most often are Yokota Sennosuke and Mori Kaku, both of whom served in the post at the height of party government in the decade of the twenties. Present-day politicians usually explain the importance and authority of these men in terms of their ability to collect funds for the party. "One important responsibility was party finance, keeping the party larder full. When the party had a leader who was weak in fund-raising abilities, the secretary general had to take on his own shoulders the burdens of party finance."[8]

Yokota Sennosuke was known as the "hidden sword" of the party president, Hara Kei. He is credited with having held the Friends of Constitutional Government Association together after half its members deserted to form their own party in 1924, and subsequently to have welded three political parties together to form the "Protect the Constitution Movement." Tsugumo Kunitoshi, a politician who was then a follower of Yokota Sennosuke, speaks of him with only the highest

[6] *Ibid.*
[7] *Ibid.*   [8] *Asahi Shimbun*, August 19, 1962, p. 2.

praise. "If it were for the party, Yokota would think nothing about incurring huge personal debt. When Yokota died, I was one of the men appointed to look after his affairs. He owed more than 850,000 yen in debts. In today's money, that's a bill of better than 1,000,000,000 yen [$2.8 million]. His wife and children were left with only the clothes on their back. It's no wonder that the party members respected him so much. Even though he was a small man—just a little over five feet tall—and he carried himself very simply, he certainly looked big."[9]

Mori Kaku was Yokota's successor and served under both Tanaka Giichi and Inukai Tsuyoshi, party presidents and ultimately prime ministers. "Because of his connections with the Mitsui *zaibatsu*, he was effective in the financial circles."[10] Hosokawa Takamoto, then a newspaperman covering the parties and now a political critic, speaks of Mori's fund raising abilities. "Mori's technique was forceful and unique. He would call a prospective company president on the phone, order him to come up with a certain sum of money on a certain day of a certain month, and then slam the phone down without bothering to wait for an answer. He really shook the businessmen. Today's politicians hang their heads and beg for money like a child for candy, but Mori confiscated it."[11] All of Mori's money went into politics and he, like Yokota, died penniless. "When Mori died, his widow had to take to door-to-door peddling to make a living," says Iwabuchi Tatsuo, another political critic.[12]

Secretary Generals of the Friends of Constitutional Government Association were in some ways more powerful than the party president. In an earlier chapter, we saw that the party president was a man who was looked on with favor by the *Genrō*, and a man who might be selected as prime minister. But the man who was responsible for pushing a prospective party president's case was often the secretary general. Yokota is credited with planning for Tanaka Giichi to suc-

[9] *Ibid.*   [10] *Ibid.*   [11] *Ibid.*
[12] *Ibid.*

ceed Takahashi Korekiyo. Mori played a central role in arranging for Inukai Tsuyoshi to succeed Tanaka Giichi. Both Mori and Yokota "shared in common the power to make kings; they were not lightweights used as the jaw of the party leader."[13] Strangely enough, fate conspired that none of the prewar secretary generals ever became prime minister in his own name. This jinx was not broken until 1957, when Kishi Nobusuke, who had served as secretary general under Hatoyama Ichirō, became prime minister.

The secretary general of the present conservative party is the inheritor of both traditions. If he is not as strong as the secretary general of the Friends of Constitutional Government Association, neither is he as weak as his predecessors in the Constitutional Democratic party. In my discussions with reporters and politicians I continually asked what the limitations are on the authority of the secretary general and the invariable answer was none. Mori Kiyoshi, a young conservative politician who leads part of the old Kōno faction, spoke for the rest when he called the secretary general, "the Almighty,"[14] a term which was used earlier to describe the prime minister. But when I asked if the secretary general acted independently of the prime minister, the answer was no. Mori Kiyoshi said, "The secretary general is the prime minister's boy."[15] Miyake Hisayuki, a reporter on the *Mainichi Shimbun*, said, "There have been secretary generals who didn't owe any particular allegiance to the prime minister. But they have been few. Prime ministers don't like them because they could easily make it impossible for the prime ministers to stay in office."[16]

The prime minister has his way in the appointment of the secretary general. Article nine of the party law decrees that "the secretary general shall be appointed by the president with the consent of the executive council."[17] Nowadays, he

13 *Ibid.*   14 Mori Kiyoshi, interview, July 6, 1966.
15 *Ibid.*   16 Miyake Hisayuki, interview, July 5, 1966.
17 Jiyūminshutō, "Tōsoku" [Party Law] in *Wagatō no Kihon Hōshin* [Basic Policies of Our Party] (Tokyo: Jiyūminshutō Kōkoku Iinkai, 1966), Art. 9.

will almost invariably choose a man from his own faction. The other faction leaders do not object. They recognize that the prime minister has a right to appoint a man loyal to him and, more importantly, that opposition on their part would probably be fruitless.

Factional loyalty is only the first of the qualifications. The secretary general must also share the thoughts and temperament of the prime minister. If the chief cabinet secretary is the closest official to the prime minister acting as head of government, then the secretary general is the closest figure to the prime minister acting as the president of the party. Given the tendency for all prime ministers to concentrate on government affairs, the secretary general does not always have the opportunity for close consultation with him and must exercise considerable initiative. If the secretary general has an inherent understanding of the prime minister's wishes, everything goes smoothly. There is a Japanese proverb, "one heart, same body [*isshin dōtai*]" and virtually every politician uses it when describing the qualifications of the secretary general. A candidate for the post of secretary general is always experienced in party affairs. Particularly, he must have a detailed understanding of each of the conservative politicians' personalities, problems, hopes, and, of course, election districts. He has been a cabinet officer in the past and is known as a good administrator. He must also be trusted by the other factions. Finally, he must have almost a pathological drive to work.

No politician would contest Tanaka Kakuei's claim that he was busy. A theme that ran through all the interviews was that the secretary general was always on the go. His formal responsibilities are vague. The party law charges him with "assisting the party president and managing party affairs."[18] The last clause gives him license to turn his hand to anything he wants to, while the first clause means that the party president will back him up. Specifically, the responsibilities of the secretary general have come to be recognized over the years

18 Jiyūminshutō, *Tōsoku*, Art. 8, sec. 1.

273

as collecting and distributing party funds, handing out posts within the party, government, and Diet, assisting in policy decisions, quarterbacking election campaigns, overseeing the party secretariat, managing legislation in the Diet, and directing the press campaign on behalf of the party.

Kawashima Shōjirō, a former vice president of the present conservative party and politician before the war, claims, "The duties of the secretary general are the same now as they were in the past."[19] Although the tasks may have remained constant, a new element has been added. Now there are separate organs in the party charged with each of these functions. A description of the secretary general must start with his division of responsibility with each of these organs.

The secretary general firmly clenches the party purse strings. Theoretically, of course, the finances of the party are subject to a variety of controls. The party conference, the supreme organ of the party, is called upon at its annual meeting to approve the next year's budget[20] and the settled accounts of the past year.[21] There is an audit board[22] composed of two members from the lower house and one member from the upper house who are charged with "overseeing regular accounts and deliberating on the budget of the party."[23] The executive council, a group of thirty politicians, bears the responsibility for making decisions in the party's name and it should be consulted about finances. There is also a finance committee, presently composed of twelve politicians, which has the task both of gathering funds and insuring their proper management.[24] Tucked away in a little box on the party organization charts is an obscure office called the financial accounts bureau. It is manned by professional accountants and headed by a politician.[25] "He's the chief cashier," explains Kosaka Zentarō, a politician who worked on party finance when Ikeda Hayato was prime minister.[26] With these

19 *Asahi Shimbun*, August 16, 1962, p. 2.
20 Jiyūminshutō, *Tōsoku*, Art. 96, sec. 2.
21 *Ibid.*, Art. 100.   22 *Ibid.*, Art. 66.   23 *Ibid.*, Art. 67.
24 *Ibid.*, Art. 12.   25 *Ibid.*, Art. 11.
26 Kosaka Zentarō, interview, May 25, 1966.

elaborate accounting procedures, overlapping organs, and division of power—particularly, with this number of politicians in the act—the conclusion might be drawn that the secretary general's powers are circumscribed. Such is not the case.

Political parties the world over are reluctant to discuss their finances, and the Liberal Democratic party is no exception. The politicians themselves claim they know none of the details. I asked several of them why they do not insist on being informed. Kuraishi Tadao, once a businessman but now an important labor expert in the party, said, "Japanese are reluctant to make a fuss about money and this seems to hang over into the political world."[27] The press does not share the politicians' sensitivities. They complain constantly and in print about the "veil of secrecy" that covers the party coffers.[28] But the complaints of the reporters have not loosened the party's tongue.

The desire to remain quiet about party finance has brought about a streamlining of procedures. Approval is asked of the party conference for past accounts and the future budget, but no detailed explanation accompanies the request. The delegates to the conference raise no objection. They cheerfully approve whatever motion is put before them. The statement to the conference is read by the audit board. This seems to be its only responsibility. The politicians claim the audit board has prestige but no real power in deciding financial matters.

The executive council is likewise rarely consulted about the finances of the party. "During the time that I was on the executive council," says Hara Kenzaburō, "I can remember discussing party finances only once or twice, and then only in the vaguest terms."[29] Thirty politicians is a large number of men and it is recognized that the press would soon be in on

27 Kuraishi Tadao, interview, July 15, 1966.
28 *Yomiuri Shimbun*, January 16, 1966, p. 1.
29 Hara Kenzaburō, interview, May 25, 1966.

275

the inner secrets of the party's finances if matters were brought before this body.

The finance committee is appointed by the president of the party.[30] All the factions are represented, and as a general rule, they are the senior members of the faction. In the finance committee of early 1966, all the members but one had been elected at least six times. There are also several politicians from the upper house to represent its interests.

The finance committee is charged with two responsibilities. One is to provide for the "powerful repletion" of the party coffers, and the other is to insure their "healthy management."[31] There is a difference of opinion among the politicians over how effectively the committee fulfills either task. With regard to the collecting of funds, Fujieda Sensuke says, "Some of the committee members work very hard for the party, others are not that interested."[32] This is a sympathetic judgment. Other politicians dismissed the committee as nothing more than a receiving window for funds from the peoples' association. With regard to management of the funds, the politicians were more or less in agreement that the committee as a whole had little power. "If the party makes a major expenditure, they are informed, but that's about it," said one politician. There were differences of opinion among the politicians over the role of the chairman of the finance committee. Some of the politicians dismissed him along with the rest of the committee as so much window dressing. Others stated him to be important. Kosaka Zentarō, who has served in the post, highly valued the position.[33] The chairman is always chosen from the prime minister's faction.

While there is a heavy turnover in the regular members of the committee each year when the terms of office for the party posts elapse, the chairman usually is reappointed. These two facts would suggest that he is more important than some politicians would like to believe. Since the finance com-

30 Jiyūminshutō, *Tōsoku*, Art. 14.   31 *Ibid.*, Art. 12.
32 Fujieda Sensuke, interview, July 14, 1966.
33 Kosaka Zentarō, interview, May 25, 1966.

mittee has been in existence only since 1961, it is perhaps too early to make a judgment.

There are no doubts among the politicians about the importance of the chief of the financial accounts bureau. They all regard him as one of the kingpins of party finance. He is appointed by the prime minister and is a member of the prime minister's faction. Perhaps he has served as its treasurer. Usually, he has the reputation of being an excellent fund-raiser, and this talent is bent to the party's behalf. Once in office, he tends to remain there as long as his faction leader is prime minister. Since he is chief cashier, he has unlimited access to and detailed knowledge of the party's financial position. As a fund-raiser, he feels free to give advice on how the funds are to be used. Since he enjoys the trust of the prime minister, his political views are important. There are no other politicians in the financial accounts bureau. The chief exercises his powers alone.

Party finance is controlled, then, by a triumvirate: the secretary general, the financial accounts bureau chief, and the chairman of the finance committee. All three men are from the same faction. Are there no checks on these men's decisions? I asked. The politicians said, no. Did the politicians wish to change the present arrangements? Fujieda Sensuke said, "There are some politicians who want more exposure of public funds. Especially in regard to regular expenditures, a detailed budget should be drawn up and followed."[34] Other politicians declared themselves satisfied with the present arrangements.

Perhaps one of the reasons why the politicians do not speak up more clearly for tighter restrictions over party funds is that the triumvirate which controls them is also the triumvirate which gathers them. Party funds can be divided into two major categories: regular operating expenses and election funds. It has been publicly stated that the Peoples' Association furnishes about 70% of the daily operating costs

[34] Fujieda Sensuke, interview, July 14, 1966.

of the party.[35] The association also makes a special assessment of its members for elections. Since no one knows how much an election costs, no precise figure can be given on how much of the election expenses are borne by the association. But the sum is substantial. There are also party dues, but the money raised through this system is not very much. The remainder of the operating costs and the election funds must be raised by the triumvirate. Fund raising remains an important responsibility of the secretary general. And since he raises the money, few in the party feel bold enough to put restrictions on the way he spends it.

There are, however, several partial and informal checks. The conservative Dietmen make up a small group. While they are not informed on the details of party finance, they talk enough among themselves so that if anything got radically out of line, they would know about it and see that it was corrected. A second check lies with the businessmen. Major party contributions usually come from the big companies, and most of these companies have vice presidents whose task it is to follow the workings of the party closely. If funds were being used incorrectly, they could also institute moves to correct whatever was wrong. The third check is the caliber of men the prime minister appoints to the three posts. They must have a reputation for fair dealing. Nishimura Eiichi, who served as financial accounts bureau chief under two Satō cabinets, is praised throughout the party for his rectitude and impartiality, even by politicians who waste no love on the Satō regime. Perhaps the greatest check is the factional system itself. It is in the interest of the prime minister to quell factional strife. There is no surer way to sound the bugles of political warfare than for expenditures to favor one faction. The prime minister and his men will insure that funds earmarked for the party are used for the party.

The secretary general keeps the job roster for the party. With the exception of a few top posts to which men are appointed by the president of the party, all the other positions

[35] *Yomiuri Shimbun*, January 16, 1966, p. 1.

are filled by men appointed by the secretary general. We have discussed these appointments at length in the chapter dealing with the executive council. We need add only a few additional comments here.

Besides the better than two hundred party posts, the secretary general also has the power to appoint men to posts in the government and the Diet.

The secretary general appoints the parliamentary vice ministers, theoretically the second-ranking man in each of the ministries. There are twenty of these posts, two in the Ministries of Finance, Agriculture and Forestry, and International Trade and Industry, and one in each of the other ministries. In the reshuffle of party posts in August 1966, five of these posts went to members of the upper house and the other fifteen went to members of the lower house. This seems to be the usual division. Appointments are made on the basis of factional balance. These posts do not entail a great deal of responsibility; the chief task seems to be squiring through the Diet legislation of interest to the ministry. "But competition for these posts is strong," notes Tanikawa Kazuo, a young conservative from Hiroshima.[36] The posts' chief attraction is that they furnish the politicians a chance to use the ministry's facilities to do favors for their constituents (thus bettering themselves in the elections), and for other politicians (thus bettering themselves in the party). "There is opinion within the party and the government that middle-grade politicians of the lower house who have won four or five elections ought to be appointed, thus giving the parliamentary vice minister the character of a 'semi-cabinet officer.' But to date, appointments of parliamentary vice minister center around the group who have won two elections."[37]

The secretary general also appoints the chairmen of the standing and special committees in the lower house. (There are also standing and special committees in the upper house, but the chairmen are appointed after consultations among

36 Tanikawa Kazuo, interview, July 28, 1966.
37 *Asahi Shimbun*, evening edition, August 2, 1966, p. 1.

the upper house leadership.) At the present time, there are sixteen standing committees and eight special committees. These committees were modeled after the committee system in the United States Congress. While they are not as powerful as their United States counterparts, they are important. All legislation will pass through these committees, important debate will take place in them rather than in the Diet plenary session, and many times the chairmen will be responsible for the compromises that must be made with the opposition to get the legislation enacted into law. In short, the posts are highly desired, and there is subtle competition among the older Dietmen to obtain them.

The parliamentary vice ministerships go to Dietmen who have won two or three elections. Most party posts go to men who have won four or five elections. The Diet chairmanships go to men who have won six or more elections. All members of the party, no matter how great their seniority, are dependent on the secretary general for posts.

The party bureaucracy is nominally under the control of the secretary general. The party law states, "There shall be a secretariat within the party headquarters with necessary personnel under the supervision of the secretary general to handle the affairs of the party."[38]

The politicians told me that there were small secretariats attached to the prewar parties. None of the history books gives them even a footnote. Instead, the parties had *ingaidan,* which literally means, "group outside the Diet." Ōno Bamboku, one of their most illustrious graduates, defines them as follows: "The *ingaidan* were men who would do anything for the sake of the party."[39] Tsuchikura Sōmei, a colleague of Ōno, defines them as "groups of politicians who did not have seats in the Diet."[40] A reporter says, "Generally speaking, they were politicians who had lost elections or young men who wanted to become politicians."[41] These defi-

---

[38] Jiyūminshutō, *Tōsoku,* Art. 101.
[39] *Asahi Shimbun,* August 26, 1962, p. 2.
[40] *Ibid.*   [41] *Ibid.*

nitions lack color. The *ingaidan* were predominantly young men eager to demonstrate their political talent either through speech or muscle, with plenty of the latter. Ōno claims in his memoirs that there is not a police station in Tokyo where he hasn't been detained for his activities.[42]

Nobody ever bothered to clarify just what the responsibilities of the *ingaidan* were. But they were not regarded as paper shufflers. "Besides serving as bodyguards for the party leaders, getting out the vote at election time, and giving warm-up talks before the main speaker at political gatherings, their job was to heckle and break up meetings of the opposition."[43] Ōno recalls, "When the opposition party held a lecture, we always put in an appearance and got rough. The *ingaidan* of the opposition party would pretend ignorance and let us raise one or two fusses. After that, well . . . nobody was ever seriously injured, but nobody ever gave up. These were the ethics of the *ingaidan*."[44]

The day of the *ingaidan* is past. Since the assassination of President Kennedy, the Japanese police have been meticulous in the protection of the prime minister. Wherever he goes, he is flanked by discreet but competent plain clothesmen. But when the prime minister makes a formal appearance, such as the opening speech of the Diet, several old gentlemen can be found leading the entourage along the faded and splotched red carpet of the Diet corridors. These are the last of the *ingaidan* and they number, I am told, about fifteen. They have a small room in the new headquarters building. But somehow the expanses of glass, the tiled floors, the low acoustical ceilings, and the recessed neon lighting have destroyed whatever flavor the *ingaidan* once brought to Japanese politics.

Young men who are full of political enthusiasm no longer join the *ingaidan* but instead become resident organizers.[45]

---

[42] Ōno Bamboku, *Ōno Bamboku Kaisōroku* [The Memoirs of Ōno Bamboku] (Tokyo: Kōbundō, 1964), p. 31.

[43] *Asahi Shimbun*, August 26, 1962, p. 2.

[44] Ōno, *Kaisōroku*, p. 31. [45] Jiyūminshutō, *Tōsoku*, Art. 78.

The party has sixty of them and plans to expand their numbers further. These are young men who have been brought to Tokyo, trained in the arts of political persuasion and organization for three months or so at a special party school and then returned to the various prefectures. "Their main job is to maintain liaison with the party headquarters and work on party organization," says Matsushita Yoshio, chief of the personnel section in the party headquarters.[46] I have talked with many of the regional organizers and some of them are impressive young men. But there are problems. Shōji Tsuyoshi, a former regional organizer in Chiba, explains, "We were told at party school in Tokyo that we were in charge of the organizational activities in the prefectures. Some of the prefectural assemblymen don't see eye-to-eye with us on this point. Occasionally, our efforts run afoul of the organizers of the support organizations. But the biggest problem, at least for me, is that the party rules prevent us from standing for elections. I became a regional organizer because I'm interested in politics and want to run for office. I finally had to quit. Now I am talking with Kawashima [the party vice president] to see if there is some way whereby I can make a bid for a seat in the prefectural assembly."[47] The party will have to give further consideration to creating a future for these young men if it wants to continue to attract a high caliber of regional organizer.

Besides the regional organizers, there are more than two hundred other bureaucrats who work for the party. Some of them are attached to the prefectural federations, but a significant number are in the party headquarters in Tokyo. When the conservative parties merged in 1955, each of them had a small group of men who worked for it and these men make up the majority of the present staff. For many years, however, the party headquarters has organized itself into divisions, bureaus, and sections, and each of these men is assigned to some special job within the structure. The party

[46] Matsushita Yoshio, interview, July 5, 1966.
[47] Shōji Tsuyoshi, interview, August 24, 1966.

has also drawn up a set of regulations, modelled closely after the regulations of the Japanese government for its civil service, and now there are ranks, a promotion system, and a retirement plan. The party workers have, in short, become full-fledged bureaucrats.

The bureaucrats stand apart from the Dietmen in the central headquarters. Despite their background, they have not become members of the various factions. Nor do they become overtly involved in the various political issues which concern the Dietmen. I asked Matsushita Yoshio how much this party bureaucracy influenced the party. He at first interpreted the bureaucratic role as subsidiary. They assisted the Dietmen, prepared research, took care of the administration. Finally he said, "The length of service for one of the Dietmen in a party post is one year. They usually have to spend six months learning the job. We try to make sure that things go smoothly during this period."[48] Although the party bureaucrats' influence on the party is limited at present, they are at least a potential countervailing power for the overwhelming influence of the Dietmen.

The party bureaucrats operate under a dual command structure. On one hand, they are variously assigned to one of the party organs, such as the finance committee, the national organization committee, the public relations committee, and so on. Each of these organs is headed by a Dietman and the party bureaucrats are under his direction. On the other hand, there is the usual pyramid of section, division, and bureau, at the top of which is the secretary general.[49] I asked how much the secretary general has to do with the running of the bureaucracy, and the consensus seemed to be that important decisions affecting the bureaucracy as a whole, upper level personnel assignments, and decisions involving considerable expenditures of money were brought to his attention. But other than this, the bureaucracy pretty much took care of itself.

[48] Matsushita Yoshio, interview, July 5, 1966.
[49] Jiyūminshutō, *Tōsoku*, Art. 11.

The secretary general also has considerable powers in managing the election campaigns. In our earlier discussions of the elections, we stressed the support organizations and the factions. But the party plays an important role in the drama too, and the chief actor is the secretary general.

An enumeration of the secretary general's powers in the elections begins with the party endorsement. This is a valuable prize which all the candidates want. Incumbent Dietmen rarely have trouble in being endorsed, but it is an open battle among the other hopefuls to receive the endorsement. Each of the candidates will have his backers urging his case upon the party. It is the task of the election policy committee to sort through all these candidates and come up with the final verdict. The party law puts the president at the head of this committee.[50] But he rarely makes an appearance. His powers are exercised by the secretary general.

The process of deciding the party endorsements starts with the prefectural federations. They will submit their recommendations to a secretariat attached to the election policy committee. This secretariat, composed of several party bureaucrats and a politician as chief officer, has been charged with watching over the fortunes and qualifications of the conservative candidates.[51] It is supposed to reach an independent judgment regarding each of them. It screens the prefectural recommendations and passes its findings on to the five deputy secretary generals. Each of these men is a representative of one of the factions and they will add the factions' views. Their deliberations will in turn be handed on to the election policy committee for final resolution.

On paper, this may appear a tidy, neat operation. But the party endorsements affect the political fortunes of the candidates, the factions, and the party. No decisions are reached easily. It is the task of the secretary general to ride herd over this operation. When he is not trying to get the prefectural federations and the party headquarters to see eye-to-eye,

---

[50] *Ibid.*, Art. 52, sec. 4.   [51] *Ibid.*, Art. 53.

then he is trying to mediate the conflicting interests of the factions. No one succeeds at this task, but it is a good measure of the secretary general's abilities to see how well he does.

The secretary general also controls the election funds of the party. Before each campaign he will give to the Dietmen and the other endorsed candidates the party endorsement fee. The amount varies with each election but it is usually in the neighborhood of $5,500.[52] "Since the Dietmen have to show up personally and sign a receipt for the money, there are a few faction leaders whose pride does not permit them to come around. But all the rest, including the ministers, never fail to put in an appearance," says Miyake Hisayuki, a reporter on the *Mainichi Shimbun*.[53] No candidate ever has enough money to run a campaign the way he wants to, and the secretary general is one of the sources he will tap again. In the closing days of the campaign, the candidates will fall into three groups: those that are bound to win, those that are bound to lose and those who are on the border. The secretary general will step into the campaigns of those on the border and supply further funds. The decision of who gets the money and how much rests solely in the hands of the secretary general.

The secretary general also has the task of overseeing all the other services that the party can provide the candidate. Selecting the major themes of the campaign (the executive council will formally approve them) falls under his jurisdiction. Arranging the tours of cabinet ministers and the other well-known men of the party is his responsibility. His twice-daily press conferences allow him to do a little campaigning on his own. Although it entails a great deal of work, a secretary general usually looks forward to a general election. It gives him the opportunity to help out a great many Dietmen. If the campaign goes well, it increases his stature in the

[52] Often the party endorsement fee is accompanied by a loan. In preparation for the general elections of January 1967, the party gave to each of its candidates an endorsement fee of $5,500 and a loan of $2,750. *Asahi Shimbun*, December 29, 1966, p. 13.

[53] Miyake Hisayuki, interview, July 5, 1966.

party. This does not do any harm if the secretary general is given the opportunity of making a bid for the presidency itself.

When the Diet is in session, the secretary general has his office in the Diet building. In addition to his duties of running the party, he also plays a major role in managing legislation.

In previous chapters, we have traced the drafting of legislation out of the ministries through the divisions and deliberation commission of the policy affairs research council up and over to the executive council, and finally into the cabinet. When the measure is sent to the Diet, other hands take over.

When introduced into the Diet, each bill is sent for hearings to one of the sixteen standing committees or one of the six special committees in the lower house.[54] For example, a labor bill goes to the standing committee on social and labor affairs; a bill dealing with subsidies for the coal industry will go to the special committee for coal policy. Above these committees is the steering committee. Its task is to prepare the legislative calendar. The steering committee and most of the special and standing committees are chaired by a conservative. LDP Dietmen comprise the majority of committee members.

The party also has its own organs which deal with the Diet. There is the Diet policy committee.[55] It is composed of one or two members from the upper house for liaison, and five members from the lower house, all from different factions, who have been elected from three to six times. Two of the lower house members will serve on the steering committee in the Diet. Above the Diet policy committee is the Dietmen's conference [Daigishikai] which is composed of all the party members of the lower house.[56]

54 This is the normal route for a cabinet bill. Bills can also be introduced into the upper house and the separate party organs of the upper house manage them. The secretary general has little to do with the legislation in the upper house other than urge its rapid passage.

55 Jiyūminshutō, *Tōsoku*, Art. 23.   56 *Ibid.*, Art. 54.

So much for the actors. Now for the action. "The main aim of the conservatives is to push the bill through the Diet as fast as possible," says Mori Kiyoshi.[57] They have already conducted all the deliberations on the measure in the party organs. What they now want is the measure enacted into law. Since the conservative party is in the majority, there would seem to be little problem. But the socialists have one great power that the conservatives have found no way to get around. The legislative load that is presented to the Diet each year is heavy. Even with the best of good will and complete cooperation on the part of the opposition, it is doubtful that all the measures could get enacted into law. The socialists have the power of delay, and they use it to the fullest. The conservatives, then, are obliged to compromise to maintain the legislative pace. The compromises can take place in any of the organs we have mentioned.

The first clash between the opposition and the conservatives will take place in the standing or special committees. The chairman may make minor compromises, but anything of substance is reported back to the conservative members of the steering committee. The conservatives in this committee will try to work out a compromise with the socialists. Minor concessions are again in order, but with anything major, the steering committee raises it with the Diet policy committee. It is here that legislative strategy is really plotted. These committee members are the men who manage the Diet on a day-to-day basis. Once their strategy is set, they will report it to the Dietmen's conference which, if the plenary session is at two o'clock, will meet at half past one. "In theory, the Dietmen's conference is called to give its approval to the legislative strategy," says Sakurauchi Yoshio. "Once in a while there are objections, but usually the Dietmen give their approval readily. The Dietmen's conference is used more to give the Dietmen a report on what has happened and what their instructions are for the day."[58] Overseeing this entire

[57] Mori Kiyoshi, interview, July 6, 1966.
[58] Sakurauchi Yoshio, interview, May 24, 1966.

287

operation is the secretary general. He will receive reports of the negotiations in the steering committee, he will be consulted on the decisions of the Diet policy committee, and, on occasion, he will undertake to secure the assent of the Dietmen's conference.

Compromise is the essence of parliamentary procedure. The threat of hamstringing legislation may appear to be just a good way for a numerically weak minority to get the conservative majority to give a little ground. But the socialists have never quite made up their mind whether they are a parliamentary party or a revolutionary party, and many times their obstruction is for the sake of obstruction. When they decide to dig in their heels they have a whole array of tricks which successfully bring the Diet to a halt. Lengthy and acrimonious debate about where and how long to hold hearings, interminable interrogations not always to the point, a series of no confidence motions—these and others are ploys that are not unheard of in other parliaments. But the socialists have added their own unique stratagems to these old standbys. "Cow tactics" is one of their ploys. All legislative action is conducted at the slowest possible speed. A vote, for example, can take many hours to complete as the socialist Dietmen inch up the aisles to the ballot box. Rushing the speaker or committee chairman and physically occupying his chair or, alternatively, barricading the committee chambers and not allowing him entrance are other tactics. Finally, boycott of the Diet proceedings is occasionally employed. (The extraordinary session of the Diet held in December 1966 to pass a supplementary budget was attended only by the conservatives. The socialists and other opposition parties were trying to force a general election. They got it.) The press is critical of these tactics. But they are aware that the conservatives hold the ultimate weapon—ramming the bill through the Diet. When the conservatives choose to use this power, the press breaks loose with its big guns. The result is that on occasion, the speaker is obliged to take responsibility and resign.

The conservatives are reluctant to use the power of forced passage. This reluctance insures that the socialists are able at almost every Diet session to bring the proceedings to a complete halt. Long talk and much haggling take place in the special, standing, and steering committees, but it is rarely to any avail. Occasionally the speaker of the house is called in to try to smooth things over, but this tactic rarely works. It is at this time that the secretary general stands forth publicly. A conference is called of all his counterparts in the opposition parties. This conference usually stretches into a series of conferences. All the arguments are dragged out and gone over again and again. When the socialists and the other opposition parties feel that they have made their point—more importantly, when they feel that they have gotten all publicity they can out of the issue—they may be willing to reach agreement. But sometimes the issues are ones on which the socialists feel that they cannot give way. The stalemate continues until the conservatives bring forth their ultimate weapon.

A price tag can be put on these services of the secretary general. The *Asahi Shimbun* made a detailed study of the financial reports submitted by the political parties to the Home Ministry in 1965. It pointed out that "when the proceedings in the Diet reach a climax, such as the forced passage of a bill through a committee or when the opposition and conservative parties are able to reach agreement, on that day or shortly before or after, the Liberal Democratic party almost invariably shells out a substantial sum of money."[59]

In another article, the *Asahi Shimbun* explains how the funds are used: "The legislative funds of the Liberal Democratic party are used within the party for consultations between interested persons and conservative members of a committee concerned with a particular bill, as encouragement for ruling party members who face Diet sessions lasting through the night, and to create the mood for ramming a bill through the Diet. But these are not the only purposes. It

[59] *Asahi Shimbun*, October 29, 1966, p. 4.

is an open secret within the Diet that substantial amounts are expended in maneuvers with the opposition."[60] The *Sankei Shimbun* adds that it often hears of cases where the members of the steering committee "during the day exchange fierce and violent arguments and part without reaching agreement, but at night meet secretly in a restaurant within the city and have another 'discussion.' Generally, they reach agreement on what the steps in the future should be."[61]

In 1965, the *Asahi Shimbun* counted 33 occasions on which the opposition and the conservatives seriously clashed, and on each of these occasions expenditures in the name of "Diet policy expenses" were recorded, for a total expenditure of $403,194. "In almost all instances, if the secretary general did not sign for these expenditures, then the chairman of the Diet policy committee did."[62]

In recent years, the party has become increasingly conscious of its public image. In 1960, the conservatives took a severe drubbing from the opposition parties over the issue of whether or not to renew a mutual security treaty with the United States. A great deal of Monday quarterbacking went on in the party after this upset, and mainly at the urging of Hashimoto Tomisaburō, a former newsman later to become the chief cabinet secretary under Prime Minister Satō Eisaku, the party decided to strengthen its public voice. Energies and funds were poured into creating and staffing a public relations committee.

Today, the public relations committee is one of the largest of the party organs. It has six bureaus, of which the chief and vice chief are all Dietmen.[63] It tries to cover the complete range of propaganda activity. On one hand there is the information bureau which gathers and analyzes data to decide where the party's effort should be directed. On the other hand, there is the publishing bureau, the party news bureau

---

[60] *Asahi Shimbun*, October 7, 1966, p. 1.
[61] *Sankei Shimbun*, November 21, 1966, p. 1.
[62] *Asahi Shimbun*, October 29, 1966, p. 4.
[63] Jiyūminshutō, *Tōsoku*, Arts. 20, 22.

and the membership center which try to keep publicity themes and materials before the eyes of the party faithful. The cultural bureau works on groups and individuals sympathetic to the party's aims. Finally, there is a people's movement headquarters which sponsors political campaigns that do not bear the party label, although this organization is not formally part of the public relations committee. Heading up this elaborate machinery is a chairman. "He's not as powerful as the vice president, the secretary general, the chairman of the executive council, or the chairman of the policy affairs research council," says Tanikawa Kazuo, a young Dietman, "But he is probably the next in line after them."[64]

The committee claims its successes. At the time of the first entry of a United States nuclear-powered submarine into the port of Sasebo, sound trucks bumped through the streets, posters were plastered on every telegraph pole, welcome demonstrations were staged, and "men of learning and culture" stood up and set forth their opinion that there should be no qualms about the safety of the vessel. The protest demonstrations fizzled. The opposition promised to start another rhubarb over the reopening of formal relations with the Republic of South Korea. The public relations committee launched another massive campaign. The protest movement of the opposition never materialized. Over the past year, the public relations committee has successfully published a party newspaper distributed in many thousands of copies. The secretary general's role in all this activity is minimal. He makes occasional suggestions and pays the bills.

Great energies of the party go into these public relations activities. But official party propaganda never has the impact on the public consciousness that it is intended to. In the case of the nuclear-powered submarine, it can be argued that the quiet notification by the mayor of Sasebo to the demonstrators that the facilities of the port—water, restrooms, shelter—would be cut off if the demonstrations got too far out of line was more effective than the sound trucks, parades, and

[64] Tanikawa Kazuo, interview, July 28, 1966.

posters. It can be argued that the reestablishment of relations with Korea went off quietly because none of the factions within the Liberal Democratic party decided to make an issue out of it. In the case of the newspaper, Kosaka Zentarō has expressed a commonly held opinion, "The party spends a fortune publishing that newspaper. The layout, articles, and distribution are, I guess, pretty good. There's only one trouble. Nobody reads it."[65]

Yet the party makes its voice heard effectively throughout Japan. Nobody remains in the dark very long about what the conservatives are thinking and what they plan to do. But rather than the public relations committee, it is the commercial press that carries the news into each Japanese home and office. Relations with the commercial press are the responsibility of the secretary general.

The age of mass media has long since arrived in Japan. The press is an immense and powerful institution. And no place is their prowess more fully demonstrated than in their coverage of domestic politics. Although the official visitor to Japan, who has seen hordes of reporters push each other around at the airport, may have reason to doubt it, the Japanese press is highly organized. At the peak of the hierarchy sit the three national newspapers—the *Asahi Shimbun*, the *Yomiuri Shimbun*, and the *Mainichi Shimbun*; the government owned but independently managed national television and radio network, the Japan Broadcasting Corporation; and the *Nihon Keizai Shimbun*, an economic newspaper which also has political coverage. On the next echelon are the *Sankei Shimbun* and the regional newspapers—the *Hokkaidō Shimbun*, the *Chū-Nichi Shimbun*, the *Tōkyō Shimbun*, and the *Nishi Nihon Shimbun*. In a special niche are the two Japanese wire services, the *Kyōdō News* and *Jiji Press*. Beneath them are the local newspapers and far, far, below them, if not in circulation then in reliability, are the weekly magazines.

The newspapers are organized in clubs and at least one of

[65] Kosaka Zentarō, interview, May 25, 1966.

these clubs can be found in every government agency, commission, or ministry. Other clubs cover the activities of the economic community, the courts, the police, and the political parties. The two clubs that are of most concern to the conservatives are the Nagata Club and the Hirakawa Club. The Nagata Club is housed in a modern building adjoining the prime minister's residence in Nagata-chō. It is the responsibility of the chief cabinet secretary. It covers the activities of the prime minister and the cabinet. If one must draw a distinction, the Nagata Club reports the news of the government rather than the news of the party, but the distinction is tenuous.

The Hirakawa Club is attached to the party and is so named for the district in which party headquarters is located. When the Diet is in session, it sits in the Diet building. It is the responsibility of the secretary general. The press members occupy the room adjacent to his chambers. The secretary general becomes involved in many activities that are not strictly-speaking directly related to the party, and the Hirakawa Club is responsible for covering these activities. But if a distinction must be made, the Hirakawa Club covers the party rather than the government or Diet.

The reporters do not restrict themselves to reporting only what the chief cabinet secretary and the secretary general tell them. With the exception of a group of young reporters in the Nagata Club who have the task of dogging the prime minister wherever he may go, all the other reporters are senior men who have been covering Japanese politics for many years and they all have close friendships with the Dietmen. Wander into either the Hirakawa or Nagata press room in the early afternoon and you will find it almost deserted. A game of *go* or poker may be going on in one corner, some reporters may be watching television, one man from each of the papers will be watching his company's phones, but all the other reporters are out talking either in the offices of the Dietmen, the committee rooms of the Diet, or the headquarters of the factions. When evening comes, they will return briefly

293

to their newspaper offices, report what they have heard, and then set out again for the Dietmen's homes, there to drink his whiskey, eat his food, and tell him what's wrong with Japanese politics. There is intimate and never-ending dialogue between the press and the politicians.

The press measures the secretary general's words against what they hear from other politicians. He meets with them twice a day and he, too, has evening sessions. While the other politicians' thoughts may be instructive, the secretary general's words are authoritative. He is the chief spokesman for the party.

The secretary general's role in making decisions for the party is not limited solely to affairs concerned with the Diet. As one of the top party officials, he is consulted on all matters that affect the party's fortunes.

The politicians are agreed that decisions are made formally, as we have described in the preceding chapter. They are also in accord that there is informal decision-making machinery within the party. Hara Kenzaburō put it most bluntly, "If you bring a matter directly to the executive council, it will get turned down. Decide the question elsewhere and then bring it to the executive council."[66]

None of the politicians could tell me just where elsewhere was. They said it depended on time, circumstance, personality, and issue. They were, however, all agreed that the favor of the top party leadership had to be obtained. Fukunaga Kenji said, "In trying to get a favorable decision from the executive council, many times a minister, if it is a bill, a party committee chairman if it is a party matter, or an individual politician if it is a personal plan, will spend the night before the executive council session on the phone asking for approval from the faction leaders and the party officials."[67] Other politicians stressed that it took a great deal longer than an evening of phone calls. Sakurauchi Yoshio said, "Policy is deliberated on two levels in the party. One level is

[66] Hara Kenzaburō, interview, May 25, 1966.
[67] Fukunaga Kenji, interview, June 3, 1966.

in the party organs. The other level is the party leadership. If I were to push a policy, I would go first to the party leadership and try to convince them."[68] Kosaka Zentarō, a former foreign minister put it slightly differently, "Pushing a plan through the party organs takes a long time. A short cut is to take your ideas to the top party leaders, get their understanding, and let them do the pushing for you."[69] Koyanagi Makie said, "Real decisions come from above, formal decisions come from below."[70]

Obtaining the support of the party leaders can be a highly informal process. The conservative politicians talk about trimming the roots: the word they use is *nemawashi*, a gardener's term whereby a trench is dug around a large tree and all the roots tied off so that the tree can be transplanted at a later date. The politicians use the term to refer to the pourparlers they must hold to get a policy decision in their interests. But part of the process of obtaining party leaders' approval has become institutionalized. There are three semi-official decision-making organs in the party and the secretary general is a member of all of them.

One is the six man conference, composed of the prime minister, the chief cabinet secretary, the vice president, the secretary general, the chairman of the executive council, and the chairman of the policy affairs research council. The second organ is the four party officials' conference, which is composed of the same men as the six man conference minus the two government leaders, the prime minister and the chief cabinet secretary. The third organ is the party officials' conference which is composed of the four top party officials mentioned above plus the chairman of the national organization committee, the chairman of the public relations committee, and the chairman of the Diet policy committee. The first two of these organs, the six man conference and the four party officials' conference, are mentioned in no party docu-

68 Sakurauchi Yoshio, interview, May 24, 1966.
69 Kosaka Zentarō, interview, May 25, 1966.
70 Koyanagi Makie, interview, May 30, 1966.

ments, yet they have been in existence for quite some time and have been used by successive prime ministers as decision-making bodies. The last organ, the party officials' conference, was created under the provisions of the party law "for the purpose of better cooperation among the various party organs and the smooth management of party affairs."[71] Nothing is said about this conference being a decision-making organ. Yet this has come to be one of its functions.

There are no firm rules about when the six man conference and the four party officials' conference meet, what they are called upon to decide and how they make their decisions. Sometimes they come together when the executive council is unable to reach a decision and passes the buck to them. But on other occasions, they convene before a matter has reached the executive council, and they reach a decision which they hand back to the executive council to rubber-stamp. Usually for a decision involving both government and party, the six man conference is called. For a decision involving the party alone, the four party officials' conference meets. The six man conference is regarded as a superior organ to the four party officials' conference, since the prime minister sits in its deliberations. Occasionally, when a party decision is deemed important enough to have the prime minister participate in its making, the six man conference will meet to discuss a party matter. But these occasions are rare. The prime minister likes to maintain the image of being a leader of government rather than of party and he is usually willing to have the secretary general represent his views.

For the past year or so, these two conferences have met very infrequently. Most of the decisions have been made in the party officials' conference. This body meets several times a week, usually at ten o'clock in the morning, just before the meeting of the executive council, which convenes at eleven o'clock. One of its functions is, as the party law states, to keep the party organs running smoothly. The secretary general informs the other chairmen of events that might affect

71 Jiyūminshutō, *Tōsoku*, Art. 25.

their committees and the other chairmen inform the secretary general of what their committees are doing. Day-to-day decisions necessary for the running of the party are made, with the secretary general doing most of the deciding. But this conference has developed into an unofficial screening body for all proposals that are to be given to the executive council. "Most matters that are going to be given to the executive council are first raised in the party officials' conference since it meets an hour before," says Fukunaga Kenji. "Usually, the committee chairmen, in particular the four senior chairmen, are able to reach an agreement on their position before the measure is introduced into the executive council."[72] If these men decide that the measure should be party policy, they will attend the executive council and urge its adoption. Their voice will usually carry the day.

Another party official who is a member of all three of these conferences is the vice president of the party. We need add some comment about his position and his relations with the secretary general.

The post of vice president is new, but not without precedent. The Friends of Constitutional Government Association had a vice president in 1921,[73] but the post is not mentioned in the party law of either of the two major prewar parties. None of the sixteen conservative parties that emerged after the war had vice presidents. The post was created when the conservative parties merged in 1955. The politicians apparently had doubts whether the post was necessary or not and they equivocated in framing the statute. The party law reads, "There may be a vice president in the party."[74]

The option of having a vice president was not exercised during the cabinets of Hatoyama and Ishibashi. Prime Minister Kishi was the first to use the position when he offered it to Ōno Bamboku in exchange for his support and assistance. Ōno accepted and on July 16, 1957 became the first vice

[72] Fukunaga Kenji, interview, June 3, 1966.
[73] Tōyama, Hikkei, p. 146.
[74] Jiyūminshutō, Tōsoku, Art. 5.

president of the party. Ōno was reappointed to the post in 1958 and again in 1959. He was to serve throughout the Kishi years as the vice president.

Ōno made his own bid for the party presidency upon Kishi's retirement. He lost in the party elections to Ikeda Hayato. However, Ikeda also recognized Ōno's immense political talents. After allowing the post to remain vacant for a year, he offered it once more to Ōno. Ōno again accepted and was to serve in this office until his death on May 29, 1964. As Ōno's successor, Ikeda appointed Kawashima Shōjirō, a faction leader and an experienced politician who had become a politician before the war and subsequently had been elected to the Diet twelve times. Satō Eisaku, when he became prime minister, offered Kawashima the opportunity to remain in the post and Kawashima served under Prime Minister Satō until December 1966. He resigned with the other party officials shortly prior to Satō's second election to the party presidency. Prime Minister Satō reappointed him in November 1967.

From this brief history, the reader can find several clues regarding the qualifications for the post. The candidate will have a strong enough political clout for the prime minister to wish to make an ally of him. This means he is a faction leader. Both Kawashima and Ōno were faction leaders.

Secondly, the candidate will probably be a politician who has risen through the party rather than a former bureaucrat. The former bureaucrat would probably prefer a seat in the cabinet, since he has more experience and interest in government. While both Kawashima and Ōno are famous for making ministers, Ōno more than Kawashima, they have chosen to sit in the cabinet only rarely themselves. Ōno was the director of the Hokkaidō Development Agency in 1953 and Kawashima was director of the Administrative Management Agency in 1955 and 1961 and Home Minister in 1955. Both these men have chosen to work largely within the party rather than in the government.

The third criterion is age. The post demands long political

experience and sufficient personal prestige so that the judgment of the vice president is not questioned. Both Ōno Bamboku and Kawashima Shōjirō were born in 1890 and have devoted their lives to politics. The vice presidency is not the job for the active young politician eager to seek out and respond to new challenges, but rather the job for the old professional, wise in the affairs of men, with limited personal ambition,[75] content to resolve the problems of others on the basis of precedent and custom. The post calls for a judge, not a warrior.

The responsibilities of the vice president are only vaguely defined. The party constitution says that the "vice president shall assist the president and act in his stead when the president is unable to discharge his duties or the seat of the president is vacant."[76]

Acting in the stead of the president does not mean that the vice president inherits the chair of the prime minister. The pertinent provision covering this eventuality is article nine of the cabinet law which states that "in the event the prime minister is unable to discharge his functions or the post of the prime minister is vacant, a minister of state designated by him in advance shall perform temporarily the duties of the prime minister."[77] The post of the "acting prime minister" is one that has seen great service since the formation of the Liberal Democratic party. Both Prime Minister Kishi and Prime Minister Ikeda appointed "acting prime ministers" on five different occasions, usually when they left the country for one reason or another. Neither Ōno nor Kawashima was appointed minister of state during the period he served as

[75] Limited personal ambition may strike the reader as a poor phrase to describe Ōno Bamboku, who made a bid for the party presidency. Ōno maintains, however, that he was first persuaded to run at the insistence of Prime Minister Kishi. Ōno wrote while he was vice president, "I have gone as far as I am capable of. My future role is to be the helmsman in the shadows, guiding party politics." Ōno, *Kaisōroku*, p. 101.

[76] Jiyūminshutō, *Tōsoku*, Art. 5.

[77] Japan, "Naikaku Hō" [Cabinet Law] in *Roppō Zensho* [Compendium of Laws] (Tokyo: Iwanami, 1960), Art. 9.

vice president of the party, and thus was ineligible for appointment to this post. Acting in the stead of the president means taking over affairs that concern the party and the party only.

The phrase, "assist the president," sets the framework for political conflict between the vice president and the secretary general, since the same clause is also used to describe the latter's responsibilities. Yet, in actuality, there have been few instances of such conflict between the two men. On occasion the two men work together, the most notable example being when Secretary General Miki Takeo and Vice President Kawashima arranged through consultations for Satō Eisaku to become Ikeda Hayato's successor to the party presidency. Both men put in appearance at the meetings of the three conferences and the executive council, though I am informed that in the executive council and in the party officials' conference, the vice president is content to remain in the background and allow the secretary general to manage affairs. There seems to be a fine line dividing the areas of responsibility of the two men. Perhaps it is fair to say that the secretary general is the regular duty officer while the vice president is the stand-by reserve of the party. When the vice president is called upon, he usually gets a task of some magnitude. Ōno, for example, was called upon to decide the yearly price of rice, a problem that always creates division within the party; Kawashima was asked to chair the foreign policy commission in the policy affairs research council when the debate within the party on Communist China began to get out of hand. Perhaps the secretary general could have performed these tasks, but he did not. In any case, the secretary general must consider the position of the vice president of the party before he chooses to act.

Finally, the faction leaders have a say in the decisions of the party. Their voices are carried to the secretary general by the deputy secretary generals. During the Ikeda cabinets, there were eight of these men, one selected from each of the factions. Nowadays, there are only five, one selected from

300

the upper house and the other four chosen from each of the major factions. The party law states that they "shall be appointed by the secretary general with the consent of the executive council"[78] and that their responsibilities are "to assist the secretary general."[79] Their informal responsibilities are to watch out for their faction's interests and their selection will be proposed by the faction leader. The interests of the faction vary from time to time and between factions. A deputy secretary general may find himself performing a variety of missions. Two of his tasks, however, deserve special mention. The cabinet formation staff, we will recall from a previous chapter, fulfilled the task of maintaining liaison with the factions and serving as a sounding board for the prime minister in the selection of a cabinet. The deputy secretary generals serve the same function for the secretary general when he makes the other appointments to the party. The route in deciding the party endorsements for a general election was described as four-staged—from the prefectural federations, through the election policy secretariat, into the hands of the deputy secretary generals, thence to the election policy committee for final resolution. None of these stages should be ignored, but most of the hard dickering and compromise between the factions has been done in the past by the deputy secretary generals.

A deputy secretary general also serves the party, his second major task being to maintain liaison with the various party committees. Usually one of the deputies covers the policy affairs research council, another works with the executive council, a third with the Diet policy committee, and the fourth with the rest of the party organs. The upper house member's task is to maintain liaison with the House of Councillors. The deputies also have the task of maintaining liaison with the ministries. Under the Ikeda and Satō cabinets, one of the Deputies came from the prime minister's faction and had responsibilities in fund raising and power to authorize minor expenditures of the party's money. It should be noted

[78] Jiyūminshutō, *Tōsoku*, Art. 10. [79] *Ibid.*, Art. 8, sec. 2.

that under the Satō cabinets the factional functions have been downplayed and the party functions have become more prominent. Moreover, in the party endorsements for the general election in 1967, the deputy secretary generals did not play an important role. The fight took place in the election policy committee secretariat. Whether these are temporary or permanent changes remains to be seen.

The deputy secretary generals are regarded as men on the way up in the party, men who will soon be appointed to an important party post or a seat in the cabinet. Setoyama Mitsuo was a deputy representing the Satō faction before becoming minister of construction. Suzuki Zenkō served for three years as a deputy representing the Ikeda faction before his appointment to the post of chief cabinet secretary and then to the post of minister of health and welfare. Tokuyasu Jitsuzō served two years as deputy before his appointment as minister of posts and telecommunications. With a little bit of luck these men may reach the top. Tanaka Kakuei was also a deputy secretary general not too many years ago.

The conservative politicians do not talk much about "reforming" the post of the secretary general. I asked many politicians how the post of the secretary general should be changed to "modernize" the Liberal Democratic party. The only politician who had clear views on the subject was Kuraishi Tadao, a former labor minister, who said, "The secretary general ought to be more forthright and vigorous in the leadership of the party."[80] The other politicians took the opposite tack, muttering something about more democracy in the party, but most of them had not given the matter any previous thought. The institution of the secretary general is above them and something, like lightning or smog, about which they can do nothing.

Nevertheless, the post of the secretary general is subject to several conflicting trends that are influencing both its authority and responsibilities. Our last task will be to try to describe these trends.

[80] Kuraishi Tadao, interview, July 15, 1966.

The party at its inception was a loose grouping of politicians who had spent ten years fighting each other as much as fighting the renovationist parties. There was little internal cohesion. Nevertheless the party survived and with the passage of time increased its strength. As the powers of the party increase, so will those of the secretary general.

If the old-timers are to be believed, the prewar secretary generals, particularly the secretary generals of the Friends of Constitutional Government Association, were head and shoulders above the secretaries of the present conservative party. But there is a difference between the two groups. The power of the prewar men rested on their personal authority and powers outside the party, and particularly on their ability to gather funds. This latter talent is not overlooked in the selection of the present secretary general, nor does any back bencher in the party get appointed to the post. But the strength of the present secretary generals comes from the position itself rather than from outside considerations. In this respect, the post of the secretary general is stronger today than in the conservative parties before the war.

A third tendency is for the present conservative party to institutionalize its functions. To be sure, the present party has many of the same institutions that the prewar parties did. The executive council and the policy affairs research council are cases in point. But like the prewar secretary generals the strength of those institutions lay in the men who occupied them rather than in the institutions themselves. Moreover, the present conservative party has created more institutions —the public relations committee and the national organization committee are examples. These new committees are growing stronger and broadening their responsibilities. Their chairmen participate more and more in the decisions of the party. Rather than a one-man proprietor, the secretary general is becoming the chairman of the board. This trend may be interpreted as a weakening in the powers of the secretary general. It would probably be more correct to regard it as a

303

change in the qualities of leadership required in the secretary general.

We will inquire more closely into these trends in the next chapter. An evaluation of the post of secretary general is, in effect, an evaluation of the conservative party. Our general conclusion at this point is, however, that the powers of the secretary general are growing and his areas of responsibility becoming more complex.

CHAPTER XI

Conclusions

THE ultimate purpose of a political party is to rule the nation. Yet when the Liberal Democratic party was formed in 1955, the conservative politicians could agree only on one aim—who was *not* to rule the nation. At its inception, the sole purpose of the Liberal Democratic party was to keep the opposition parties—the socialists, in particular—out of power.

To be sure, an elaborate institutional fretwork decorated this simple political scheme. The conservative politicians made provision in the new party for a party president, a secretary general, an executive council, and a policy affairs research council. All the conservative parties had had these offices at least since the decade of the twenties and the new conservative party was to be no different. Each of these offices was given its traditional responsibilities. But real political power rested in a handful of individual politicians whose strength was derived from their ability to assist other politicians. By late 1957 they had institutionalized this strength in the factions. The Liberal Democratic party became an arena in which the various conservative factions vied for the right to rule the nation. The factions were the basic political unit. They were parties within a party.

The factions have become essential to the political process. They choose who will rule the nation. If they did not exist, it is hard to imagine how the prime minister would be elected, how the cabinet would be chosen, how the other government and party positions would be filled. Without the factions, political funds would be much scarcer. Without the factional teams barnstorming their members' districts, elections would become even more parochial than they are. Without the fights between the factions to liven things up and maintain public interest, Japanese politics might well devolve into a

305

series of intricate problems comprehensible only to the bureaucrats and of interest only to the pressure groups.

But whether or not they are essential, nobody says anything good about the factions. They are uniformly castigated.

The press was the first to take out after the factions. The power of the faction leaders was drawn too much from the purse. The blind loyalties of the faction members smacked too much of the feudal past. The factions fought over the personal ambitions of the politicians, while the press wanted debate over the destiny of the nation. The factions, in short, belied the ideals of government which the press had long championed.

The economic community also turned against the factions. Its concern was building and protecting a modern capitalist system and this concern could best be fulfilled with a single conservative party wielding a solid majority. Factions pitted conservative against conservative. The economic community found itself financing all camps in the factional wars with little benefit accruing to its fundamental interests. The factions were too expensive.

The conservative politicians also spoke out against the factions. The constant infighting among the factions undermined the validity of conservative rule. The politicians regard themselves the leaders of Japanese society, but the factions clearly relegated some of them to the role of followers. The factions were closed corporations dedicated to the care and feeding of the politicians themselves; they had neither the vision or the ideals to attract the support of the voters. The factions cast the shadow of history while the nation was concerned with pressing on into the future.

Prime ministers did not like the factions, either. After each prime minister had attained office, he found it to his interest to enhance the strength of the party which was under his control and weaken the powers of the factions from which the challenge to his rule would come. Under the prime ministers' leadership, and with the tacit backing of the other conservative politicians, the voluble urgings of the press, and the backstage maneuverings of the economic community, political power has begun to swing away from the factions and over to the party.

This movement should not be overestimated. It has been most gradual. There have been few advances and many retreats. Nonetheless, a change is under way. It can be seen along several fronts.

First of all, the existing organs of the party have been strengthened. The policy affairs research council is the clearest example. Historically, this organ was not important. One of the prewar parties did not even bother to mention it in its party law. The chairman was occasionally a party leader. More often, he was not. Although the divisions were supposed to follow the activities of the ministries, they rarely did so. Responsibility was limited to formulating arguments with which to attack the government and the other parties. Today, the policy affairs research council is one of the most important organs in the party. The list of the council's members is a required reference work in every large business firm. Its chairman has great political prestige and is one of the four senior officials in the party. It has acquired an infrastructure consisting not only of the divisions, but also special committees and investigative commissions, a deliberation commission, and vice chairmen, and most, though not all of these sub-organs have real duties. The task of the council is no longer grinding out political rhetoric, but rather fashioning the stuff of government. Nothing becomes policy in the party or law in the nation without passing through the council.

A second example is the office of the party vice-president. This is a new office that was born with the Liberal Democratic party. During the first two years of the position's existence, no politician occupied its chair nor did anyone particularly want to. Yet during the past ten years, the post has come to have power. Perhaps the most interesting development was in the last months of 1966, when a move started within the party to enforce the provisions of the party law and have the vice-president elected. Political observers suggest that the

307

move was generated less out of consideration for the party law than for a desire to deny Prime Minister Satō the power to gain some faction leader's support in the upcoming party presidential election by promising him this post. The prime minister apparently accepted this interpretation because his response was to accept the incumbent vice president's resignation, and then to reappoint him the following year when there was no party presidential election. It is argued that the party vice president is unimportant because the post is vacant almost as often as it is filled. But it should be noted that the prime minister went to quite elaborate lengths to maintain his power to appoint a man to this post rather than allow him to be elected. The post of the vice president has come to have political importance, and this importance comes from the party.

The party bureaucracy is a third case. Each of the pre-1955 parties had men who ran errands, answered phones, and tended to the menial tasks in return for being allowed to sit near the edges of political power. Some were salaried, most were not; all depended on the favor of the party leader. When the Liberal Democratic party was formed, these men were gathered together and called the party bureaucracy. They were simply a group of men who had served some of the political leaders in the past, and nobody knew what to do with them.

Today, however, a real bureaucracy is beginning to take shape. Formal regulations have been drawn up giving those men ranks, establishing chains of command, providing for leave privileges, retirement benefits, travel allotments. The party bureaucrats now have defined duties and responsibilities. A nine-story modern office building has been constructed to serve as party headquarters and it is indistinguishable from any of the government offices. In short, the paid party workers have all the accoutrements of a modern professional bureaucracy.

The strengthening of the existing organs of the party has not taken place across the board. The prefectural federations are little stronger than when they were first formed. The executive council has not been able to realize its great potential. Some of the major debates over policy do not take place in the policy affairs research council. The debate over Japan's relations with Communist China, for example, is taking place in ad hoc groups outside the formal structure of the party. In the case of the bureaucracy, a positive policy of recruiting superior talent has yet to be developed. There are problems with the regional organizers. But the trend is clear.

Not only have the existing organs of the party become stronger, but new organs have been created. Some of these new organs are to be found outside the formal structure of the party. Examples are the *kōenkai* of the various conservative politicians and the people's association. Others are within the party structure. Examples are the cabinet formation staff, the party officials' conference, the national organization committee, and the public relations committee. Several reasons can be advanced for their emergence.

Changes in Japanese society brought about some of the new institutions. An example is the development of the *kōenkai* of the conservative politicians in their election districts. There was no need for this institution before the war. The nation, particularly the rural area, was tightly and hierarchically organized. The basic unit was, first, the family and then the village. To gather the vote, the Japanese politician had only to reach agreement with the leading local families and with the village bosses. Today, however, substantial changes are taking place in Japanese society. The movement of workers to the cities, the changes in ownership of the land, the development of new agricultural techniques, marketing, and finance have begun to break down the solidarity of the village. Changes in social values, particularly the greater respect given the individual in Japanese society, has broken the solidarity of the family. The politician can no longer manipulate the traditional social structure to win elections. He has had to create his own vote-gathering mechanism, the *kōenkai*, and he is beginning to have to form a separate *kōenkai* for each member of the voter's family. The calculus of the *kōenkai* is clear to all the conservative politicians. Those who have a strong *kōenkai* win elections; those who have no *kōenkai* or a weak *kōenkai* lose elections. It is a safe prediction that the *kōenkai* will continue to grow in importance.

If the breakdown of the social hierarchy on the local level produced the *kōenkai*, then the breakdown of the financial hierarchy on the upper levels produced the people's association. Before the war there had been a measure of order. The large financial houses, the *zaibatsu*, aligned themselves with each of the conservative parties, and they could be counted upon for a steady supply of political capital. After the war, the fragmentation of the *zaibatsu* produced a gap which the politicians tried to fill through informal arrangements. The personal ties between the businessmen and the politicians became all-important.

This arrangement, however, left a great deal to be desired. The businessmen found that their funds were being used to divide the conservatives into warring factions rather than to unite them to protect and promote business interests. The politicians found that they were being placed under obligation both to businessmen and other politicians, obligation which they did not always wish to incur. The need for an impersonal, formal organization was apparent to all.

Early organizational efforts failed and the present organization leaves a lot to be desired. The funds collected are not sufficient. Divergent and private interests among the businessmen apparently make them reluctant to entrust their fortunes to a single organization. The politicians worry that the organization may be manipulated by the factions, particularly the prime minister's faction. The present organization has not inspired the electorate to open its purse strings. Further experimentation and adjustment of the internal processes and structure of the people's association are in order, although the creation of a completely satisfactory organization is probably impossible.

A third motive encouraging the development of new organs

310

has been the desire to inject the party into processes that heretofore had been subject to personal caprice. The creation of the cabinet formation staff is a case in point.

The fight for high office occupies the energies of many politicians and the making of cabinets forms a fat volume in Japanese political history. The postwar chapter is chiefly the story of attempts by the other conservative politicians to curb the clear constitutional right of the prime minister to exercise this power. The use of this power has passed through three stages. Yoshida Shigeru, during the years when he was prime minister, used the power to create a group of politicians personally loyal to him. The formation of the Liberal Democratic party and the subsequent growth of the factions saw the use of this power expand informally to the other faction leaders, whose aim in recommending men to cabinet posts was to reward loyalty to the faction. It was Prime Minister Kishi Nobusuke who recognized that the party should have a voice in these matters, that the awarding of cabinet posts should be used to cement, not divide, the party. He created the new office of the cabinet formation staff.

The performance of the cabinet formation staff has been ragged. Its prerogatives and responsibilities are loosely defined. Each prime minister has used the staff in different ways: Prime Minister Ikeda relied greatly on it in forming his latter cabinets; Prime Minister Satō has virtually ignored it in making his cabinets. The staff seems to have been more concerned with adjudicating factional claims than with representing the party. Nevertheless, the party now has some role, although it is a very minor one, in deciding appointment to the high political offices.

The changing concept of what a political party is and what a political party is supposed to do has brought about the creation of other organs in the party, such as the national organization committee and the public relations committee. Historically, political parties in Japan have been parliamentary clubs. They have been used as a way of ordering and controlling the Diet. The acceptance of the idea that the strength

311

of a political party lies in its popular support, and the growing belief that this support can be gained through modern communication techniques, accounts for the emergence of these new committees.

None of the earlier conservative parties had organizations of this type. Today, these two committees are the largest in the Liberal Democratic party and account for a substantial portion of its budget. The concepts which launched these committees seem to have been accepted throughout the party, particularly since several opposition parties have used them effectively to launch mass demonstrations of popular protest. But the committees still have to prove their worth, and in terms of political prestige, their chairmen are still juniors.

The expansion of the functions of the party and the increase in its powers have brought about the creation of still other new institutions. One is the party officials' conference. When the Liberal Democratic party was first formed, there was neither a party officials' conference nor any equivalent entity. With the passage of time, the expansion of functions, and the increase of power, the need for such a body became apparent; the right hand needed to know what the left hand was doing, and the chairmen of the various committees began meeting informally and irregularly to exchange views. Chance meetings with informal chatter hardened into regular meetings with an agenda, and finally, in 1961, the conference received formal mandate when its existence was written into the party law. "The party officials' conference has been meeting for quite some time," says Fukunaga Kenji, a conservative politician who has served in many high posts in the party. "It was only considerably after the fact that somebody remembered to stick it in the party law."[1]

Not all the moves towards the creation of new institutions within the party have been successful. Concerned that the young Dietmen had no way to gain political experience in party affairs, the conservative politicians created posts for secretaries within the party. These posts were placed in the

[1] Fukunaga Kenji, interview, June 3, 1966.

party hierarchy below the secretary general and the five deputy secretary generals. Their purpose is to assist these men in running the party. The secretary general appoints secretaries each year when the posts in the party are switched around, but he has yet to use these men in running the party. "The secretaries are important in name only," says Harada Ken, a former deputy secretary general. "They were an idea of the party which did not work out."[2]

Concerned that the regional politicians were not consulted in the making of policy, in May 1966 the conservative politicians set up a discussion council which was to meet once a month at the party headquarters in Tokyo to give regional politicians the opportunity to question the top leaders of the party. The council has yet to hold its first meeting.

Apprehensive that the Dietmen were too dependent on the bureaucracy for policy innovations, the conservative politicians made provision in the party law for the creation of a general institute of policy studies within the policy affairs research council "for the purpose of studying fundamental problems of democratic government and basic policies of the party, as well as collecting and filing various research materials."[3] The institute has yet to be formed.

To add a measure of rationality to appointments within the government and party, the conservative Dietmen directed that a section be set up in the personnel affairs division of the party secretariat to draft comprehensive statements on the background and experience of each of the party members, particularly the Dietmen. These curricula vitae have been prepared but there is no sign that any prime minister or secretary general has used them in making his appointments. Not all the innovations that the party has tried out have been successful. But again, the trend is clear.

As the existing organs of the party have been strengthened

2 Harada Ken, interview, June 6, 1966.
3 Jiyūminshutō, "Tōsoku" [Party Law] in *Wagatō no Kihon Hōshin* [Basic Policies of Our Party] (Tokyo: Jiyūminshutō Kōkoku Iinkai, 1966), Art. 49.

313

and new organs created, the politicians have come to rely more on them than they did in the past. The third change, then, has been the institutionalization of the processes of party, although this development is not as marked as in the case of the party organs.

A specific example can be found in the award of party endorsements for elections. This power is lodged in the election policy committee, and initially its members were the faction leaders themselves. Today these men have been replaced by the committee chairmen of the party. This is not to say that the faction leaders are no longer important in deciding the party endorsements. Even though they are no longer physically present, they still have ways of making their voices heard. But the power of decision gradually seems to be swinging over to the committee chairmen and the secretary general.

The decision-making process offers another example. The executive council, from the beginning, has been used chiefly to make ceremonial or formal decisions. Recall the statement of Hara Kenzaburō: "Decide the matter elsewhere, then bring it to the executive council." The politicians could not be precise on where elsewhere was: it depended on time, place, personality, and issue. But several of them said that they would try to get the concurrence of the leaders before tangling with the policy affairs research council. Initially these leaders were the faction chiefs. But in time they were, if not supplanted, at least supplemented by the four senior chairmen of the party—the secretary general, the chairman of the executive council, the chairman of the policy affairs research council, and the vice president (if there was one). These men gathered only for the most important decisions and then they met in the six man conference or the four party officials' conference, both highly informal bodies. After a while, the chairman of the public relations committee and the chairman of the national organization committee were added and the new group, the party officials' conference, began meeting on a regular basis. Although decision-making is not one of its assigned duties, this has come to be one of its principal functions. The voice of the faction leaders is still important if they choose to speak. The six man conference and the four party officials' conference is still occasionally called upon for its deliberations. But the trend is clear. Decisions that formerly rested with a few politicians outside the party structure generally are made now by a larger group of men who have formal position within the party.

The Liberal Democratic party is slowly losing its character as an alliance. The old organs of the party are becoming stronger and in some cases broadening their function. New organs are being created to fulfill new-found political needs. The politicians are beginning to take their own party seriously and rely upon it, at least in part, to carry out the processes of government. The party is gradually assuming the power to rule in its own right.

What does the future hold for the conservative party? Are the factions doomed to eventual extinction? Will the conservative party hold together or will it split again? What are the major challenges facing the Liberal Democratic party?

Our answers must be speculative, but one fact is clear. The factions should not be counted out. The factions and the party are mutually antagonistic, but at present, the party cannot exist without the factions and the factions cannot exist without the party.

The factions were created to fulfill the political needs of the politicians which the party could not or would not satisfy. The party presidential elections, the selection of cabinet officers, the appointment of party officials, the competition for political funds, the fight for party endorsement, the general elections are all processes within the party which pit conservative against conservative and have brought about the factions. So long as the party does not find ways of eliminating the competition among the conservative politicians and satisfying their needs, the factions are going to continue to play a major role in conservative politics.

On the other hand, the factions could not exist without the

party. No faction has enough members to elect the prime minister by itself. It must rely on coalitions. The party provides the framework within which the coalitions are formed.

In theory, coalition is not restricted to factions within the Liberal Democratic party. Factions and other groupings also exist within the renovationist camp, and the conservative factions could align with some of them. From time to time, usually just after a conservative faction leader has lost a battle with the prime minister, the press reports that this faction leader is plotting to bolt the party, ally with one of the renovationist parties or several of the renovationist factions, and take over the country.

But it never happens. One reason is ideology. The Communist party has recently tried to assume an independent stance, but it clearly is a Marxist party. So, too, is the Socialist party: several of its factions often find themselves further to the left than the Communist party because of their close identification with Mao. The conservatives are vague about what they stand for, but they are very voluble about what they are against. They are anti-Marx, anti-communist, anti-red—the words vary with the speaker. Though capable of considerable compromise, even the conservative politicians would be unable to work with these parties. So long as the socialists or the communists adhere to their doctrines, the conservative factions will abjure alliance with them.

But not all the parties of the renovationist camp have a dogma. The Democratic Socialists preach a pragmatic socialism. The intent of the Clean Government party, according to its 1967 platform, is to build a "new society of peace and plenty by following the middle way";[4] it avoids any further ideological commitment. Certainly, it is argued, the conservative factions could reach a meeting of the minds with either of these parties.

This argument overlooks the fact that the conservative party is a ruling party. And all the forces in the nation that

[4] *Asahi Nenkan* [Asahi Yearbook] 1968 edition (Tokyo, Asahi, Newspaper Co., 1968), p. 280.

316

want to share in the benefits and prerogatives of rule are aligned with it. The bureaucrats look to the party for future employment, the businessmen hope for favorable policy decisions, the local politicians want the bridges and the dams to hold their constituencies together. Any conservative politician who leaves the party to form an outside coalition runs the risk of seriously diminishing or, in fact, losing the support of these groups. It is far easier and less dangerous to take over the government by working from within the party. The outlook is that the party will stay together.

The greatest challenge that the present conservative party faces is to secure the support and participation of the electorate. It is not a new challenge; all Japanese political parties have been built from the top and none of them has been able to establish roots among the people. Today's politicians are working hard to create a popular party. Hardly a year goes by without a drive being launched by the party headquarters to recruit party members. Each conservative Dietman dutifully instructs the members of his *kōenkai* to register with the party and usually finds himself in the position of paying all the party dues for these new members himself. By the time the next year rolls around, these new members have forgotten they ever joined. The Japanese citizen still regards a political party as the bauble of the Dietmen, not an integral part of the democratic system in which he must participate fully.

Who will correct this concept is anybody's guess. The politicians seem to have done their part. The press can probably do more; it can create an atmosphere in which membership in a political party is not regarded as a crime but a civic responsibility. But the rest is up to the people themselves. Until such time as they join a party, the nation is not going to have the politics to which it aspires. Tanaka Kakuei said it as well as anyone else in a speech he made while he was secretary general of the party: "When a person asks me when we are going to modernize the party, I answer as soon as we are able to get him to join the party. I don't know but

317

what he's going to get a little splattered with the mud that's thrown around. But until the people join, we are not going to have a party worthy of the name." The future of the party lies with the people.

Glossary of
Offices and Organizations

Administrative Management Agency	Gyōsei kanri chō
Assembly of the Members of Both Houses of the Diet (LDP)	Ryōin giin sōkai
Assembly of the Members of the House of Councillors (LDP)	Sangiin giin sōkai
Assembly of the Members of the House of Representatives (LDP)	Shūgiin giin sōkai
Audit Board (LDP)	Kaikei kantoku
Ayame Club	Ayame kai
Azabudai Club	Azabudai kurabu
Blue Cloud School	Sei'un juku
Cabinet	Naikaku
Central Academy of Politics (LDP)	Chūō seiji daigaku
Chairman of the Executive Council (LDP)	Sōmukai chō
Chairman of the National Organization Committee (LDP)	Zenkoku soshiki iinkai chō
Chairman of the Policy Affairs Research Council (LDP)	Seimu chōsakai chō
Chairman of the Public Relations Committee (LDP)	Kōkoku iinkai chō
Chief Cabinet Secretary	Naikaku kanbō chōkan
Chōei Society	Chōeikai
Clean Election Federation	Kōmei senkyo renmei
Clean Government Party	Kōmeitō
Comradery of Youths	Seinen Dōshikai
Constitutional Association	Kenseikai
Constitutional Democratic Party	Rikken minseitō
Constitutional Progressive Party	Rikken kaishintō
Defence Agency	Bōeichō
Democratic Party	Minshutō

319

GLOSSARY

Democratic Socialist Party	Minshu shakaitō
Deliberation Commission (LDP)	Shingikai
Dietmen's Conference (LDP)	Daigishikai
Diet Policy Committee (LDP)	Kokkai taisaku iinkai
Division (LDP)	Bukai
Economic Planning Agency	Keizai kikaku chō
Economic Reconstruction Conference	Keizai saiken kondankai
Executive Council	Sōmukai
Executor; First Executor	Sōmu; Hittō sōmu
Federation of Economic Organizations	Keizai dantai rengōkai (keidanren)
Federation of Housewives' Associations	Shufu rengōkai
Finance Committee (LDP)	Zaimu iinkai
Financial Accounts Bureau (LDP)	Keirikyoku
Four Party Officials' Conference	Tōyonyaku kaigi
Friends of Constitutional Government Association	Rikken seiyūkai
General Federation for the Renovation of Political Conditions	Seikyoku isshin sōrengō
General Institute of Policy Studies	Sōgō seisaku kenkyūjo
Green Breeze Society	Ryokufūkai
Hokkaidō Development Agency	Hokkaidō kaihatsu chō
House of Councillors	Sangiin
House of Representatives	Shūgiin
Imperial Rule Assistance Association	Taisei yokusankai
Investigative Commissions (LDP)	Chōsakai
Japan Broadcasting Corporation	Nihon hōsō kyōkai (N.H.K.)
Japan Chamber of Commerce	Nihon shōkō kaigisho (nisshō)
Japan Committee for Economic Development	Keizai dōyūkai
Japan Communist Party	Nihon kyōsantō

GLOSSARY

Japan Federation of Employers' Organizations	Nihon keieisha dantai renmei (Nikkeiren)
Japan Liberal Party	Nihon jiyūtō
Japan Medical Association	Nihon ishikai
Japan Progressive Party	Nihon shimpotō
Japan Socialist Party	Nihon shakaitō
Kōchi Society	Kōchikai
Konwa Society	Konwakai
Liberal Democratic Party	Jiyūminshutō
Liberal Party	Jiyūtō
Life Insurance Federation	Seimei hoken kyōkai
Ministry of Agriculture and Forestry	Nōrinshō
Ministry of Construction	Kensetsushō
Ministry of Education	Mombushō
Ministry of Finance	Ōkurashō
Ministry of Foreign Affairs	Gaimushō
Ministry of Health and Welfare	Kōseishō
Ministry of Home Affairs	Jichishō
Ministry of International Trade and Industry	Tsūshō sangyōshō (Tsūsanshō)
Ministry of Justice	Hōmushō
Ministry of Labor	Rōdōshō
Ministry of Posts and Telecommunications	Yūseishō
Ministry of Transportation	Unyushō
Mizuho Club	Mizuho kurabu
National Capital Region Development Commission	Shutoken seibi iinkai
National Diet	Kokkai
National Organization Committee (LDP)	Zenkoku soshiki iinkai
National Public Safety Commission	Kokka kōan iin
Office of the Prime Minister	Sōrifu
Organization Research Committee (LDP)	Soshiki chōsakai
Ōsaka Taxi Federation	Ōsaka takushii kyōkai

321

GLOSSARY

Party Conference	Tōtaikai
Party Discipline Committee	Tōki iinkai
Party Officials' Conference	Tōyakuinkai
People's Association	Kokumin kyōkai
People's Cooperative Party	Kokumin kyōdōtō
Personnel Affairs Division (LDP)	Jinji kyoku
Policy Affairs Research Council (LDP)	Seimu chōsakai
Prefectural Association	Todōfuken shibu rengōkai
President (LDP)	Sōsai
Privy Council	Sūmitsuin
Public Relations Committee	Kōhō iinkai
Sake Brewers' Federation	Jōzō kumiai
Sankin Society	Sankinkai
Science and Technology Agency	Kagaku gijutsu chō
Secretary (LDP)	Kanji
Secretary General (LDP)	Kanjichō
Seishin Club	Seishin kurabu
Six Man Conference (LDP)	Rokusha kaidan
Speaker of the Upper House	Sangiin gichō
Special Committee (LDP)	Tokubetsu iinkai
Spring and Autumn Society	Shunjūkai
Sumire Club	Sumire Kai
Third Thursday Society	Sammokukai
Value Creation Society	Sōka gakkai
Vice President (LDP)	Fukusōsai

322

Appendix

CONSERVATIVE MEMBERS OF THE LOWER HOUSE OF THE DIET,
DIVIDED BY FACTION, JULY 1968

	Electoral District	Age	Occupation	Education	No. Times Elected
MATSUMURA					
Matsumura Kenzō	Toyama 2	84	Party official	Waseda U.	13
Kawasaki Hideji	Mie 1	55	Writer	Waseda U.	9
Furui Yoshimi	Tottori	64	Public corporation executive	Tokyo U.	7
Sasayama Shigetarō	Akita 5	65	Public corporation executive	Tokyo U.	6
MURAKAMI					
Murakami Isamu	Ōita 1	64	Public corporation executive	Technical	10
Kanda Hiroshi	Shizuoka 1	63	Businessman	Hōsei U.	7
Tokuyasu Jitsuzō	Tottori	66	Businessman	Business school	7
Fukuda Tokuyasu	Tokyo 7	70	Public corporation executive	Tokyo U.	7
Harada Ken	Ōsaka 3	47	Party official	Meiji U.	6
Tamura Hajime	Mie 2	42	Businessman	Keiō U.	5
Ōno Akira	Gifu 1	38	Businessman	Keiō U.	2
Inamura Sakonshirō	Ishikawa 2	50	Businessman	Technical	2
Mihara Asao	Fukuoka 2	57	Party official	Meiji U.	2
Satō Bunsei	Ōita 2	47	Public corporation executive	Meiji U.	1
MATSUDA—SONODA GROUP					
Matsuda Takechiyo	Ōsaka 5	78	None	New York U.	11
Sonoda Sunao	Kumamoto 2	53	Agriculture	Middle school	9
Nemoto Ryūtarō	Akita	59	Public corporation executive	Kyoto U.	8

SOURCE: *Asahi Shimbun*, July 19, 1968, p. 18; Japan, Jichishō Senkyo Kyoku, *Shūgiin Giin Sōsenkyo, Saikō-Saibansho Saibankan Kokumin Shinsa Kekka Shirabe* [Survey of Results of the General Elections of the House of Representatives and Peoples' Judgment of the Legal Officers of the Supreme Court] (Tokyo: Jichishō Senkyo Kyoku, 1967), pp. 212-240.

	Electoral District	Age	Occupation	Education	No. Times Elected
Takahashi Seiichirō	Niigata 1	56	Businessman	Kyoto U.	7
Nakagawa Shunji	Hiroshima 2	64	Public corporation executive	Chūō U.	7
Shigemasa Seishi	Hiroshima 3	69	Businessman	Tokyo U.	6
Shirahama Nikichi	Nagasaki 2	58	Public corporation executive	Jikei U.	6
Uemura Sen'ichirō	Aichi 5	55	Party official	Waseda U.	3
Uno Sōsuke	Shiga	44	Party official	Kōbe U.	3
Fujio Masayuki	Tochigi 2	50	Businessman	Jōchi U.	2
Fujinami Takao	Mie 2	34	Businessman	Waseda U.	1
FUNADA					
Funada Naka	Tochigi 1	71	Educator	Tokyo U.	12
Hara Kenzaburō	Hyōgo 2	59	Writer	Waseda U.	10
Mizuta Mikio	Chiba 3	63	Minister	Kyoto U.	10
Kawano Hōman	Miyazaki 1	68	Businessman	Keiō U.	9
Nakayama Masa	Ōsaka 2	76	Public corporation executive	Wesleyan U.	8
Horikawa Kyōhei	Hyōgo 4	72	Businessman	Waseda U.	8
Fukuda Hajime	Fukui	64	Businessman	Tokyo U.	7
Kamoda Sōichi	Saitama 3	60	Party official	Tokyo U.	4
Watanabe Eiichi	Gifu 1	49	Public corporation executive	Nagoya H.S.	2
Nakagawa Ichirō	Hokkaidō 5	41	Businessman	Kyūshū U.	2
Utsumi Hideo	Miyagi 2	44	Businessman	Chūō U.	1
Aoki Masahisa	Saitama 4	44	Agriculture	Tokyo	1
Hanashi Nobuyuki	Ibaragi 1	38	Businessman	Hokkaidō U.	1
ISHII					
Tanaka Isaji	Kyoto 1	61	Lawyer	Ritsumei U.	10
Sakata Michita	Kumamoto 2	50	Agriculture	Tokyo U.	10
Ishii Mitsujirō	Fukuoka 3	77	Public corporation executive	Business school	9
Hata Bushirō	Nagano 2	63	Businessman	Tōhoku U.	8
Hirose Masao	Ōita 1	60	None	Kyūshū U.	7
Nadao Hirokichi	Hiroshima 1	67	Public corporation executive	Tokyo U.	7
Nakagaki Kunio	Aichi 4	55	Businessman	Tōyō U.	7
Hasegawa Takashi	Miyagi 2	54	Party official	Waseda U.	5
Furukawa Jōkichi	Ōsaka 4	62	Businessman	Tokyo U.	5

APPENDIX

	Electoral District	Age	Occupation	Education	No. Times Elected
Tanaka Eiichi	Tokyo 1	65	Public corporation executive	Tokyo U.	4
Ōtsubo Yasuo	Saga	67	Lawyer	Tokyo U.	4
Shintō Kazuma	Fukuoka 1	63	Businessman	Waseda U.	3
Tsukada Tōru	Niigata 4	32	Businessman	U. of San Francisco	2
Abe Kigen	Ehime 3	43	Businessman	Waseda U.	1

FUJIYAMA

Waseda Ryūemon	Aichi 2	66	Businessman	Elementary	10
Nanjō Tokuo	Hokkaidō 4	71	Lawyer	Tokyo U.	10
Esaki Masumi	Aichi 3	51	Party official	Nippon U.	9
Endō Saburō	Shizuoka 2	62	Public corporation executive	Tokyo U.	8
Tokonami Tokuji	Kagoshima 1	62	Educator	Tokyo U.	8
Nagata Ryōichi	Hyōgo 2	55	Businessman	Keiō U.	7
Morita Jūjirō	Aomori 1	76	Lawyer	Teachers' school	6
Nakayama Eiichi	Ibaragi 1	71	Businessman	Waseda U.	6
Ikeda Kiyoshi	Kagoshima 2	66	Lawyer	Tokyo U.	6
Sunahara Kaku	Hiroshima 1	64	Businessman	Elementary	5
Fujiyama Aiichirō	Kanagawa 1	69	Party official	Keiō U.	4
Takeuchi Reiichi	Aomori 2	40	Writer	Tokyo U.	2
Tamura Ryōhei	Kōchi 1	49	Agriculture	Waseda U.	2

KAWASHIMA

Kawashima Shōjirō	Chiba 1	76	Educator	Senshū U.	13
Yamaguchi Kikuichirō	Wakayama 1	69	Party official	Waseda U.	11
Akagi Munenori	Ibaragi 3	62	Agriculture	Tokyo U.	9
Shinoda Kōsaku	Hokkaidō 4	67	Businessman	Waseda U.	8
Hasegawa Shirō	Gumma 2	62	Businessman	Elementary	8
Arafune Seijūrō	Saitama 3	59	Businessman	Meiji U.	8
Akita Daisuke	Tokushima	61	Party official	Tokyo U.	8
Fujieda Sensuke	Gumma 1	59	Minister	Tokyo U.	7
Kikuchi Yoshirō	Tokyo 5	76	Educator	Nippon U.	7
Hamano Seigo	Tokyo 9	68	Businessman	Chūō U.	6
Shiina Etsusaburō	Iwate 2	69	Public corporation executive	Tokyo U.	5
Okazaki Eijō	Tokyo 4	66	Party official	Tokyo U.	5
Ogasa Kōshō	Tokushima	62	Businessman	Tokyo U.	5

325

	Electoral District	Age	Occupation	Education	No. Times Elected
Matsuzawa Yūzō	Yamagata 2	56	Public corporation executive	High school	5
Yamamura Shinjirō	Chiba 2	34	Businessman	Gakushūin U.	2
Mizuno Kiyoshi	Chiba 2	41	Businessman	Tōhoku U.	1
Furuya Tōru	Gifu 2	58	Lawyer	Tokyo U.	1
NAKASONE					
Nakamura Umekichi	Tokyo 5	65	Lawyer	Hōsei U.	10
Nakasone Yasuhiro	Gumma 3	48	Writer	Tokyo U.	9
Ōishi Buichi	Miyagi	57	Physician	Tōhoku U.	8
Inaba Osamu	Niigata 2	57	Lawyer	Chūō U.	8
Sakurauchi Yoshio	Shimane	54	Party official	Keiō U.	8
Noda Takeo	Kumamoto 1	71	Businessman	Waseda U.	7
Yamanaka Sadanori	Kagoshima 4	45	Agriculture	Taipei Teachers School	6
Yagi Tetsuo	Ehime 2	50	Public corporation executive	Business high school	4
Kurauchi Shūji	Fukuoka 4	48	Party official	Tokyo U.	4
Kuranari Tadashi	Nagasaki 1	48	Public corporation executive	Tokyo U.	4
Amano Kōsei	Fukushima 1	59	Businessman	Elementary	3
Tagawa Seiichi	Kanagawa 2	48	Businessman	Keiō U.	3
Satō Takayuki	Hokkaidō 3	38	Public corporation executive	Meiji U.	2
Watanabe Michio	Tochigi 1	43	Tax accountant	Tokyo Business U.	2
Sakamura Yoshimasa	Gumma 2	53	Public corporation executive	Tokyo U.	2
Shinomiya Hisakichi	Tokyo 8	71	Lawyer	Meiji U.	2
Ōtake Tarō	Niigata 4	61	Businessman	Tokyo U.	2
Ōishi Hachiji	Shizuoka 1	58	Public corporation executive	High school	2
Kibe Yoshiaki	Shizuoka 2	40	Party official	Chūō U.	2
Sunada Shigetami	Hyōgo 1	49	Businessman	Rikkyō U.	2
Minato Tetsurō	Fukushima 1	47	Agriculture	Tokyo U.	2
Mutō Kabun	Gifu 1	40	Businessman	Kyoto U.	1
Nakao Eiichi	Yamanashi 1	37	Public corporation executive	Aoyama U.	1
MIKI					
Miki Takeo	Tokushima	59	Minister	Meiji U.	12
Matsuura Shūtarō	Hokkaidō 2	70	Businessman	Elementary	10

APPENDIX

	Electoral District	Age	Occupation	Education	No. Times Elected
Ide Ichitarō	Nagano 2	55	Businessman	Kyoto U.	10
Shiga Kenjirō	Iwate 2	63	None	Waseda U.	9
Hayakawa Takashi	Wakayama 2	50	Minister	Tokyo U.	9
Nohara Masakatsu	Iwate 1	60	Public corporation executive	High school	8
Kōmoto Toshio	Hyōgo 4	55	Businessman	Nippon U.	8
Yamate Mitsuo	Mie 1	55	None	Kyoto U.	8
Nakamura Torata	Fukuoka 1	64	Agriculture	High school	8
Honna Takeshi	Hokkaidō 5	55	Party official	Technical	7
Usui Sōichi	Chiba 1	64	Businessman	Waseda U.	7
Kitsukawa Kyūe	Nagano 3	61	Public corporation executive	Meiji U.	7
Kanno Watarō	Ōsaka 1	71	Minister	Kyoto U.	7
Akazawa Masamichi	Tottori	59	Businessman	Tokyo U.	7
Moriyama Kinji	Tochigi 1	50	Public corporation executive	Tokyo U.	6
Niwa Hyōsuke	Aichi 2	57	Businessman	Kansaigakuin U.	5
Fujita Yoshimitsu	Kumamoto 1	55	Public corporation executive	Chūō U.	5
Fujimoto Takao	Kagawa 1	36	Party official	Waseda U.	4
Mōri Matsuhei	Ehime 3	53	Businessman	Keiō U.	4
Kan Tarō	Ehime 1	62	Businessman	Tokyo U.	4
Shibuya Naozō	Fukushima 2	50	Businessman	Tokyo U.	3
Kaifu Toshiki	Aichi 3	55	Businessman	Kansai U.	3
Fujii Katsushi	Okayama 2	51	Public corporation executive	Tokyo U.	3
Tanigawa Kazuo	Hiroshima 2	36	Public corporation executive	Keiō U.	3
Kumagai Yoshio	Aomori 1	61	Fishery	Meiji U.	2
Noro Kyōichi	Mie 2	47	Public corporation executive	High school	2
Nishioka Takeo	Nagasaki 1	30	Public corporation executive	Waseda U.	2
Itō Sōichirō	Miyagi 1	42	Public corporation executive	Tōhoku U.	2
Kujiraoka Hyōsuke	Tokyo 8	51	Businessman	Waseda U.	2
Momiyama Hide	Fukushima 1	60	Businessman	High school	2
Suganami Shigeru	Fukushima 3	53	Physician	Shōwa medical	1
Niwa Kyūshō	Aichi 1	52	Businessman	Elementary	1
Sakamoto Misoji	Ishikawa 2	44	Businessman	Tōhoku U.	1

327

APPENDIX

	Electoral District	Age	Occupation	Education	No. Times Elected
Murakami Shinjirō	Ehime 2	48	Public corporation executive	Tokyo U.	1
Hashiguchi Takashi	Kagoshima 3	53	Public corporation executive	Tokyo U.	1
Katsuragi Tetsuo	Ishikawa 1	46	Businessman	Waseda U.	1
Shionoya Kazuo	Shizuoka 3	47	Writer	Waseda U.	1
MAEO					
Masutani Shūji	Ishikawa 2	79	None	Kyoto U.	13
Shimamura Ichirō	Tokyo 10	72	Businessman	Chūō U.	10
Kosaka Zentarō	Nagano 1	55	Educator	Tokyo Business U.	10
Kodaira Hisao	Tochigi 2	56	Businessman	Tokyo Business U.	9
Suzuki Zenkō	Iwate 1	56	Public corporation executive	Technical	9
Maeo Shigesaburō	Kyoto 2	61	Businessman	Tokyo U.	8
Sutō Hideo	Yamaguchi 1	69	Public corporation executive	Tokyo U.	8
Fukunaga Kenji	Saitama 1	56	Party official	Tokyo U.	8
Araki Masuo	Fukuoka 3	65	Public corporation executive	Tokyo U.	8
Sasaki Hideyo	Hokkaidō 5	57	Businessman	Technical school	7
Kurogane Yasumi	Yamagata 1	56	Accountant	Tokyo U.	7
Ogawa Heiji	Nagano 3	57	Businessman	Tokyo U.	7
Ōhira Masayoshi	Kagawa 2	56	None	Tokyo Business U.	7
Koyama Osanori	Miyazaki 2	61	Lawyer	Tokyo U.	7
Niwa Kyōshirō	Ibaragi 3	62	Businessman	Tokyo U.	6
Amano Kimiyoshi	Tokyo 6	45	Businessman	Tokyo U.	6
Uchida Tsuneo	Yamanashi	59	Public corporation executive	Tokyo U.	6
Takami Saburō	Shizuoka 1	63	None	Teachers' school	6
Kaji Ryōsaku	Toyama 1	71	Lawyer	Meiji U.	6
Yoshida Shigenobu	Kumamoto 2	57	Agriculture	Tokyo U.	6
Hatsuta Sadayoshi	Fukushima 2	57	Educator	Nippon Medical U.	5
Ōkubo Takeo	Kumamoto 1	63	Public corporation executive	Tokyo U.	5
Saitō Kunikichi	Fukushima 3	57	Lawyer	Tokyo U.	4
Kusano Ichirobei	Shiga	61	Party official	Middle school	4

328

	Electoral District	Age	Occupation	Education	No. Times Elected
Kameyama Kōichi	Okayama 1	66	Public corporation executive	Tokyo U.	4
Kaneko Iwazō	Nagasaki 2	59	Businessman	Elementary	4
Tazawa Kichirō	Aomori 2	49	Party official	Waseda	3
Sasaki Yoshitake	Akita 1	57	Public corporation executive	Tokyo U.	3
Ozawa Tatsuo	Niigata 1	50	Party official	Tokyo U.	3
Urano Sachio	Aichi 4	53	Businessman	Nippon U.	3
Kaneko Ippei	Gifu 2	53	Party official	Tokyo U.	3
Imura Shigeo	Ishikawa 1	64	Physician	Medical school	3
Tanigaki Sen'ichi	Kyoto 2	55	Public corporation executive	Tokyo U.	3
Shōji Keijirō	Wakayama 2	55	Public corporation executive	Tokyo U.	3
Tosaka Jūjirō	Ibaragi 3	62	Businessman	Middle school	2
Murayama Tatsuo	Niigata 3	51	Research institute director	Tokyo U.	2
Tanaka Rokusuke	Fukuoka 4	44	Party official	Waseda U.	2
Kubota Fujimaro	Mie 1	49	Public corporation executive	Tokyo U.	2
Kino Haruo	Ōsaka 5	47	Research institute director	Tokyo U.	1
Masuoka Hiroyuki	Hiroshima 2	43	Businessman	Waseda U.	1
Miyazawa Kiichi	Hiroshima 3	47	Party official	Tokyo U.	1
Furuuchi Hirō	Miyagi 1	59	Businessman	Tokyo U.	1
SATŌ					
Satō Yōnosuke	Ibaragi 3	72	Businessman	Keiō U.	10
Tanaka Kakuei	Niigata 3	48	Educator, businessman	Technical	9
Matsuno Raizō	Kumamoto 1	49	None	Keiō U.	9
Hori Shigeru	Saga 1	65	Educator	Chūō U.	9
Kimura Takeo	Yamagata 1	65	Businessman	Meiji U.	8
Hashimoto Tomisaburō	Ibaragi 1	65	Party official	Waseda U.	8
Tsukahara Toshirō	Ibaragi 2	56	Minister	Tokyo U.	8
Masuda Kaneshichi	Nagano 4	68	Lawyer	Kyoto U.	8
Kanbayashiyama Eikichi	Kagoshima 1	63	Educator	Nippon U.	8
Nishimura Naomi	Shizuoka 1	61	Public corporation executive	Tokyo U.	8

329

APPENDIX

	Electoral District	Age	Occupation	Education	No. Times Elected
Hisano Chūji	Aichi 2	56	Businessman	Middle school	8
Nakano Shirō	Aichi 4	60	Public corporation executive	Middle school	8
Satō Eisaku	Yamaguchi 2	65	Prime minister	Tokyo U.	8
Takahashi Eikichi	Ehime 3	69	Lawyer	Nippon U.	8
Ueki Kōshirō	Fukui 1	68	Businessman	Tokyo U.	7
Nakamura Yōichirō	Chiba 3	70	Businessman	Senshū U.	7
Sakata Eiichi	Ishikawa 1	69	Public corporation executive	Tokyo U.	7
Tsubokawa Shinzō	Fukui 1	57	Party official	Teachers' school	7
Kimura Toshio	Mie 1	58	Party official	Tokyo U.	7
Nishimura Eiichi	Ōita 2	69	Minister	Tōhoku U.	7
Aikawa Katsuroku	Miyazaki 1	75	Lawyer	Tokyo U.	7
Setoyama Mitsuo	Miyazaki 5	63	Agriculture	Meiji U.	7
Chūma Tatsui	Kagoshima 2	50	Businessman	Kyoto U.	7
Nikaidō Susumu	Kagoshima 3	57	Minister	U. of California	7
Naitō Takashi	Toyama 1	73	Party official	Waseda U.	6
Adachi Tokurō	Shizuoka 3	56	Public corporation executive	Kyoto U.	6
Ihara Kishitaka	Ehime 2	65	Agriculture	Elementary	5
Aichi Kiichi	Miyagi 1	59	Public corporation executive	Tokyo U.	5
Shiseki Ihei	Chiba 1	59	Lawyer	Tokyo U.	5
Fukui Isamu	Aichi 5	63	Businessman	Shizuoka U.	5
Kitazawa Naokichi	Ibaragi 3	65	Public corporation executive	Tokyo Business U.	5
Ōno Ichirō	Niigata 3	56	Businessman	Business high school	5
Inō Shigejirō	Chiba 2	65	Public corporation executive	Tokyo U.	4
Kanemaru Shin	Yamanashi 1	52	Businessman	Tokyo Agricultural U.	4
Takeshita Noboru	Shimane 1	42	Public corporation executive	Waseda U.	4
Okamoto Shigeru	Nara 1	68	Public corporation executive	Kyoto U.	4
Kameoka Takeo	Fukushima 1	47	Public corporation executive	Military academy	3
Kariya Tadao	Kōchi 1	53	Agriculture	Elementary	3
Hosoda Kichizō	Shimane 1	54	Public corporation executive	Tokyo U.	3

330

APPENDIX

	Electoral District	Age	Occupation	Education	No. Times Elected
Ozawa Tarō	Yamaguchi 2	62	Public corporation executive	Tokyo U.	2
Obuchi Keizō	Gumma 3	29	Businessman	Waseda U.	2
Komiyama Jūshirō	Saitama 2	39	Educator	Waseda U.	2
Koyama Shōji	Tokyo 7	70	Businessman	Technical high school	2
Hashimoto Ryūtarō	Okayama 2	29	Public corporation executive	Keiō U.	2
Sekō Masataka	Wakayama 2	45	Businessman	Tokyo U.	1
Yamada Hisanari	Tokyo 8	61	Party official	Tokyo U.	1
Minowa Noboru	Hokkaidō 1	42	Physician	Hokkaidō U.	1
Watanabe Hajime	Niigata 2	28	Political secretary	Keiō U.	1
Yamashita Motoyoshi	Shiga 1	45	Public corporation executive	Tokyo U.	1
Ōmura Jōji	Okayama 1	47	Research institute director	Tokyo U.	1

NON-FACTION

	Electoral District	Age	Occupation	Education	No. Times Elected
Tsuji Kanichi	Aichi 6	62	Businessman	High school	9
Ishida Hirohide	Akita 1	53	Writer	Waseda U.	9
Ōhashi Takeo	Shimane 1	63	Lawyer	Tokyo U.	8
Utsumiya Tokuma	Tokyo 5	61	Businessman	Kyoto U.	7
Katō Tsunetarō	Kagawa 2	61	Public corporation executive	Harbin Foreign Language	7
Noda Uichi	Gifu 1	63	Party official	Tokyo U.	6
Shiroki Matsutarō	Toyama 2	81	Businessman	Tokyo U.	5
Kaya Okinori	Tokyo 3	78	Public corporation executive	Tokyo U.	4
Chizaki Usaburō	Hokkaidō 1	48	Businessman	Ritsumeikan U.	2
Okuno Seisuke	Nara 1	55	None	Tokyo U.	2
Kōno Yōhei	Kanagawa 3	31	Businessman	Waseda U.	1
Yamaguchi Toshio	Saitama 2	27	Public corporation executive	Meiji U.	1

FUKUDA

	Electoral District	Age	Occupation	Education	No. Times Elected
Chiba Saburō	Chiba 3	73	Educator	Tokyo U.	10
Yamaguchi Shizue	Tokyo 6	50	Businessman	High school	10
Morishita Kunio	Tochigi 2	70	Businessman	Waseda U.	9
Koizumi Junya	Kanagawa 2	64	None	Nippon U.	9
Kuraishi Tadao	Nagano 1	66	Minister	Hōsei U.	9

331

	Electoral District	Age	Occupation	Education	No. Times Elected
Ogawa Hanji	Kyoto 1	57	Public corporation executive	Ritsumeikan U.	9
Nagayama Tadanori	Hiroshima 3	69	Public corporation executive	Chūō U.	9
Fukunaga Kazuomi	Kumamoto 2	59	Party official	Tokyo Foreign Language U.	8
Fukuda Takeo	Gumma 3	62	Public corporation executive	Tokyo U.	7
Arita Kiichi	Hyōgo 5	65	Businessman	Tokyo U.	7
Bō Hideo	Wakayama 1	62	Minister	Tokyo U.	7
Kishi Nobusuke	Yamaguchi 2	70	None	Tokyo U.	7
Miike Makoto	Saga 1	66	Businessman	Kyūshū U.	7
Tanaka Tatsuo	Yamaguchi 1	56	Public corporation executive	Tokyo U.	6
Tokai Motosaburō	Hyōgo 3	51	Party official	Kyoto U.	5
Tanaka Masami	Hokkaidō 3	51	Businessman	Tokyo U.	5
Ichimada Hisato	Ōita 1	73	Public corporation executive	Tokyo U.	5
Saitō Kenzō	Akita 2	68	Businessman	Waseda U.	5
Komine Ryūta	Tokyo 4	58	Businessman	Hitotsubashi U.	5
Kano Hikokichi	Yamagata 1	62	Businessman	Kyoto U.	4
Fuke Toshiichi	Kagawa 1	54	Businessman	Waseda U.	4
Kubota Enji	Gumma 1	63	Businessman	Technical school	3
Abe Shintarō	Yamaguchi 1	42	Public corporation executive	Tokyo U.	3
Shiokawa Masajūrō	Ōsaka 4	45	Businessman	Keiō U.	1
Mitsubayashi Yatarō	Saitama 4	48	Agriculture	Teachers' school	1
Hirokawa Shizue	Tokyo 3	54	Educator	High school	1
Katō Mutsuki	Okayama 5	42	Businessman	High school	1

Bibliography

This bibliography is broken down into five categories: articles and books, interviews, serials, party documents, and official documents.

ARTICLES AND BOOKS

Borton, Hugh. *Japan's Modern Century*. New York: Ronald Press, 1955.

Duverger, Maurice. *Political Parties*. 2nd English ed. revised. New York: John Wiley and Sons, Inc., 1959.

Fujiwara Hirotatsu, and Tomita Nobuo. "Kokumin Seiji Ishiki no Kichō to Henka no Taiyō" [The Basis and Mode of Change of the Political Consciousness of the People], *Seikei Ronsō*, Vol. 31, No. 6 (January 1964).

Fukumoto Kunio. "Kansai Zaikai no Shisō to Kōdō" [Thought and Activities of the Kansai Business Community] *Chūō Kōron* (April 1964).

Fukutake Tadashi. "The Communal Character and Democratic Development of Farming Villages," *Journal of Social and Political Ideas in Japan*, Vol. 2, No. 3 (December 1964).

Hatoyama Ichirō. *Kaikoroku* [Memoirs]. Tokyo: Bungei Shunjūsha, 1957.

Hayakawa Takashi, *Shin-Hoshushugi no Seiji Rinen* [Political Ideals of the New Conservatism]. Tokyo: [n.p.], April 1965.

Ishikawa Tatsuzō. *Kinkanshoku* [The Corona of Gold]. Tokyo: Shinchō-sha, 1966.

Itō Hirobumi. *Kempō Gikai* [Commentary of the Constitution]. 15th ed. revised. Tokyo: Maruzen, 1935.

Kikuoka Yaozō, ed. *Kokkai Binran* [Parliamentary Handbook]. 42nd ed. Tokyo: Nihon Seikei Shimbun Shuppan-bu, 1967.

Kiya Ikusaburō, *Seikai Gojūnen no Butai Ura* [Fifty Years Behind the Political Scenes]. Tokyo: Seikai Odrai Sha, 1965.

Kōno Ichirō. *Kōno Ichirō Jiden* [The Autobiography of Kōno Ichirō]. Tokyo: Tokuma Shoten, 1965.

Kokumin Seiji Kenkyūkai. "Kanjichō Shian to Tōkindaika" [The Secretary General's Proposal and the Modernization of the Party], *Getsuyōkai* [Monday Club Report] (October 11, 1965). Mimeo.

Masumi Junnosuke. *Nihon Seitōshi-ron* [A History of Japanese Political Parties]. Vol. 1. Tokyo: Tokyo Daigaku Shuppan-kai, 1965.

Masumi Junnosuke. "Sen-kyūhyaku-gojūgo-nen no Seiji Taisei" [The Political Structure of 1955], *Shisō* (June 1964).

BIBLIOGRAPHY

Matsushita Keiichi. *Gendai Nihon no Seijiteki Kōsei* [Political Structure of Contemporary Japan]. Tokyo: Tokyo University Press, 1962.

Miyamoto Ken'ichi. "Kusa no Ne Hoshushugi" [Grassroots Conservatism], in *Machi no Seiji, Mura no Seiji* [Town Politics, Village Politics]. Tokyo: Keisō Shobō, 1965.

Nagai Yōnosuke. "Structural Characteristics of Pressure Politics in Japan," *Journal of Social and Political Ideas in Japan*, Vol. 2, No. 6 (December 1964).

Nakamura Kikuo. *Gendai Seiji no Jittai* [The True Conditions of Present Day Politics]. Tokyo: Yūshindō, 1965.

———. *Senkyosen* [The Election War]. Tokyo: Kōdansha, 1965.

———. *Shindan-Nihon no Seiji Taishitsu* [The Japanese Body Politic —A Diagnosis]. Tokyo: Ronsō-sha, 1961.

Nakasone Yasuhiro. "Seiji o Kokumin no Naka e" [Put Politics into the Hearts of the People]. *Nihon oyobi Nihonjin* (October 1963).

——— et al. *Warera Taishōkko* [We Children of the Taishō Era]. Tokyo: Tokuma Shoten, 1961.

Nihon Kindai-shi Jiten [A Dictionary of Modern Japanese History]. Tokyo: Tōyō Keizai Shinpōsha, 1958.

Nihon-shi Jiten [A Dictionary of Japanese History]. Ōsaka: Sōgensha, 1961.

Ōnishi Yutaka. "Sūji de miru Seitō Shiji no Suii" [Numerical Analysis of Changes in Party Support], *Asahi Jānaru* (September 1965).

Ōno Bamboku. *Ōno Bamboku Kaisōroku* [The Memoirs of Ōno Bamboku]. Tokyo: Kōbundō, 1964.

Ōyama Ryōichi. "Saikyō Pawā Eriito—Zaikai" [The Economic Community—The Strongest Power Elite], *Ekonomisuto*, Vol. 42, No. 15 (April 10, 1964).

Reischauer, Robert K. *Japan: Government—Politics*. New York: Thomas Nelson and Sons, 1939.

"Satō Eisaku-shi o Meguru Jimmyaku" [When Surrounding Mr. Satō Eisaku], *Top Research* (Special Spring Issue 1966).

Scalapino, Robert. *Democracy and the Party Movement in Prewar Japan*. Berkeley: University of California, 1953.

Scalapino, Robert A., and Masumi Junnosuke. *Parties and Politics in Contemporary Japan*. Berkeley and Los Angeles: University of California Press, 1962.

Suzuki Yukio. *Seiji o Ugokasu Keieisha* [Business Executives Who Move Politics]. Tokyo: Nihon Keizai Shimbun-sha, 1965.

Takayanagi Kenzō. "A Century of Innovation: The Development of Japanese Law, 1868-1961," in *Law in Japan*, ed. by Arthur Taylor von Mehren. Cambridge: Harvard University Press, 1963.

BIBLIOGRAPHY

Togawa Isamu, *Seiji Shikin* [Political Funds]. Tokyo: Uchida Rōkakuho, 1961.

Tōyama Shigeki and Adachi Yoshiko. *Kindai Nihon Seiji-shi Hikkei* [A Handbook of Modern Japanese Political History]. Tokyo: Iwanami Shoten, 1961.

Tsuchiya Shōzō. "Senkyo Seido no Kaisei Mondai ni tsuite" [Concerning the Reform Problem of the Electoral System], *Shinseikai* No. 190 (August 1, 1966).

Tsuji Kiyoaki, ed. *Shiryō—Sengo Nijūnen-shi* [History of the Twenty Years After the War—Documents]. Vol. 1. Tokyo: Nihon Hyōronsha, 1966.

Waseda Daigaku Shakaikagaku Kenkyūjo. "Tōhyō Kōdō no Kenkyū" [A Study of Voting Behavior], *Shakai Kagaku Tōkyū*, Vol. 4, No. 1/2 (March 1959).

Watanabe Tsuneo. *Daijin* [Minister]. Tokyo: Kōbundō, 1959.

———. *Habatsu* [Factions]. 2nd revised, ed. Tokyo: Kōbundō, 1963.

———. *Seiji no Misshitsu* [The Backroom of Politics]. Tokyo: Sekkasha, 1966.

———. *Tōshu to Seitō* [Party Leaders and Political Parties]. Tokyo: Kōbundō, 1961.

Yanaga Chitose. *Japan Since Perry*. New York: McGraw-Hill Book Company, 1949.

Yashiro Kenzō. "Seizaikai no Jimmyaku o Saguru" [Probing the Human Sources of the Political and Economic Community], *Ekonomisuto*, Vol. 42, No. 15 (April 10, 1964).

Yomiuri Shimbun Seiji-bu. *Seitō* [Political Parties]. Tokyo: Yomiuri Shimbun-sha, 1966.

Yoshimura Tadashi. *Nihon Seiji no Shindan* [A Diagnosis of Japanese Politics]. Tokyo: Shinshin Shobō, 1964.

———. "Sengo ni okeru Wagakuni no Hoshutō" [Conservative Parties in Japan After the War], *Shakai Kagaku Tōkyū*, Vol. 1, No. 1 (January 1956).

———. "Shō-senkyoku-sei-ron no Munashisa" [The Emptiness of the Argument concerning the Small Electoral System], in *Shōsenkyokusei* [The Small Election District System], by Rōyama Masamichi, *et al.* Tokyo: Ushio Shuppan-sha, 1966.

———, ed. *Shushō Kōsen-ron* [Discussion of the Public Election of the Prime Minister]. Tokyo: Kōbundō, 1964.

INTERVIEWS

Aoki Kazuo. Member of the Diet. January 19, 1966.

Arakawa Hiroshi. Editorial writer for the *Sankei Shimbun*. November 22, 1966.

BIBLIOGRAPHY

Fujieda Sensuke. Member of the Diet. February 23, 1966; April 25, 1966; and July 14, 1966.

Fukunaga Kenji. Member of the Diet. June 3, 1966.

Gotō Ichirō. Professor at Waseda University. October 24, 1966.

Hara Kenzaburō. Member of the Diet. May 25, 1966.

Harada Ken. Member of the Diet. June 6, 1966.

Hasegawa Shirō. Member of the Diet. February 28, 1966.

Hayakawa Takashi. Member of the Diet. February 24, 1966.

Hayashi Shin'ichi. Counselor of Cabinet. January 5, 1966.

Hori, Shigeru. Member of the Diet. January 12, 1966.

Ikeda Kanjō. Reporter for *Asahi Shimbun*. October 15, 1965 and February 14, 1966.

Imai Kazuo. Independent critic, former official of the Finance Ministry. November 11, 1966.

Iwano Miyoji. Secretary to member of the Diet. May 13, 1966.

Kobayashi Katsumi. Secretary to member of the Diet. April 13, 1966; August 6, 1966; and August 15, 1966.

Kōno Kenzō. Member of the Diet. January 25, 1966.

Kosaka Zentarō. Member of the Diet. May 25, 1966.

Koyanagi Makie. Member of the Diet. May 30, 1966.

Kurogane Yasumi. Member of the Diet. February 22, 1966; April 21, 1966; May 18, 1966; August 23, 1966.

Matsuda Takechiyo. Member of the Diet. May 23, 1966.

Matsushita Yoshio. Official in the Liberal Democratic party. July 5, 1966.

Masutani Shūji. Member of the Diet. April 12, 1966.

Miura Kineji. Director for the National Education Television Network. October 15, 1965.

Miyake Hisayuki. Reporter for the *Mainichi Shimbun*. October 1, 1966.

Mizuta Mikio. Member of the Diet. January 10, 1966.

Mori Kiyoshi. Member of the Diet. July 6, 1966.

Nabeshima Naokatsu. Member of the Diet. February 3, 1966.

Nakamura Eiichi. Member of the Diet. August 8, 1966.

Nakasone Yasuhiro. Member of the Diet. June 3, 1966 and October 31, 1966.

Nemoto Ryūtarō. Member of the Diet. February 5, 1966 and May 18, 1966.

Ogata Akira. News executive for the Japan Broadcasting Corporation. April 1, 1965.

Ōhira Masayoshi. Member of the Diet. April 26, 1966.

Okamoto Masao. Official in the Liberal Democratic party. October 19, 1966.

Okino Mitsu. Reporter for the *Sankei Shimbun*. May 18, 1966.

336

BIBLIOGRAPHY

Ōkuma Ryōichi. Official in the Liberal Democratic party. June 4, 1966.

Onozato Hiroshi. Secretary to member of the Diet. August 7, 1966.

Ōta Takeo. Secretary to member of the Diet. August 6, 1966.

Ōwada Toshio. Reporter for the *Sankei Shimbun*. November 22, 1966.

Sakata Michita. Member of the Diet. May 18, 1966.

Sakurauchi Yoshio. Member of the Diet. May 24, 1966.

Senda Wataru. Reporter for the *Sankei Shimbun*. November 6, 1965.

Shiina Etsusaburō. Member of the Diet. October 13, 1965.

Shōji Tsuyoshi. Regional organizer for the Liberal Democratic party. August 24, 1966.

Soga Yoshiharu. Official in the Liberal Democratic party. October 19, 1966.

Sutō Hideo. Member of the Diet. January 18, 1966.

Tanaka Tatsuo. Member of the Diet. November 17, 1965.

Tanikawa Kazuo. Member of the Diet. July 28, 1966.

Tomita Nobuo. Professor at Meiji University. October 12, 1966.

Watanabe Tsuneo. Reporter for the *Yomiuri Shimbun*. January 22, 1966.

Yamamoto Katsuichi. Member of the Diet. June 6, 1966 and October 24, 1966.

Yamamuro Hideo. Reporter for the Japan Broadcasting Corporation. April 6, 1966.

Yamashita Seiichi. Managing Director for the Japan Committee for Economic Development. November 22, 1966.

Yoshimura Katsumi. Assistant Managing Editor for the *Sankei Shimbun*. June 3, 1966 and June 24, 1966.

SERIALS

Asahi Evening News. October 25, 1966.

Asahi Jānaru. 1960-1968.

Asahi Nenkan [Asahi Yearbook]. Tokyo: Asahi Shimbun Co., 1966, 1968.

Asahi Shimbun. 1945-1968.

Ayamekai-hō [Report of the Ayame Society]. January 1, 1966.

Mainichi Shimbun. 1964-1968.

Nihon Keizai Shimbun. October 31, 1963.

Sankei Shimbun. 1962-1968.

Tokyo Shimbun. September 20, 1964.

Yomiuri Shimbun. 1963-1968.

337

BIBLIOGRAPHY

PARTY DOCUMENTS

Jiyūminshutō. *Jiyūminshutō Jūnen no Ayumi* [Ten Years of Progress with the Liberal Democratic Party]. Tokyo: Jiyūminshutō Kōkoku Iinkai. 1966.

Jiyūminshutō. *Seimu Chōsakai Meibo* [Membership List of the Policy Affairs Research Council]. December 1, 1965.

Jiyūminshutō. "Sōsai Kōsen Kitei" [Rules for the Public Election of the Party President], in *Wagatō no Kihon Hōshin* [Basic Policies of Our Party]. Tokyo: Jiyūminshutō Kōkoku Iinkai, 1966.

Jiyūminshutō. *Soshiki Chōsakai Tōshin* [Report of the Organization Investigation Commission]. Tokyo: Jiyūminshutō, 1963.

Jiyūminshutō. *Tōkindaika ni Kansuru Kanjichō Shian* [Proposal of the Secretary General Concerning the Modernization of the Party]. September 25, 1965.

Jiyūminshutō. "Tōsoku" [Party Law], in *Wagatō no Kihon Hōshin* [Basic Policies of Our Party]. Tokyo: Jiyūminshutō Kōkoku Iinkai, 1966.

Rikken Seiyūkai. "Kaisoku" [Association Rules], in *Rikken Seiyūkai Shi* [History of the Friends of Constitutional Government Association], by Kobayashi Yūgo, Vol. 1. Tokyo: Rikken Seiyūkai Shi Shuppan Kyoku, 1923, pp. 31-32.

Rikken Minseitō. "Tōsoku" [Party Law], in *Gendai Seijigaku Zenshū* [Collection of Studies on Modern Politics], by Takahashi Seigo, Vol. 10. Tokyo: Nihon Hyōronsha, 1930, pp. 510-511.

OFFICIAL DOCUMENTS

A. JAPANESE GOVERNMENT

Gumma Ken. Senkyo Kanri Iinkai. *Senkyo no Kiroku* [Election Proceedings]. [N.p.], November 21, 1963; January 29, 1967.

Japan. Jichishō Senkyo Kyoku. *Shūgiin Giin Sōsenkyo, Saikō-Saibansho Saibankan Kokumin Shinsa: Kekka Shirabe* [Survey of Results of the General Elections of the House of Representatives and Peoples' Judgment of the Legal Officers of the Supreme Court]. Tokyo: Jichishō Senkyo Kyoku, 1953, 1955, 1958, 1960, 1963, 1967.

Japan. "Kokka Gyōsei Soshiki Hō" [National Government Organization Law] in *Roppō Zensho* [Compendium of Laws]. Tokyo: Iwanami, 1960, pp. 145-148.

Japan. "Kokkai Hō" [National Diet Law], in *Roppō Zensho* [Compendium of Laws]. Tokyo: Iwanami, 1960, pp. 19-24. Amended, in *Roppō Zensho*. Tokyo: Yūhikaku, 1967, pp. 61-65.

Japan. *Kokkai Tōkei Teiyō* [Statistical Abstract of Japan]. Tokyo: National Diet Library, 1965.

BIBLIOGRAPHY

Japan. "Kōshoku Senkyo Hō" [Public Offices Election Law], in *Roppō Zensho* [Compendium of Laws]. Tokyo: Iwanami, 1960, pp. 44-104.

Japan. "Naikaku Hō" [Cabinet Law], in *Roppō Zensho* [Compendium of Laws]. Tokyo: Iwanami, 1960, p. 145.

Japan. "Nippon Koku Kempō" [Japanese National Constitution], in *Roppō Zensho* [Compendium of Laws]. Tokyo: Iwanami, 1960, pp. 1-11.

Japan. Shūgiin and Sangiin, ed. *Gikai-seido Nanajū-nen-shi: Kensei-shi Gaikan* [An Outline of Constitutional History: The Seventy Year History of the Parliamentary System]. Tokyo: Insatsu kyoku, 1965.

Japan. Shūgiin Giin Jimukyoku. *Shūgiin Giin Sōsenkyo Ichiran* [A Conspectus of the 30th General Elections of the House of Representatives]. Tokyo: Ōkurashō Insatsu Kyoku, 1964.

Japan. "Teikoku Kempō" [Imperial Constitution], in *Roppō Zensho* [Compendium of Laws]. 5th rev. ed., Tokyo: Iwanami, 1934, pp. 1-13.

"Japanese Government Documents: Memorial on the Establishment of a Representative Assembly" [tr. by W. W. McLaren], *Transactions of the Asiatic Society of Japan*, Vol. 42, pt. 1 (1914), p. 428.

B. QUASI-GOVERNMENTAL BODIES

Kempō Chōsakai Jimukyoku. *Kempō Kaisei-ron oyobi Kaisei Hantai-ron ni okeru Kihonteki Tairitsuten—Kaisetsu to Shiryō* [Basic Points of Conflict Regarding the Arguments Favoring Constitutional Revision and Arguments Opposing Constitutional Revision—Documents and Analysis]. Tokyo: [n.p.], 1962.

Kōmei Senkyo Renmei. *Sōsenkyo no Jittai* [True Conditions of the General Elections]. Tokyo: [n.p.], 1958, 1960, 1963, March 1964, March 1967.

Rinji Gyōsei Chōsakai. "Naikaku no Kinō ni kansuru Kaikaku Iken" [Reform Opinion regarding the Functions of the Cabinet]. Tokyo: [n.p.], September, 1964. Mimeo.

Senkyo Seido Nanajū-nen Kinenkai. *Senkyo-hō no Enkaku* [The History of the Elections Laws]. Tokyo: Daiichi Hōki Shuppan K. K., 1959.

Senkyo Seido Shingikai. *Dai-ichiji Senkyo Seido Shingikai Kōmei Senkyo Suishin Undō ni kansuru Iinkai (Dai-san Iinkai) oyobi Senkyoku-betsu Teisū ni kansuru Iinkai (Dai-yon Iinkai) Giji Sokkiroku* [Transcript of the Proceedings of the Committee Concerned with the Movement Urging Clean Elections (No. 3 Committee)

339

and the Committee Concerned with Establishing the Number of Election Districts (No. 4 Committee) of the First Election System Deliberation Commission]. Tokyo: [n.p.], 1961.

Senkyo Seido Shingikai. *Dai-niji Senkyo Seido Shingikai Giji Sok-kiroku* [Transcript of the Proceedings of the Second Election System Deliberation Commission]. Tokyo: [n.p.], 1963.

Senkyo Seido Shingikai. *Dai-sanji Senkyo Seido Shingikai Giji Sok-kiroku* [Transcript of the Proceedings of the Third Election System Deliberation Commission]. Tokyo: [n.p.], 1964.

Senkyo Seido Shingikai. *Senkyo no Jittai ni kansuru Seron Chōsa* [Public Opinion Survey Concerning the Actual State of the Elections]. [n.p.]: August 1965.

C. SCAP DOCUMENTS

Supreme Commander of the Allied Powers. *Political Reorientation of Japan.* Washington, D.C.: U.S. Printing Office, 1950.

Index

Adachi Kōichi, 82
Adachi Tadashi, 67
Afro-Asia Study Group, 48
Agricultural Cooperatives Association, 222, 224-25
Akasaka, 58
Akita Daisuke, 47
Amami Ōshima, 114, 143-44
American occupation, 7; economic policies, 8-9; land reform, 10; and party president, 151; purge, 7-8, 88
Annaka, 89, 99-101
Anzai Hiroshi, 65
Anzai Masao, 61, 67
Aoki Kazuo, 201-2, 260
Aoki Masashi, 142, 170-71
Arafune Seijūrō, 32-34, 128-29
Arakawa Hiroshi, 63, 69
Asahi Shimbun, 292
Ashida Hitoshi, 11
Asia Study Group, 48
Automobile Manufacturers' Association, 69
Ayame Club, 93, 97
Azabudai Club, 66

Beer Federation, 73
Blue Cloud School, 90
Bridgestone Tire Company, 61
Buddhists, 13
bureaucrats, and policy-making, 225-26, 228-29; retirement, 226-28

cabinet, 193; announcement of, 200-1; authority of, 201-2; cabinet formation staff, 184-85, 311; candidates, 191-92, 199-200; criticisms of, 202-5; high turnover, 202-4; number of

new ministers, 181-82; "one-lunged," 188; posts in, 185-86, 197-99; reasons for changes in, 182-83; "of strong men," 188
Central Academy of Politics, 83, 262
Chiba prefecture, 85
chief cabinet secretary, 193, 293; duties, 186-87
chinjōdan, 223-24
Chōei Society, 65-66
Chōshū, 4, 150n
Chū-Nichi Shimbun, 292
Chūo University, 3, 12
Clean Elections Federation, 107
Clean Government party, 134-35, 316; formation, 13
communists, *see* Japan Communist party
Comradery of Youths, 93, 96
constitution, of 1889, 5; post-war, 7
Constitutional Association, 5; and Mitsubishi, 8; secretary general, 269. *See also* Constitutional Democratic party
Constitutional Democratic party, 5, 8, 60, 269; decision-making, 238-39; factions in, 18; organization, 82; policy-making, 208
Constitutional Progressive party, 4

Daiei Motion Pictures, 61, 67
deliberation councils, of ministries, 64
Democratic party, 151; merger, 11
Democratic Socialist party, 316; in elections, 13; formation, 12; legislation, 221

341

Fujioka, 89, 100-1
Fujiwara Hirotatsu, 109
Fujiwara Setsuo, 124
Fujiyama Aiichirō, 12, 64, 77;
  faction of, 17, 52; and presi-
  dential election, 148-49, 161,
  170-71, 173, 188
Fukuda Takeo, 67, 98-102;
  election, 135
Fukuda Tokuyasu, 201
Fukunaga Kenji, 238, 256, 262,
  265, 294, 297, 312
Funada Naka, 20, 24, 67
Furui Yoshimi, 165, 178

General Federation for the
  Renovation of Political
  Conditions, 163
genrō, 150
Gotō Ichirō, 86, 87
governor, 160-61
Green Breeze Society, 51
Grumman, 70
Gumma, 89, 98-102

Hagiwara Kichitarō, 67
Hamaguchi Ōsachi, 6
hanashiai, 251, 253, 265
Hara Kei, 270
Hara Kenzaburō, 249, 263-65,
  275, 294, 314
Harada Ken, 313
Hasegawa Shirō, 261
Hashimoto Tomisaburō, 290
Hatoyama Ichirō, 3, 11, 19
  139, 151, 163, 165, 166, 170,
  250, 272, 297; purged, 10;
  resignation, 153
Hayakawa Takashi, 177, 219-20,
  236
Hayashi Senjūrō, 112
Hayashi Shin'ichi, 186
Hirakawa Club, 293
Hiroshima, by-elections, 86-87
Hokkaido Mining and Shipping,
  67

Hokkaidō Shimbun, 292
Honda, 63
Hori Shigeru, 180
Hoshijima Nirō, 19, 243
Hosokawa Takamoto, 271
Hotta Shōzō, 62
House of Councillors, elections,
  50-51; and executive council,
  256-57; factions in, 48-53;
  leadership, 52; members in
  cabinet, 193-94; members of,
  49-50; powers, 49
House of Peers, 238

Ibaraki prefecture, 85
Idemitsu Oil Company, 61, 73
Idemitsu Sazō, 61
identity, need for, 39
Ikeda Hayato, 46, 53, 198-99,
  311; on cabinet, 189-90, 195;
  death and succession, 24, 26,
  300; and economic community,
  66, 73, 79; election, 129-30;
  faction of, 52; presidential
  election, 148-49, 158-60, 163,
  165, 166, 170, 172-73; resignation, 153, 187; selection of
  cabinet, 185, 190, 197; and
  vice president, 298
Ikeda Kanjō, 212, 216
Imai Kazuo, 227
Imperial Rule Assistance
  Association, 150
Inayama Yoshihiro, 61
ingaidan, 280-81
Inomata Kōzō, 136-37
International Motors, 62
Inukai Michiko, 223
Inukai Tsuyoshi, 19, 271-72
Ishibashi Shōjirō, 61
Ishibashi Tanzan, 51, 53, 146,
  164, 168-70, 172, 178, 297;
  cabinet, 191, 195, 197;
  resignation, 153

INDEX

Ōno Bamboku, 3, 46-47, 111,
164, 280-81; on cabinet, 195;
and cabinet recommendations,
192, 197; death and succession,
24; faction, 52; and formation
of Liberal Democratic party,
11-12; party presidential
election, 169-73, 176-77; vice
president, 297-300
Ōno Ichirō, 133-34
Onozato Hiroshi, 92, 96
Ōsaka Taxi Association, 62, 73
Osano Kenji, 61
Ōsawa Yūichi, 175
Ōta Takeo, 90, 93-96
Ōtake Tarō, 137
Ōwada Toshio, 62, 68, 74
Ozaki Yukio, 18

parliamentary vice ministers,
279-80
parties, political, between wars,
5-6; popular attitude toward,
107-10; weakness after World
War II, 8-10
People's Association, 72-73, 80-
81, 242, 277-78
policy affairs research council of
the Liberal Democratic party,
64, 183, 257, 261, 307; and
bureaucracy, 225-26, 228-29,
232; chairman, 218-19; criticisms, 229-36; deliberation
commission, 216-17; divisions,
210-11; and economic com-
munity, 233; function, 207;
investigative commissions, 211-
14, 215n; policy sources, 219;
and press, 234-35; research
staff, 216; special committees,
211-14, 215n; vice chairmen,
218
political fund regulation law, 77
political funds, 72-81

press, and cabinet, 187; and economic community, 64-65; and
legislation, 214; and Liberal
Democratic party, 292-94; and
parties, 109; and policy affairs
research council, 234-35; and
secretary general, 293-94
pressure groups, 219, 221, 224-25,
234
prime minister, "acting prime
minister," 299; between wars,
5; election of, 49; and elections, 112-13; and factions, 21,
55-56; office of, 185n; powers
of appointment, 180; protection of, 281; qualifications,
152; selection of cabinet, 194-
201
Protect the Constitution Movement, 270
public offices election law, 122

Reischauer, Robert K., 4, 6
rice deliberation council, 222
Rōyama Masamichi, 178
Russo-Japanese War of 1905, 59

Saigō Takamori, 132
Sakarauchi Yoshio, 287, 294
Sakata Michita, 46, 237, 248,
249, 253, 259, 265
Sake Brewers' Federation, 62, 70
Sakurauchi Yoshio, 250
Sankei Shimbun, 292
Sankin Society, 66-67
Satō Eisaku, 53, 199, 243, 248,
300, 308, 311; and business
community, 65-66; and elections, 122; faction, 16, 48, 51;
on *kōenkai*, 88; on political
funds, 76; presidential election,
148-49, 161-62, 165, 166, 175,
177; selection of cabinet, 185,

347